RESEARCHING AND WRITING HISTORY

RESEARCHING AND WRITING HISTORY

A guide for local historians

DAVID DYMOND

Carnegie Publishing Ltd,
in association with
The British Association for Local History, 2009

Researching and writing history: A guide for local historians

Copyright © David Dymond, 1981, 1999, 2009

First published by The British Association for Local History, 1999

Third edition published in 2009 by
Carnegie Publishing Ltd
in association with The British Association for Local History

Carnegie Publishing Ltd
Carnegie House
Chatsworth Road,
Lancaster LA1 4SL
telephone: 01524 840111
www.carnegiepublishing.com

ISBN 978-1-85936-196-2

British Library Cataloguing-in-Publication data
A catalogue record for this book is available from the British Library

Designed and typeset by Carnegie Book Production, Lancaster
Printed and bound in the UK by Short Run Press, Exeter

Contents

Illustrations

Plates (between pages 80 and 81)

Abbreviations

BALH	British Association for Local History
BPP	British Parliamentary Papers
CBA	Council for British Archaeology
CUP	Cambridge University Press
CORAL	Conference of Regional and Local Historians (now merged with BALH)
FACH	*Family and Community History*
FACHRS	Family and Community History Research Society
HMC	Historical Manuscripts Commission
JORALS	*Journal of Regional and Local Studies*
LHM	*Local History Magazine*
LPS	*Local Population Studies*
LPSS	Local Population Studies Society
OUP	Oxford University Press
PRO	Public Record Office (now TNA)
REED	*Records of Early English Drama*
TNA	The National Archives (Kew, London; formerly PRO)
TLH	*The Local Historian*
TRHS	*Transactions of the Royal Historical Society* (RHS)
UP	University Press (e.g. Exeter, Hertfordshire, Leicester)
VCH	*Victoria County History*
WEA	Workers' Educational Association

Preface

THE British Association for Local History first published this book in 1981, over a quarter of a century ago, under the title *Writing Local History*. It was substantially revised in 1999, and to reflect the contents more accurately the title was then changed to *Researching and Writing History*. To the author's surprise, although several thousand copies have been sold over the years, it is still selling in 2007 and stocks are again almost exhausted. As in 1999, it is obvious that a simple reprint is not enough, because developments in the theory and practice of local history have recently come thick and fast. The decision has therefore been made to undertake another revision, and to float it under a third title, this time *Researching and Writing History: A Guide for Local Historians*.

As was said in the first version, I do not propose to discuss historical sources in any detail, or to introduce special historical techniques such as oral recording and diplomatic. Good advice on these matters can be found in other publications, and more will doubtless appear. Nor, at the other end of the subject, am I much concerned with the business of actually getting into print because, again, others have written on the subject. The central purpose of this book, as in the two previous editions, is to investigate how we discipline ourselves to write better. How do we find and interpret evidence and then convert our thoughts, through our pens or word-processors, into a reasoned yet imaginative reconstruction of the past? In thinking about the challenge of writing, one inevitably has to reconsider the earlier processes of research as well, a point which was conceded in the title of the second edition. Curiously this is a subject which has been largely avoided by other authors, even though several of them have incorporated the word 'Writing' in their titles.

The arrangement of the book has not been changed. An introductory chapter debates 'Local history now' (that is, in 2007–8). Thereafter, twelve sections review the various processes involved in researching and writing history. They are followed by nineteen appendices giving more detailed information, examples of writing and practical exercises. Originally produced as teaching-aids, the latter are offered in the hope that they give practical help to actual and would-be writers, and give to teachers at various levels ideas worth adapting to their own circumstances.

I hope that readers will not find too many flaws and inconsistencies in the following pages. The danger of writing a didactic book of this kind is that one risks breaking rules and recommendations as one makes them. Comments and criticisms will always be gratefully received, in case a fourth version ever sees the light of day!

Acknowledgements

I am grateful to the British Association for Local History, an organisation with which I have been closely involved since its foundation in 1982, for giving me the chance to update this book yet again. In particular I should like to mention the following colleagues and friends who have given me useful criticisms and practical help in revising both text and appendices: Peter Bysouth, John Chandler, Claire Cross, Gill Draper, Heather Falvey, Simon Fletcher, Tim Lomas, Evelyn Lord, Jo Mattingly, Dennis Mills, Peter Northeast, Ken Sneath and Nigel Tringham. In the final shaping of the book, the encouragement of Alan Crosby, editor of *The Local Historian*, has been simply invaluable. As always in my work, I have been hugely dependent on the helpful staff and rich resources of Cambridge University Library.

Confession

Unfortunately the English language has no singular pronoun covering male and female, a fact which casts shame on Anglo-Saxon and Middle-English attitudes. As a result I have sometimes been forced to refer to the local historian as 'he'. Endless repetition of the only alternatives ('he or she', 'he/she' and the ugliest of all 's/he') would have been tedious to everyone. So in practice I have found myself resorting wherever possible to the plural 'they' or 'we' and to the indeterminate 'you' or the regal 'one'. In acknowledgement of this verbal injustice, I wish to assert here and now that women are *at least* as important as men in this branch of history – just as they were in the past itself.

David Dymond
Bury St Edmunds
June 2008

Thoughts on local history

'I have confessed to you that I am fond of local histories. It is the general execution of them that I condemn, and that I call *the worst kind of writing*. I cannot comprehend but that they might be performed with taste.' (Horace Walpole in letter to Revd William Cole, 1780)

'The historian should look first at the manor house and the parsonage, which were the principal seats of local power and leadership from the Norman Conquest to the reign of Victoria. He should not neglect the cottage, the workshop and the market-place but he should not allow himself to be excessively preoccupied by them ...' (W. R. Powell, *Bulletin of the Institute of Historical Research*, xxxi, 1958, p. 48)

'Eventually indeed, when the history of English towns and villages has been written as it ought to be, the study of English history itself will also be revolutionised.' (Alan Everitt, *Ways and Means in Local History*, 1971, p. 5)

'Ultimately there is no distinction between local and national history' (Philip Styles, quoted by E. A. O. Whiteman in *Studies in Seventeenth Century West Midlands History*, 1978, p. xv)

'The study of chosen themes in their local settings ought eventually to lead to the writing of a new kind of national history, which will incorporate and explain the rich variety of regional and local experiences.' (J. K. Walton and J. Walvin, *Leisure in Britain, 1780–1939*, 1983, p. 2)

'What distinguishes a significant from an insignificant piece of historical research is not the size of the unit of investigation, whether in time or space, but the ends in view and the methods used.' (E. A. Wrigley, *The Local and the General in Population History*, 1985, p. 1)

'I have always believed that through local history we can develop a new version of national history: local history should never simply illustrate national history, or take it as given, it should point to new interpretations.' (Asa Briggs in foreword to G. Mayhew, *Tudor Rye*, 1987)

'A good national history of inclosure will refer to Widmerpool [Notts] or other places in order to show how real people were affected. A good local history of the inclosure of Widmerpool will show that what happened there was part of a national pattern, not a wholly unique experience.' (Christopher Lewis, *Particular Places*, 1989, p. 48)

'But local history is frequently the nursery for ideas that are developed on the national stage, its seeds are germinated into the lawns of history.' (William Gibson in *Archives*, xxiii, 98, Apr. 1998, 68)

'One of the most striking developments of the late twentieth century in the historiography of Tudor and Stuart England has been its localisation.' (P. Collinson and J. Craig, *The Reformation in English Towns, 1500–1640*, 1998, p. 1)

'… the use of small-scale research to ask, and to answer, big questions.' (Pat Hudson, *FACH*, May 1999, 5)

'In both countries [*UK and USA*] local history has become one of the principal laboratories for social history … Local history has to be rooted in particulars – they provide some of its obvious distinctiveness – but it does not have to be confined by them.' (R. C. Richardson, *The Changing Face of English Local History*, 2000, pp. 199, 211)

'[*History*] was too important to be confined to the intra-mural disputes of the professionals.' (Simon Schama in obituary for Sir John Plumb, *The Independent*, 27 Oct. 2001)

'Tragic problems of alienation can arise for people growing up in an incoherent pattern-less environment … History cannot remain an academic preserve. Ordinary people have been taking hold of history. This puts an increased responsibility on academics ...' (M. Reeves, *The Historian*, 74, 2002, 6–10)

'The extent of localization is so compelling that it forces a rethinking of any conception of a "rural England" ... we need to replace it with rural Englands.' (Barry Reay, *Rural Englands*, 2004, pp. 205–6)

'Through detailed research into relatively small geographical areas or communities, micro-history can provide much valuable information on the "macro-questions" of life, work and death.' (Christopher French, *TLH*, 36, 1, Feb. 2006, 17–28)

'Although some economic and social historians still look askance at the study of a single place, such intensive research remains the only way to address key questions and to test theoretical perspectives.' (H. R. French and R. W. Hoyle, *The Character of Rural Society: Earl's Colne 1550–1750*, 2007, p. xxiii)

'What we have to develop is a shared agenda of academic and lay practitioners, in which the professionals recognise the contribution of the enthusiastic amateurs, and the amateurs have at least some understanding of the seemingly arcane disputes about what is local and what is regional which often threaten to pass them by ... The key issue is to avoid ending up with several local history communities, not always talking to each other.' (John Beckett, *Writing Local History*, 2007, pp. 191, 210)

'British local history is unashamedly holistic and inclusive.' (Kate Tiller, *TLH*, 37, 4, Nov. 2007, 250)

Sir William Dugdale, 1605–86, Garter King of Arms, pioneering antiquary and local historian, whose writings include *Antiquities of Warwickshire* (1656), *The History of St Paul's Cathedral* (1658) and the monumental *Monasticon Anglicanum* (with Roger Dodsworth, 1655–61). Looking at this portrait, modern historians and archivists can only boggle at the chaotic tables and shelves, the use of ink beside original documents, and the need to write history with a hat on! Today's researchers expect high standards of conservation and use sophisticated technology, but the basic intellectual responsibilities are much the same as in earlier generations. Our constant task as historians is to think both critically and imaginatively, and to write with lucidity and elegance.

(Drawn and engraved by Wenceslaus Hollar, 1655)

1

Local history today

If you understand the atom, you understand the universe.

(Michio Kaku in broadcast, 4 June 2008)

T HOSE not familiar with the subject will often ask, 'What *is* Local History, and how do you define it?', but no easy answer leaps to mind. Perhaps we should simply say, as Kate Tiller has suggested, that the two essential ingredients of this kind of history are 'people and place'. That is incontestable but it does not, of itself, constitute a satisfactory definition. Clearly we use 'place' as the physical setting of our studies and as important evidence in itself (whether it be, for example, buried archaeology, vernacular buildings or complete landscapes), but beyond that we are soon driven to acknowledge that the central emphasis must always be, unequivocally, on human beings. Alan Rogers put this point well by saying that, for the local historian, the 'subject is not a place, a village, parish or town, but a group of people'. So perhaps the least unsatisfactory definition we can offer is that local historians study the lives of the great mass of ordinary men, women and children in their social and physical environments.[1] Put at its simplest, we are concerned with 'people *in* their place'.

Seeking greater precision we could argue for ever over such slippery words as 'locality', 'ordinary' and 'community'. It is surely better to accept that local

---

[1]   In John Beckett's words, any proposed definition of local history soon 'squirms, wriggles and escapes our grasp'; Herbert Finberg thought it futile to seek a definition at all: J. Beckett, *Writing Local History* (Manchester UP, 2007), p. 189; H. Finberg and V. Skipp, *Local History: Objective and Pursuit* (David and Charles, 1967), p. vii; Kate Tiller, *English Local History: an Introduction* (Alan Sutton, 2002), p. 1; Alan Rogers, *Approaches to Local History* (Longman, 1977), p. 6. In championing 'community history', Dennis Mills still insists that local historians emphasise places rather than people; see his *Rural Community History from Trade Directories* (Hertfordshire UP, 2001), p. 9.

history does not have, and can never have, exact limits. On one side it overlaps with biography and with family and population history, and on the other merges seamlessly with landscape, economic, urban, social, religious and cultural history. We are therefore on safer ground seeing local history not as a discipline with precise boundaries but as a major *emphasis* within the broad spectrum of historical studies. It lies at the opposite end from World History and International History because it deals with human life almost microscopically and within much tighter spatial limits. In that sense our work is akin to those sciences which deal with the smallest and most fundamental bits of life and matter. Therefore, we cannot be altogether surprised that some contemporary historians use the term 'microhistory' in preference to 'local history'.

Definable or not, local history is widely pursued for its own rewards, and has been repeatedly justified as having value in its own right.[2] In every corner of Britain we see popular enthusiasm for the subject, for it has become generally agreed that 'everywhere has an interesting past' and that 'anyone can have a go'.[3] Battersea, Cleethorpes and Tow Law are just as 'historical' as Totnes, York and Alnwick, and the Black Country and Tyneside now receive at least as much attention, rightly, as the Kentish Weald and the Lake District. Other touchstones of the subject's vitality include the number of visitors at record offices and specialised libraries, attendances at courses and membership of voluntary societies. We could also weigh in well-attended exhibitions, the holding of competitions and giving of prizes, and of course the rising tide of publication, both printed and electronic. Last and by no means least, history (often with a local focus) now enjoys unprecedented popularity on radio, television and the internet.[4] Paradoxically, this huge public appetite for the past has recently stimulated a new academic specialisation known as 'Public History'. Its practitioners investigate how history is portrayed to, and consumed by, the contemporary non-academic world. One of their most important challenges must surely be to explain why history has particular appeal when it is localised.[5]

All these are encouraging general trends, but the true rewards and challenges of local history call for deeper scrutiny. This is best done by distinguishing 'consumers' from 'activists'. The first group is very large indeed and comprises all

---

[2] For example, Finberg and Skipp, *Local History, Objective and Pursuit*, p. 32; C. Phythian-Adams, *Re-thinking English Local History* (Leicester UP, 1987), p. 2.

[3] C. P. Lewis, *Particular Places: An Introduction to English Local History* (British Library, 1989), p. 9; Beckett, *Writing Local History*, p. 206.

[4] As witnessed, for example, by the success of the BBC's publishing ventures, *The BBC History Magazine* and *Who do you think you are?*

[5] First developed in this country from 1996 at Ruskin College, Oxford.

who, for example, enjoy visiting National Trust properties, following 'Timewatch' on TV and dipping into volumes of the *Victoria County History*. They are not concerned with research into the past but are happy to learn about it from others. The second group includes all those, whether professional or amateur, who have actively sought original evidence and pondered over its significance. These are the coal-face workers who, for instance, find and exploit new sources; who widen, if only slowly, the chronological range of local history to include most of the twentieth century; and who open up previously neglected themes – migration, charity, medicine, food, leisure, popular religion, literacy, the role of women, and many others.

The values of local history

Some cynics will always claim that to study local history is to wallow myopically in meaningless trivia. We should not waste our time on 'minor lives' because real history, they insist, must be concerned with higher matters such as war and peace, statecraft and national politics.[6] This view, however, overlooks the symbiotic relationship which has always existed between the nation and thousands of diverse local communities and networks. Indeed, it deliberately ignores the vast majority of humanity who in every generation, with all their differences, have given shape to the nation. If these men, women and children are to be rescued, in Edward Thompson's famous phrase, 'from the enormous condescension of posterity', they need at least as much historical attention as the great and powerful.[7] Quintessentially, therefore, the mission of the local historian is to attempt to rediscover for particular areas and periods how ordinary people lived as individuals and as groups. In particular we must try to unravel the tangle of human networks which our ancestors built up for dozens of different purposes – while recognising, of course, that each individual necessarily belonged to more than one group.

Not only does this approach to the past illuminate the basic human condition in all its rich diversity, but it can prove liberating and energising for individuals immersed in it. It can, as Alan Everitt wrote in 1971, 'both broaden the mind and deepen the sympathies in very much the same way as travelling in a distant country'.[8] In other words, by studying local history (an emphasis which in no way

---

[6] David Starkey thinks that local history is 'a very limited thing': *The Historian*, 71 (Autumn 2001), 15.

[7] E. P. Thompson, *The Making of the English Working Class* (Penguin, 1968), p. 13.

[8] A. Everitt, *Ways and Means in Local History* (NCSS, 1971), p. 50. In a similar vein, John Marshall talked of 'the most magnificent liberal education' afforded by local and regional history: *Amateur Historian*, 6, 1 (Autumn 1963), 11–17.

denies the validity of national history), we come to appreciate the complicated legacy of previous generations which surrounds our daily lives – and over which we ourselves have but a brief stewardship, for better or worse. Within this perspective, our own individual lives do indeed acquire a greater and deeper meaning.

It follows, although this dimension is still not recognised widely enough, that local history also has genuine social and communal value. It can help to erode the educational, class and ethnic barriers still so deep-rooted in British society, by bringing together people of different ages and backgrounds: witness the understanding and human warmth generated when schoolchildren interview the elderly, or when projects are devised specifically for people who would never dream of attending a university course or joining the National Trust. Since World War II it has been shown in many places that historical study can promote a genuine sense of local involvement, togetherness and indeed pride, even in apparently unpromising and unglamorous places, and its effect is particularly strong when practical recording and elementary research are undertaken by well-motivated and well-led groups. For instance, small teams of local volunteers have recently studied a working-class suburb of the 1860s in Swindon and a council estate of the 1930s in Lancaster. With the support of English Heritage and its Outreach Strategy, participants have learnt basic skills, recorded oral and photographic evidence, and assembled documentary archives: 'people were involved in different ways, as sources, as audience, as researchers, and as authors'.[9] This approach might yet involve larger proportions of people in seriously deprived areas, as presaged in a new social study of London's East End in the second half of the twentieth century, which involved the interviewing of 799 local residents.[10] 'Democratising' initiatives of this kind deserve to be regarded with the greatest respect: they can lead to genuine 'People's History' and 'Community History' whereby local volunteers collect evidence in varying forms and relay the results of their labours to their neighbours in the form of talks, exhibitions and publications.[11]

On a political plane too, local knowledge helps to make grass-root democracy more informed, sensitive and effective – even if it also exposes the extreme difficulty of influencing the decisions of local authorities. Although the pace of modern change is frenzied, citizens are more likely to appreciate their own cultural

[9]   K. Tiller, 'Local history brought up to date', *The Local Historian* (*TLH*) (2006), 150–54. Contrast the nineteenth century when local history was largely the preserve of the gentry, clergy and leisured classes, and confined to studying the upper echelons of society.

[10]   G. Dench, K. Gavron and Michael Young, *The New East End: Kinship, Race and Conflict* (Profile Books, 2006).

[11]   The Community Archives Development Group brings the support of professional archivists to such projects.

and environmental 'heritage' and are better able both to defend *and* improve it, if they have access to good, de-mythologised local history on matters such as demography, living standards, vernacular architecture, dialect, place-names, traditional industries, leisure patterns and religious traditions. Going further, Alan Crosby argues that all local history societies should concern themselves with present-day issues, and if necessary become involved in active lobbying and campaigning. Why should they stand back, risking the danger of appearing pedantic and remote, when their knowledge and expertise could be used to inform and influence the future?[12]

It is no exaggeration to say that, when sound localised research is made available to a wider public, the life of the relevant community can never be the same again: it now knows more about itself, and about its place in time and in the wider world. An excellent example is provided by the Cogenhoe and Whiston Heritage Society which was founded in 2001 to serve two adjacent Northamptonshire villages: not only has it run regular talks, an annual lecture and excursions (locally and abroad), but organised research projects (for example on oral history and house history) and published the results. Among its achievements to date are a hardback book and CD on twentieth-century life, a photographic exhibition, and the establishment of a lively newsletter and website.[13] If all local societies could show such vitality and leadership, and were able to sustain them, the impact and status of local history both in local communities and in the national and academic worlds would be far greater than they are today. Meanwhile, in all parts of the globe, the increasing interest in political devolution and citizenship will in part depend on a deepening public consciousness of local and regional character, and on the successful identification of human groupings, large and small, past and contemporary, long-lasting and ephemeral, affluent and deprived.[14] In these and other ways, local history should be regarded not just as an academic subject, important though that is, but as a form of public knowledge which will

---

[12] Alan Crosby, private correspondence, 2008. For decades Enfield's Preservation Society has published local history, done voluntary work and applied political pressure: V. Carter, *Fighting for the Future: the Study of Enfield Preservation Society, 1936–96* (Enfield Preservation Soc., 1997).

[13] S. Hollowell, *A Century of Change: Cogenhoe 1901–2000* (Cogenhoe and Whiston Heritage Soc., 2003).

[14] For an example of a local historian contributing to this debate, see J. Chandler, *A Sense of Belonging: History, Community and the New Wiltshire* (Ex Libris, 1998). 'Who do we think we are?' is a new initiative of the Historical Association, Royal Geographical Society and Dept for Children, Schools and Families to explore 'identity, diversity and citizenship' by, among other methods, the study of local history and archives.

be increasingly deployed in the social and political debates of the twenty-first century.[15]

As for its strictly academic value, local 'bottom up' history acts as a vital seed-bed and test-bed for history as a whole. Not only do its practitioners constantly find new riches in their exploration of local archives, but they generate ideas which test the broader generalisations of those 'top down' historians working at national level. Sometimes they clarify and refine those generalisations, but more often than not they complicate and thicken them by bringing new evidence to bear on poorly-founded assumptions.[16] Furthermore they frequently discover entirely new issues which have the potential to become national or even global. For example, the pioneering local historian W. G. Hoskins was one of the first to draw attention to the value of investigating regional surnames and vernacular buildings, and now both studies are specialisms in their own right. These attributes mean that the word 'microcosmic' might seem a better description of local history than 'microscopic'.[17] The influences, however, are not simply one-way. While deeply involved in their chosen fields, perceptive local historians by wide reading absorb the ideas of other historical specialists. These upward and downward trends mean that local history and national history are now utterly dependent on each other: they perpetually collide in a creative way, illuminating and transforming each other.

Divisions within local history

One of the best-known divides of recent years has been between 'local' and 'family' history. The latter is a massive popular movement, which in three or four decades has boosted the number of searchers in record offices and gained far more converts than has local history. At first the two groups were deeply suspicious of each other, although their interests obviously overlap (families and kinship are basic to any kind of social history, and no individual or family can be understood without reference to a surrounding community and society). Local historians tended to regard family historians as mere name-hunters, ancestor-worshippers

---

[15]   Alan Rogers argued that 'local history belongs to the people and should be restored to them – not just by the presentation of the findings of scholars through public lectures but by opening the doors to the people to research their own past': *JORALS*, 15, 1 (Summer 1995), 1–14. Dennis Mills appealed for the writing of 'outline histories' of individual parishes: *TLH*, 24, 4 (Nov. 1994), 225–8.

[16]   Using a different metaphor, Margaret Bonney talks of the local historian's opportunity 'to muddy the water': *TLH*, 24, 1 (1994), 2–3.

[17]   M. M. Postan, *Essays on Historical Method* (CUP, 1971), pp. 20–1.

and constructors of family trees. Slowly, however, the two groups are showing a greater willingness to live together, to learn from each other and to merge their interests. In recent decades the development and maturing of demographic history has undoubtedly assisted in this process of reconciliation. Here the influence of the Local Population Studies Society, the Family and Community History Research Group and carefully designed university courses has been pivotal in helping family historians to get beyond the mere collecting of names and family-trees, and to find out how life was actually lived in local communities.[18] In the course of personal development a good family historian will inevitably become a local historian – and *vice versa*. Even if progress seems slow, we must hope that the two subjects continue to overlap and fuse.[19]

Within the world of local history itself, those of us who are activists vary considerably in our approaches to the past. Too often we divide into interest-groups blithely pursuing our own priorities and tending to ignore those of others. For example, rifts still exist between parochialists and regionalists, and between those who prefer short chronologies and those who prefer long. Few would deny that contacts need strengthening between those who focus on early periods and those whose interests are modern; between those who study documents and those concerned with buildings, landscapes and artefacts; between those who investigate rural areas and those who work on towns and industrial conurbations. Of course, in one sense variety invigorates the subject, and in practice some individuals and groups undoubtedly cross these boundaries. Nevertheless, only a minority of local historians seem prepared to discuss co-operation, objectives and standards, and they are mainly professionals. The overall result is that local research and writing is not as comparative and cumulative as it ought to be, and effort is unnecessarily wasted. Obviously we need to review our institutional structures and improve the channels of communication between local historians of all kinds at local, county, regional, national and even international levels.[20]

---

[18] Particularly important has been the contribution of the Open University with courses like DA301.

[19] One of the best symbols of this reconciliation is the work of David Hey of Sheffield University: he is the only person in England to have held an academic chair in Local and Family History; see his *Family History and Local History in England* (Longman, 1987), and *The Oxford Companion to Local and Family History* (1996, 2008). Some have seen recent trends differently. 'Local history societies have opened their doors to family historians, to the extent that there is a danger that the difference between the two may be becoming increasingly blurred': N. Goose, *Archives*, xxii, 97 (Oct. 1997), 101.

[20] Kate Tiller has argued that local and county groups could do more to cooperate with each other, and might even merge their memberships: *TLH*, 37, 4 (Nov. 2007), 254. Initiatives

CHANNELS INTO LOCAL AND REGIONAL HISTORY

i) FOR CONSUMERS

SCHOOLS - lessons, projects & local visits provide an early stimulus to historical awareness.

POPULAR MEDIA - television, radio, newspapers, periodicals, guide books, etc. have never before devoted so much time to history.

OUTDOOR LEISURE - visits to historic towns & villages, stately homes, ancient monuments & heritage centres reflect great mobility & access for all classes; trails & other forms of interpretation enhance the experience.

PRIVATE COLLECTING - paintings, engravings, maps, antiquarian books, postcards, personal correspondence, archaeological artefacts (detectorism), etc. can be more than mere investments.

MUSEUMS - the attraction of man-made artefacts, large and small, displayed and interpreted; temporary exhibitions frequently offer diversity.

FAMILY HISTORY - many genealogists go beyond the individual and family, to consider the social and economic life of the surrounding area and community.

SOCIETIES (local & county) - organise programmes of lectures, guided excursions & exhibitions (NB: the more enterprising societies undertake research & publication).

ii) FOR ACTIVISTS

LIBRARIES (public, local studies & academic) - offer printed sources & secondary history, as well as other forms of local study.

RECORD OFFICES (national, county, diocesan and other) - offer manuscript & printed sources, secondary history, aids to research; sometimes involved in educational classes.

SPECIALIST SOCIETIES - provide for their membership lectures, excursions, conferences, projects, newsletters, journals and record publications.

ADULT & CONTINUING EDUCATION - provides general, localised & methodological courses; accredited courses, certificates, diplomas, first degrees, higher degrees.

GROUP RESEARCH PROJECTS - involving academic & lay cooperation in the investigation of documentary, oral & topographical themes.

Figure 1. Channels into local and regional history.

And the divisions go deeper than mere cliquishness. Local historians have been told often enough that they do not devote sufficient thought to the basic philosophy of their subject. As long ago as 1964 Herbert Finberg asserted that local history suffered 'from a lack of theoretical discussion'. He saw his contemporaries as neglecting the units of study, themes, sources and methods which help to distinguish local from national history.[21] These are basic issues to which leading local historians have returned at frequent intervals. In the meantime, however, many students of the subject have been far too absorbed in their practical research to pay much attention to theoretical debates.

Nor were most local historians perturbed when in 1999 George and Yanina Sheeran deplored the lack of a philosophy of local history, and in starkly postmodernist terms attacked the 'realist' assumptions made by most of us.[22] To them, historians 'do not and cannot observe the past', and sources are no more than 'traces' which we connect together 'by the power of imagination'. The end result is not so much a reconstruction of the past as a 'literary process'. The main defence against this depressing nihilism must be that the past, to some extent at least, *is* recoverable by the scrupulous and subtle use of verbal, physical and other evidence. As our knowledge accumulates, it gets increasingly nuanced and subject to vigorous debate and revision – which does not make us writers of literary fiction. In rediscovering the past we are indeed frequently obliged to use our imaginations, but only when rooted in hard evidence and supported by careful thought and transparent writing.[23] The vast majority of working historians, consciously or unconsciously, embrace a realist position but postmodernist grizzling can have at least one beneficial effect. It should make us ever more careful in our handling of evidence, and ever more critical in our attempts to extract meaning from it.

Before leaving the subject of disunity, it is worth mentioning those individuals

---

at national level already include the Local History Day organised annually by BALH, and the Local History and Community Month. Seminars at the Institute of Historical Research in London are open to all interested individuals; one devoted to 'Locality and Region' encourages cooperation with local societies and heritage organisations. Much could be learnt by developing stronger links with local historians in other countries and continents.

[21]   H. P. R. Finberg, *Local History in the University: An Inaugural Lecture* (Leicester UP, 1964), p. 17.

[22]   G. and Y. Sheeran, 'Reconstructing Local History', *TLH*, 29, 4 (Nov. 1999), 256–62, followed by *TLH*, 30, 2 (May 2000); TLH, 31, 1 (Feb. 2001). See also Keith Jenkins, *Re-thinking History* (Routledge, 1991).

[23]   A brave exploration of the boundaries of historical imagination, in relation to local history, can be read in J. Hatcher, *The Black Death: An Intimate History* (London, 2008).

and groups who deliberately use and corrupt local history for largely commercial purposes. They put entertainment before education, insisting that their purpose is to 'make history come alive', but in reality they are battening on the great popular hunger for historical knowledge. Many of us cringe when we encounter feeble or phoney history, for example in newspapers, glossy county magazines and television, or witness the silliest excesses of the burgeoning 'heritage industry'.[24] I particularly abominate books which exploit the supposedly popular appetite for local spookiness. This includes ghost and graveyard trails in which 'Equity qualified guides' promise 'a spine-tingling experience that will haunt you for years'. Distortions of this kind are not merely irritating and embarrassing, but make the serious historian's task more difficult by perpetuating local myths and encouraging fabrications. Furthermore they compete with perfectly genuine attempts to re-enact the past, as happens for example with experimental archaeology and modern performances of medieval tournaments, music and drama.

Professionals and non-professionals

For generations the most persistent divide has been between, on the one hand, full-time academic researchers and teachers and, on the other hand, part-time lay people who are motivated simply by their love of the subject ('amateurs' in the best sense of the word). Indeed, some fear that the divide between these two groups may recently have widened still further.[25] Many professionals have castigated lay historians for adopting a heaping approach to the past, writing in an uncritical, anecdotal and sentimental way, failing to give references and refusing to engage with broader ideas.[26] The pejorative words most commonly used are 'antiquarian' and 'parochial'. These were the criticisms, for example, in the mid-1960s when a vigorous controversy broke out in the pages of *The Amateur Historian*.[27] The argument has rumbled on ever since, and received another boost in 1997 with

---

[24]   Edward Royle has referred to the 'vapid commercial candy-floss of the heritage industry': TLH, 28, 3 (Aug. 1998), 178. This whole area falls under the scrutiny of the new specialists in 'Public History' (see p. 2).

[25]   In this book I use the word 'professional' to mean a full-time specialist employed in an academic institution, and 'lay' or 'amateur' to mean a dedicated part-timer. See Tiller, *TLH*, 36, 3 (Aug. 2006), 157 for the fear that the divide between professional and lay historians may have actually 'opened up again'.

[26]   K. Schurer, 'The future for local history: boom or recession?', *TLH*, 21, 3 (Aug. 1991), 99–108.

[27]   *The Amateur Historian*, 6, nos 1, 2, 4, 6, 7, 8 (1963–4)

LOCALITY & THE WIDER WORLD

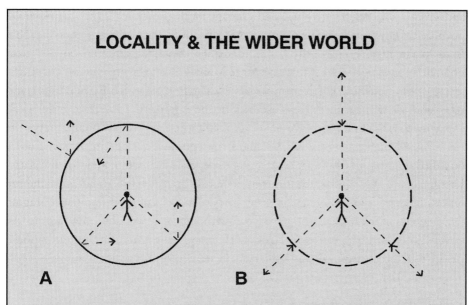

A   B

This diagram attempts to illustrate a crucial choice faced by the local historian who prefers to work on a basic administrative unit such as a parish or township. Standing, as it were, in the centre of his chosen place, he can regard the boundary in one of two ways: as an impenetrable physical and mental barrier, a sort of Berlin Wall (A); or as porous in both directions (B). The first approach is blinkered and will certainly not reveal the true significance of local life. The second will give much better shape and meaning to research and writing, because it acknowledges that every community contributes to the life of other broader groupings and in turn is affected by them. These vital and illuminating connections with the wider world can take many different forms, but will be of three main kinds which are given here in order of (arguably) ascending importance:

Administrative & Legal	Geographical & Economic	Personal & Cultural
hundred, wapentake, deanery	hinterland of town	kinship network
archdeaconry, diocese	landed estate	social contacts
Quarter Sessions district	working zone	religious bonds
Poor Law union	farming region	cultural links
shire	industrial region	shared dialect
nation	'province'	mental maps

Figure 2. Locality and the wider world.

the publication of John Marshall's *Tyranny of the Discrete*.[28] The basic charge is undoubtedly correct. Too often published local histories are uncritical and shapeless, relying heavily on miscellaneous and undigested bits of evidence (see Pl. 2 between pp. 80 and 81). They are frequently nostalgic in tone, painting the picture of a contented stable world and tending to neglect less palatable subjects such as disease, injustice, crime and rioting. The fact has to be faced that local communities at all periods were *not* perpetually stable and harmonious. Indeed, as the result of internal pressures, external influences and various misfortunes, they were quite commonly riven by social, economic, political and religious controversy. Paradoxically, while some historical trends undoubtedly led to integration and better understanding, others generated conflict and even violence.[29]

Another justified criticism is that non-professional historians often ignore the inward and outward movement of people and influences, and overlook those links with the outside world which help to make sense of what is found locally. They give the impression that the locality being studied is unique and self-contained, 'the centre of the universe'. In other words, the parish boundary has become a mental barrier, an intellectual Berlin Wall or Iron Curtain. In fact, one's community or locality can be properly understood only when it is viewed as a significant part of the wider world. The choice is very clearly presented by David Hey:

> Nothing is more difficult for a local historian who is deeply immersed in all the minutiae of the history of his particular place than to raise his sights beyond the local boundaries, so as to place his findings in a wider context. Only by being aware of what is happening elsewhere will he understand what is special and what is typical about his chosen subject.[30]

Whatever our chosen territory, we as historians must always put it into a broader setting and thereby acknowledge the flow of influences in and out. Any territory should in particular be related 'to the broader area or areas immediately above it'.[31] This awareness of an outside world can be gained in various ways: for example, by

---

[28]   J. D. Marshall, *Tyranny of the Discrete: a Discussion of the Problems of Local History in England* (Scolar, 1997). See David Hey's review in *TLH*, 28, 2 (May, 1998), 123–4.

[29]   See A. Wood, *The Politics of Social Conflict: The Peak Country, 1520–1770* (CUP, 1999); J. Walter, *Understanding Popular Violence in the English Revolution: The Colchester Plunderers* (CUP, 1999); R. Lee, *Unquiet Country: Voices of the Rural Poor, 1820–1880* (Windgather, 2005).

[30]   Review in *TLH*, 30, 3 (Nov. 1990), 141.

[31]   Marshall, *Tyranny of the Discrete*, p. 89.

looking at wide-ranging primary sources such as tax returns and census abstracts, by consulting data collected in major published surveys (those, for example, listing all known chartered markets, or estimating the populations of English towns at various dates), and above all by conscientiously reading the published work and critical interpretations of other historians.

However, some professional criticism of the work of amateurs has not been totally fair, and the gulf between the two groups is not as wide as is sometimes pretended. Yes, the flow of uncritical and nostalgic local history is certainly on the increase, but the dangers of sub-standard research and writing are now more widely recognised, and have been stressed by most teachers of local history in the last generation. *At its best*, the writing of non-professional local history is no longer 'amateurish' but is indeed critical, cumulative and comparative, just as critics have long demanded.[32] Furthermore it too is increasing in volume, partly because of the training now available in formal courses (see pp. 17–18 below) and in well-planned research projects of regional and national scope. Popular local history surely needs to be judged by its successes, and by what it offers large numbers of people actually and potentially. Although at times wasteful and unpredictable, it promotes a great deal of activity, opens up new subjects, exposes new sources and, most important of all, unearths a flow of new talent. Therefore, in spite of the wide range of standards prevailing in the subject today, we should surely applaud the broad amateur and voluntary base of local history, and not regard it *ipso facto* as embarrassing or regrettable.

In every region of Britain individuals and groups are fired by the desire to learn more about their own social and physical surroundings, and indeed to make their own contribution to knowledge. These activists are, in Kate Tiller's apt phrase, 'local local historians'.[33] They are not too troubled by definitions and philosophical theories such as postmodernism, but 'are all determined to get on with it'.[34] This is the popular, practical and empirical approach to the past which develops out of a natural fascination with aspects of life that, in one sense, are familiar and 'everyday' and, in another sense, are past, elusive and not wholly recoverable. From such activities local people obviously derive pleasure and profit: exploring the dimension of time with its multiple layers, and probing into the lives of those

[32]   To justify the coining of a new term, Dennis Mills unfairly equated all bad practice with *local* history and all good with *community* history: *Getting into Community History* (LPSS, 1995), 7–16. He even implied that 'the typical local historian' still prefers to study 'important' people.

[33]   K. Tiller, *TLH*, 36, 3 (Aug. 2006), 156.

[34]   *Report of the Committee to Review Local History* [Blake report] (London, 1979), pp. 99–108.

who preceded them in a particular place or social context. They enjoy the thrills of unearthing evidence, of questioning and detection, and of using their eyes to delve behind surface appearances. Not infrequently such exploration leads to the production of books and other forms of publication, which find a ready market among both residents and visitors.[35]

It cannot be denied that since World War II professional academics have galvanised the study of local history, mostly at postgraduate level.[36] A major influence for more than half a century has been the Department (now Centre) of English Local History which William Hoskins founded at Leicester University in 1948. Scholars at Leicester, or connected with it, have consistently followed Hoskins in integrating the study of documentary evidence with the landscape. In other words they have attempted to bring together people and place, society and environment, history and archaeology. Often adopting wide chronologies in their research, they have also encouraged new thinking around broad concepts such as community, society, kinship-networks and regions – mostly concentrating on rural contexts before the nineteenth century.[37] Meanwhile about a score of other universities scattered around the country have established centres to foster the deeper study of their own regions, whether rural, industrial or a mixture of the two. In spite of serious funding problems, they have initiated important research, published on a variety of themes, deliberately fostered an interdisciplinary approach, and successfully drawn together professionals and non-professionals.[38]

In more direct contact with the non-academic adult public and with voluntary societies, other specialist local historians have worked in university departments of adult education, the WEA and occasionally in local education authorities. Over more than fifty years these pioneers have done more than any other group in spreading the gospel of practical and participatory history in local villages, towns

---

[35] The only attempt to assess the activities of local historians nationally came in the early 1980s, when David Hayns wrote his reports as Field officer of BALH: see *Field Officer's Report* (BALH, 1982–3, 1983–4).

[36] Local history can of course be part of first degrees in combined studies. Various certificate and diploma courses can also count towards undergraduate degree programmes, as at Kent.

[37] See M. Tranter *et al.*, *English Local History: the Leicester Approach; a Departmental Bibliography and History 1948–1998* (Friends of the Dept of English Local Hist., 1999).

[38] For example, at Birmingham, Central Lancashire, Essex, Exeter, Hertfordshire, Keele, Kent, Lancaster, Leicester, London (Inst. of Historical Research), Manchester Metropolitan, East Anglia, and West of England. The North-East England History Institute (NEEHI) was formed in 1995 by a consortium of five universities associated with Beamish Museum, community organisations and individuals.

and regions but, sadly, the number of appointments in this field has declined markedly since the 1980s (see p. 17).

Finally, it is important to recognise that universities now contain a much larger body of academics who, while not calling themselves local historians, use the local approach in their detailed investigation of major themes.[39] Up to the 1950s, professional historians tended to show interest in the local scene only if it exemplified history at the national level. In the last few decades, however, attitudes have changed enormously. Nowadays, established academics and postgraduate students, trained in national and international history, frequently and deliberately choose to study local subjects and sources. They realise that this approach opens up a vast quarry of evidence and human experience.[40] In reality they are practising local history but would not dream of calling it that, preferring labels such as 'social', economic', 'ecclesiastical' and 'legal' or inventing new concepts such as 'community history' and 'microhistory'. It is satisfying to note that the study of localities is increasingly seen as academically correct, so long as the troublesome title of Local History is avoided with its strong connotations of 'antiquarianism' and 'parochialism'.[41] But looking ahead, I do not doubt that one day a national historian of note will proclaim, 'We're all local historians now'. So far the nearest to that is Patrick Collinson's admission that, 'One of the most striking developments of the late twentieth century in the historiography of Tudor and Stuart England has been its localisation', and Barry Reay's judgement that 'In the end, all history is microhistory'.[42]

In practice localised research done by academics is conducted on three main levels. First, large numbers of places and local records are combed to find detailed evidence for wide-ranging topics. Good examples are Eamon Duffy's work on traditional religion before and after the Reformation, and Steve Hindle's probings

---

[39] Already in 1994 it was calculated that 50 percent of Ph.D.s in modern English history were concerned with local communities and local sources: R. C. Richardson, 'English Local History and American Local History' in *The Changing Face of English Local History* (Ashgate, 2000), p. 198.

[40] 'One obvious reason for the boom in local history is the rise of the Ph.D. industry': John Morrill, *Seventeenth Century Britain, 1603–1714* (Dawson, 1980), p. 124. Typically, Heather Falvey's recent Ph.D. at the University of Warwick was entitled 'Custom, Resistance and Politics: Local Experiences of Improvement in early modern England' (2007).

[41] Is the very term Local History under threat from trendy new coinages like Community History? My guess is that it will outlive most of its competitors, because it is inclusive and conveys a broad if imprecise meaning.

[42] P. Collinson and J. Craig, *The Reformation in English Towns, 1500–1640* (Macmillan, 1998), p. 1; B. Reay, *Microhistories: Demography, Society and Culture in Rural England, 1800–1930* (CUP, 1996), p. xv.

into the workings of the Old Poor Law in the sixteenth to eighteenth centuries.[43] Second, a natural region or administrative county is chosen as a convenient scale for the investigation of significant historical trends. Thus, in his study of the Vale of Berkeley (Glos), David Rollison pondered on the rise of industrial capitalism in a rural setting, while J. M. Neeson used Northamptonshire to assess the loss of common rights as a result of enclosure.[44] Third, a single rural or urban community can be intensively studied for a particular period, especially if it has above-average or exceptional sources which enable an historian to develop a new emphasis or concept. Influential examples are Levine's and Wrightson's work on Whickham (Co. Durham) as it transformed itself into a mining community in the period 1560–1765, and Robert Lutton's challenging study of late-medieval religion and heresy in the parish of Tenterden (Kent).[45] The latter is described by its author as 'an unashamedly local study' yet with nationwide implications for the study of pre-Reformation piety. It is also worth remembering that those who have the courage to call themselves local historians, have also produced work at the same three levels, but from a perspective that is more obviously 'from below'. If the end-result is good history, does it really matter from which direction people are coming? In the meantime, relations are improving in other ways. For instance, the more that research projects are planned deliberately to involve both professionals and part-time volunteers, the more the barriers between them are eroded. In a sense this trend legitimises and democratises scholarship at a crucial time when universities are wrestling with chronic financial shortages.

The teaching of history

While history has never been more popular, serious teaching of the subject is languishing at several levels. Its place in schools is under greater pressure than ever before, mainly because those who shape the National Curriculum do not rate it a 'core subject'. Less and less time is devoted specifically to history from primary level onwards, and its teaching is frequently done by non-specialists. As a result the great majority of children drop the subject at the age of 14 or even

---

[43] E. Duffy, *The Stripping of the Altars* (Yale, 1992); S. Hindle, *On the Parish? The Micropolitics of Poor Relief in Rural England, c.1550–1750* (Clarendon, 2004).

[44] D. Rollinson, *The Local origins of Modern Society: Gloucestershire, 1500–1800* (Routledge, 1992); J. M. Neeson, *Commoners: Common Right, Enclosure and Social Change in England, 1700–1820* (CUP, 1996).

[45] D. Levine and K. Wrightson, *The Making of an Industrial Society: Whickham 1560–1765* (Clarendon, 1991); R. Lutton, *Lollardy and Orthodox Religion in pre-Reformation England: Reconstructing Piety* (Boydell, 2006).

13, and leave school with little connected sense of the past and its relevance to contemporary life, and with no inkling of the way historians work.[46] For a smaller number of pupils, history does remain a popular option at A-level, but even here the emphasis is drifting further from the local approach. Twenty years ago, as part of their A-levels, sixth-formers often visited record offices and undertook practical research on local themes, but such opportunities are fast diminishing as curricula are re-written.[47]

Similarly, changes in public funding mean that the number of adult students is also in decline. Many university departments of adult or continuing education have been closed and their staffs either axed or redeployed internally. Furthermore, those departments which survive, and voluntary bodies such as the WEA, employ fewer well-qualified part-time tutors and sponsor fewer classes of traditional kinds. The emphasis has changed to accumulating credits and to dodgy concepts such as Learning Outcomes and Personal Statements of Learning. From 2008 no funding is available for students who are working at levels equivalent to, or lower than, those for which they are already qualified. All this is particularly unwelcome, given that local history has for generations been one of the most popular forms of adult education, and thousands of students have embraced the subject from all sorts of academic and professional backgrounds. Many communities are therefore left without the guidance which they would previously have had in local classes or participatory projects,[48] and that in turn makes it more difficult for individuals to get on the ladder of progressive learning. These trends in education are particularly regrettable at a time when history has become so generally popular, and when thousands of people yearn to learn more about the past in general, and about their own communities in particular. Although 'edutainment' supplied by the media undoubtedly stimulates curiosity, it is no substitute for sustained teaching and properly designed syllabuses.

All, however, is not gloom. A recent development in higher education may have the potential to revolutionise the practice and status of local history. Wanting to go further, but not wishing to become fully professional, a growing minority of

[46] See Chris Culpin's Medlicott Medal Lecture in *The Historian*, 95 (Autumn 2007), 6–14; also *The Historian*, 96 (Winter 2007), 18–19. The new requirement for children up to the age of 16 to have five hours a week of 'culture' *could* give more space to the teaching of history, but plenty of competition will come, for example, from media studies, music and drama.

[47] See the new syllabuses for A-level History produced in 2007 by the three exam boards in England: Edexcel, OCR and AQA.

[48] To some extent this vacuum is now being filled by outreach activities, including training courses, organised by record offices – which are themselves under pressure to create income.

activists of all ages and backgrounds now seek formal historical training, and are willing to invest money and spare time to acquire it.[49] They enroll for a shifting variety of certificates, diplomas, first degrees and higher degrees dealing with various aspects of local and regional history (and other closely related subjects such as demographic, economic and landscape history). Higher education of this sort is on offer from over fifty different academic institutions across the country, and is also available online.[50] Indeed, over the years these students tend to progress from one kind of course to another, and their projects, dissertations and theses steadily increase the volume and quality of local historical knowledge. After undergoing such training, which may be on a part-time basis over ten or more years, some of these individuals remain committed to the subject and form an important middle group between full-time academics and 'local local historians'. Not only are they often compulsive researchers who contribute to a variety of publications, but increasingly they transmit their enthusiasm to others as freelance lecturers and as leading members of local societies.[51]

In the light of this development, some critics assert that local history is now 'too much of a top-down driven activity ... obsessed with courses and qualifications'.[52] In fact, the proliferation of examined courses at different levels has been a direct response to genuine outside pressure, because most local historians want to learn more and deepen their involvement in a subject which fascinates them. They are not content to stand still. Regrettably, however, some courses are now being withdrawn, and the overall provision of this kind of higher education has peaked since the 1990s. The reasons appear to include fewer applicants, rising fees, internal staff shortages and financial cuts imposed by the ever-changing priorities of central government.[53]

---

[49]   Such activists do not necessarily have relevant backgrounds: frequently they are graduates in other disciplines such as English or the sciences; a few have no formal qualifications but are simply driven by their interest in history.

[50]   For example, online courses are offered by the universities of Oxford and Central Lancashire.

[51]   Indeed, at meetings of activists (for example, at seminars, symposia and conferences) it is often difficult to distinguish full-timers from part-timers, academics from lay people. What really matters on these occasions is the quality of the history being discussed, not the precise status of each contributor.

[52]   *Local History News*, 84 (Summer 2007), 17.

[53]   Kate Tiller's valuable list of all courses leading to qualifications in Local History and related subjects can be found on www.uall.ac.uk. See also Robert Howard's article in *LHM*, May/June 2008, 14.

Regional history

A very important concept, especially among professionals, is Regional History which emphasises that previous generations did indeed have horizons wider than the parish, manor or town.[54] For centuries people of all social levels, for a whole variety of personal, economic and cultural reasons, walked and rode beyond their local boundaries, and thereby forged broader links, allegiances and affinities (Fig. 2, p. 11). Although some historians have defined regions by reference to permanent geographical features such as watersheds and major rivers, it becomes clearer by the day that regions are definable in many different ways. They can coalesce temporarily and then dissolve, overlap in complicated ways, vary greatly in size, and need not have any connection with administrative boundaries. If a river valley, for example, is seen in one sense as a boundary, in another sense it can be viewed as an entity in itself. Examples of larger-scale regions postulated by historians have included the economic hinterlands of great cities, areas dominated by particular heavy industries, and distinctive countrysides with their own characteristic types of farming and land-use. On a smaller scale, other scholars have talked of 'neighbourhoods' centring on the households of particular landlords, of 'societies' defined by the dominance of certain 'core' families, and of nonconformist congregations 'gathered' from miles around. Furthermore, regions and sub-regions can be defined by reference to fiction and other forms of literature, or in purely personal terms which vary over time according to factors like wealth, education, leisure, friendship and the ability to travel.[55] As A. J. Pollard has memorably expressed it, 'The region in history, like Aristotle's womb and Cuthbert's remains, wanders'.[56] The great justification of this approach is that it forces us to think much more carefully about the definition of 'communities' and 'boundaries', and about the characteristics which linked and

---

[54] Awareness of English regionalism has been stimulated by the appearance of *Northern History* (founded 1966), *Midland History* (1971) and *Southern History* (1981). Nevertheless, such journals contain many studies of individual communities, both towns and rural parishes. Longman's series of Regional Histories was never completed; although individual volumes contained much useful work, the series was marred by its arbitrary definition of regions and an equally arbitrary division of history at AD 1000.

[55] C. Phythian-Adams (ed.), *Societies, Culture and Kinship, 1580–1850: Cultural Provinces in English Local History* (Leicester UP, 1996); S. Trezise, *The West Country as a Literary Invention: Putting Fiction in its Place* (Univ. of Exeter Press, 2000); A. R. H. Baker and M. Billinge (eds), *Geographies of England: The North-South Divide, Imagined and Material* (CUP, 2004).

[56] A. J. Pollard in C. D. Liddy and R. H. Britnell (eds), *North-east England in the Later Middle Ages* (Boydell, 2005), p. 12.

divided people in the past. By doing so, it provides an important connection between local and national history.[57]

Confusion arises when the promoters of regional history, terrified by anything which smacks of parochialism, appear to condemn totally the study of basic localities such as villages and towns, parishes and townships. Like it or not, such histories will continue to be written by both lay people and professionals – because those units were historically real, created their own administrative records, and can be studied manageably. Villages and towns have undeniably retained their importance and relevance across the centuries. Indeed, recent research has re-emphasised the importance of the parish in human consciousness, and the writing of a parish history is an acknowledgement that a community of some kind still exists today.[58] Of course, everything possible should be done to ensure that these studies are critical and comparative, and that they always connect with an outside world. Today nobody really doubts 'that local studies should be set in the wider context of the neighbourhood'.[59] There are, after all, some good models to emulate. Where would English history now be without the classic studies of Myddle, Terling, Havering, Whickham, Morebath, Colyton and Elmdon, each of which was put into a broader setting?[60] Admittedly these were written by academic specialists, are not concerned with major towns and mostly stop short of the nineteenth century. However, none of them is in any sense final because they can be questioned, modified and even replaced. Their great value lies in the stimulus which they can give both to local studies *and* to national history, to professionals *and* amateurs.[61]

---

[57]   See the series on 'Regions and Regionalism in History', published by the AHRC Centre for North-East England History (NEEHI), and another called 'Explorations in Local and Regional History' published by the University of Hertfordshire Press, which is a relaunch of 'Occasional Papers' previously published by the University of Leicester.

[58]   For example, Hindle, *On the Parish?* (2004); K. Snell, *Parish and Belonging: Community, Identity and Welfare in England and Wales, 1700–1950* (Cambridge, 2006).

[59]   D. Hey in *TLH*, 28, 2 (May 1998), 123.

[60]   D. G. Hey, *An English Rural Community: Myddle under the Tudors and Stuarts* (Leicester UP, 1974); K. Wrightson and D. Levine, *Poverty and Piety in an English Village: Terling, 1525–1700* (Clarendon, 1999); M. K. McIntosh, *A Community Transformed: The Manor and Liberty of Havering, 1500–1620* (CUP, 1991); D. Levine and K. Wrightson, *The Making of an Industrial Society: Whickham, 1560–1765* (Oxford, 1991); P. Sharpe, *Population and Society in an East Devon Parish: Reproducing Colyton, 1540–1840* (Univ. of Exeter Press, 2002); Jean Robin, *Elmdon: Continuity and Change in a North-west Essex Village, 1861–1964* (CUP, 1980).

[61]   John Beckett writes of such studies giving relatively obscure communities 'celebrity status' among historians, while local people may have known nothing of the research then or even later: *Writing Local History*, p. 197. This comment highlights the importance of effective voluntary societies which bridge the gap between professionals and amateurs.

Postscript

The personal relationship between local and other historians raises a deeper philosophical problem concerning the 'particular' and 'general'. In 1965, in defence of local history, W. G. Hoskins quoted William Blake's maxim that 'To generalize is to be an idiot; to particularize is the alone distinction of merit'. In so doing he was doubtless showing his characteristic relish for the lives of ordinary people, particularly the yeomen and shopkeepers who were his ancestors.[62] However, the quotation could be taken to imply that facts are more important than generalisations: our job, antiquarian rather than historical, is to enjoy the piling up of information without worrying about its broader significance. This seemed confirmed more recently when another distinguished historian, Patrick Collinson, complained that 'the difficulty with local and regional history is that everywhere is different, so that the subject by its very nature courts particularism and resists treatment on a general or national scale'.[63] With respect, I would like to suggest that these remarks in truth reveal both the problem and the answer.

Local history is indeed full of fascinating 'particulars', probably more so than any other form of history except biography, and in the last resort every human community is inescapably unique. The more we know about local life, the more varied, intricate and complicated it becomes. But if we are to make any sense of local history, we must acknowledge that 'some places are less different than others'.[64] We are impelled to seek patterns of similarity and contrast, to attempt broader judgements and generalisations, and to relate our work to models of human development produced by other specialists such as anthropologists and social scientists. After all, as Pat Hudson memorably put it, we are embarked on 'the use of small-scale research to ask, and to answer, big questions'.[65] In the reverse direction, national historians should not be afraid to face the particularism of local history, which is always refining or undermining their broader sweeps of judgement. The purpose of comparison and generalisation is to establish what was normal in the past, and what was unusual or even unique. That, in Margaret Spufford's words, is the problem that 'bedevils or should bedevil all local historians'.[66] If all

---

[62] Hoskins, *Provincial England: Essays in Social and Economic History* (Macmillan, 1962), p. v; Chris Lewis pointed out the irony that Hoskins undermined Blake's opinion 'with every word that he has written' (*Particular Places*, p. 45).

[63] Patrick Collinson, *The Birthpangs of Protestant England* (Macmillan, 1989), p. 49.

[64] Lewis, *Particular Places*, p. 35.

[65] P. Hudson, *FACH*, 2.1 (May 1999), 5.

[66] M. Spufford, 'The total history of village communities', *TLH*, 10, 8 (Nov. 1973), 400.

this makes the job of the local historian more demanding, it does however offer a further prize of immense worth.

The great virtue of local history is that it resists fragmentation and over-specialisation, and encourages an interdisciplinary and participatory approach. Local historians, as Hoskins argued in a medical analogy, are more like general practitioners than consultants, prepared to show the connectedness of things and to follow where evidence leads. They are not inclined to divide their subject up into short arbitrary periods and small thematic specialisations or 'tunnels', a process which Keith Wrightson has lamented as 'a trend towards chronological, thematic and conceptual enclosure'.[67] We all know that concepts like 'social man' and 'economic man' are unreal abstractions, and that our proper task is to reconstruct human lives as sympathetically and completely as possible, given the evidence to hand. As local history becomes steadily more critical and comparative (not necessarily professional), one hopes that it will be seen as spearheading the fight against endless subdivision and over-specialisation. Surely, as Charles Phythian-Adams predicted in 1993, it is fast becoming 'one of the most promising and exciting growth-points in the discipline of history as a whole'.[68] Although it may be some time before our successors see the final shape of a new landscape in which the 'local' and 'regional' have as much prominence as the 'national' and 'international', the tectonic plates of history are undoubtedly shifting.

---

[67] W. G. Hoskins, *English Local History: The Past and the Future* (Leicester UP, 1966), p. 21; K. Wrightson, 'The Enclosure of English Social History', *Rural History*, 1, 1 (April 1990), 80.

[68] Phythian-Adams (ed.), *Societies, Culture and Kinship,* p. xii.

RESEARCH

1. CHOOSE SUBJECT to investigate (adjusting the three dimensions of theme, place and period); be prepared to revise as work proceeds.

2. FIND SOURCES AND EVIDENCE

books & articles	primary documents	material evidence	oral evidence
references	transcribing	fieldwork	transcribing
more reading	abstracts, extracts	maps	

3. AMASS AND CONTROL INFORMATION
Notes, transcripts, facsimiles and references stored in files, card-indexes, databases, spreadsheets, etc.

4. ANALYSE EVIDENCE, both words and numbers, by using carefully designed forms, spreadsheets, etc.; thereby creating new evidence and generalisations.

5. RE-READ AND SORT all evidence before writing; reject that which is inessential.

6. QUESTION SOURCES to weigh their relative strengths and weaknesses.

7. SYNTHESISE and INTERPRET: survey evidence in the light of other historians' work (secondary sources), and think out the historical argument to be presented. This process should have begun at the start, but climaxes here as one prepares to write.

> Constantly question and compare the primary and secondary evidence, as it accumulates.
>
> Continue to look for new evidence and comparative studies.
>
> Talk to other historians.

WRITING

8. WRITE PLAN OF TEXT, in skeletal form, establishing order of presentation (chapters, sub-headings, etc.) and main twists and turns of argument.

9. WRITE FIRST DRAFT: keep the prose flowing by writing quickly; amendments, improvements and references can be added later.

10. RE-DRAFT as many times as necessary; this often involves substantial alteration and compression. Seek the criticism of others.

11. PREPARE ALL PLATES, FIGURES, MAPS, etc. with explanatory captions.

12. PUBLISH: deal with editors, printers and publishers, or be your own desk-top publisher.

Figure 3. Processes of research and writing: a summary.

2

The challenge of writing

T HIS BOOK is intended for those who find themselves tempted or expected
to write history, especially local and regional history, but who for various
reasons are held back by hesitations and doubts. It is aimed at those who enjoy
research but have never committed their ideas to print, at those who have been
through the academic mill and want to put their work into published form, and
at the burgeoning numbers of students who are required to write essays, dissertations and theses.[1] The message is simple. Accept the challenge of writing history
– but take the task very seriously. Admittedly, encouragement of this kind runs
the risk of criticism from at least two directions. Beginners may object to advice
which to them seems pedantic and over-demanding, while those with academic
training are easily annoyed by an approach which may appear populist and not
sufficiently critical. My firm belief, nevertheless, is that by deliberately focusing
on the fundamental processes of research and writing, we can all achieve higher
standards whether we be novices, students or professionals.

The fact that this book, originally written in 1981, has sold thousands of copies
and now has had to be revised for a second time, convinces me that more people
than ever are anxious to write history, and to write it better. Behind this growth are
factors such as increased leisure (at least for some), longer retirement, the boom in
family history, new educational qualifications from certificates to higher degrees,
and the extraordinary amount of history (good and bad) in the media. We now
seem less intimidated by the *thought* of writing, partly because of the practical
advantages offered by modern computers, digitised images, desk-top publishing
and the seething cauldron of the internet. But of course computers do not create

---

[1] Local history may be the subject, solely or partly, of dissertations at various academic
levels. It features not only in those written for higher degrees (M.Phil., Ph.D., etc.), but also
forms a part of many first-degree courses. Unfortunately the number of A-level students
presenting dissertations in local history has declined in recent years.

good history by themselves. While modern technology has made our work easier in several senses, especially in the storage, indexing and analysis of huge amounts of miscellaneous data, it has made even harder the task of writing well. A sentence written by three academics in a recent journal makes the point well enough: 'Although the notion of pro-adult-male gender bias in resource allocation in nineteenth-century households is in keeping with contemporary anecdotal evidence, recent anthropometric work has struggled to identify a correlation.'[2] Tormented prose of this kind shows that the value of clear and humane writing never enters the minds of many academically well-qualified people. It is also ignored in new manuals on 'computing and history'. To their authors, 'style' means no more than formatting the layout of documents.

With the exception of students at school and university, whose written work is not intended for publication, most people who write about history hope to see their efforts in print. However, they are often confused by the fact that published history takes many different forms ranging from 'academic' to 'popular', and they are not sure where to pitch their own contributions. At one end of the scale, needing major commitments of time and effort, are full-blown specialist books or monographs, articles in hundreds of peer-reviewed journals (regional, national and international), conference proceedings, *festschriften* in honour of distinguished scholars, edited sources and academic reviews.[3] Less intimidating at the other end of the scale are the newsletters of local societies, guide-books, collections of historical photographs and contributions to newspapers and glossy commercial magazines. Those who lack experience or special training are probably best advised to start by tackling something which is limited and manageable. A few hours in a local-studies or university library will reveal the range of outlets available. In particular one will soon identify the periodicals which abound in all counties and regions, the balance of their contents, and what they require of writers submitting contributions.

Faced with so many outlets, beginners rightly ask: for whom are we writing, or for whom *should* we write? To an extent the answer depends on the medium with which they feel most comfortable. An article in a 'learned' journal will be written for people with a specialised interest, while a newspaper article or an historical

---

[2] *Local Population Studies*, 79 (Autumn 2007), 68.
[3] Theses and dissertations are regarded as 'unpublished' because only a few copies are produced. It is often highly desirable that studies of this sort be subsequently reworked as books or articles. Details of completed theses and dissertations can be found in some journals, e.g. *Urban History*. The Institute of Historical Research (Univ. of London) publishes an annual *Historical Research for Higher Degrees in the UK* (listing work completed and in progress).

trail will be aimed at a more mixed and general audience. But, because all such groups overlap, the differences in writing should be of degree only, not of kind: they concern the length and elaboration of the text, and the extent of technicalities such as footnotes and bibliographies. They should not involve changes in the actual style of writing which in its clarity, coherence and elegance should always be capable of appealing to the widest possible audience. As R. M. Robbins wrote in 1988, 'the more people read a piece of published work, the better … The audience, or the readership, that we seek must be the largest that the subject can possibly be made to interest.' More recently, fellows of the Royal Historical Society have been reminded that 'the freedom of writing for a wider audience is exhilarating'.[4] Furthermore, all kinds of written history should assume interest and intelligence on the part of readers, but not necessarily prior knowledge and experience. Some of our most eminent historians write not only for their colleagues and peers (important though that is, mainly through established journals), but also find time to communicate with the general public through newspaper articles, reviews, radio and television. They may be partly motivated by tasty fees, but at the same time are acknowledging a broader educational responsibility felt towards their contemporaries.

When one consciously aims at a wide readership, the writing of history is certainly not easy. An obvious proof today is that good research is often divorced from good writing, and *vice versa*. On the one hand, many writers do not communicate their thoughts with sufficient directness and lucidity. Consequently their readers have to struggle through passages several times before getting even the gist. This failing can be found in all kinds of writing, but is very common in the work of academics and bureaucrats. On the other hand, a lot of writing relies on the uncritical collection and chronological arrangement of historical facts, snippets and quotations. This offence must be laid at the door, almost exclusively, of amateur local historians. Four short examples will illustrate the differences.[5]

The first two were written by academics of some eminence, one in the 1970s and the other in 2006. The first was discussing an important problem familiar to all practising historians, the difficulty of using two or more documents which *may* be referring to the same historical individual. The second was trying to explain a major characteristic of towns in the late Victorian and Edwardian period.

From this claim, if it stands, it follows that historical existence claims,

---

[4]   *Antiqs Jour.*, lxviii, pt 1 (1988), 3–4; *RHS Newsletter* (Autumn/Winter 2006), 7. It is, of course, interesting that historians should need to be reminded of these truths!

[5]   References have been omitted for diplomatic reasons.

historical predicate corroboration and the growth of historical knowledge in general, presuppose historical record linkage.

Degenerationism as a fully fledged ideological ensemble, emphasizing difference and the commonsensical naturalness of self-replicating urban social segregation, attained its zenith between 1880 and 1914.

One can understand how educated people may produce such foggy verbosity in preliminary drafts, but how can they in good conscience submit it for publication? How can writing of this sort be accepted by editors and publishers, as happened in the two cases above? Is it deliberately done to flaunt esoteric learning and to deter 'the great unwashed'? We are surely forced to conclude that something is wrong not only with our standards of basic education, but also with the way in which academics are trained (or not trained) to turn their thoughts into publishable prose.[6] Of course, the complexities of history inevitably demand effort of both writer and reader, but the historian's use of language should never be allowed to compound those difficulties.

The next two examples are utterly different in flavour, and were written by well-meaning enthusiasts who wanted to contribute to the history of their own communities:

For many years I have been collecting snippets of history and doing research on [Ambridge]. The aim of this publication has been to put this all together to tell the story … over the centuries.

It seemed such a pity to have all these bits and pieces lying about, so I decided to put them in chronological order.

These sad confessions remind us of the plight of many writers and published authors. The burgeoning popularity of the subject means that an ever-increasing number of people amass information on their chosen topics but unfortunately make little creative use of it. They assume that their readers only want to be diverted by quaint facts and colourful anecdotes, dutifully arranged in chrono-logical order. Some of these writers have genuine critical and literary ability, but have never been helped sufficiently to write or to face the challenges of evidence

6   As editor of *The Local Historian* for eight years, I soon got used to receiving articles from academics which contained frequent stylistic and grammatical errors, as well as elementary spelling mistakes. The present incumbent of that seat tells me that not much has changed!

and historical debate. It is now easier than ever before to be overwhelmed and buried by the information one finds, and therefore to regard the mechanical accumulation of so-called 'facts' as *the* purpose of history.

The danger, therefore, is that writers of history often find themselves torn between two false ideals – academic incomprehensibility and undemanding readability. The situation is made worse by those publishers who abuse the popular appeal of the subject by commissioning inadequate books from ill-prepared authors.[7] Editors of some journals must also accept their share of blame.[8] In every area of history and in every British region, we see the publication of badly prepared and inferior history, which in turn makes it harder for others to teach the subject effectively. Although professionals regularly castigate amateur historians for their myopic antiquarianism, the latter are surprisingly reluctant to criticise professionals for their frequent abuse of language. In fact, both faults are serious and fundamental. And another danger has caught up with us in recent decades, for the computing revolution is already creating a new kind of antiquarianism with its own special jargon and obtuseness of language. The point is made in this fairly typical sentence published in 2006: 'Other facilities will include image zooming, rotation and download in high resolution TIF and PNG format and the download of a selection of tables in XLS and other formats.'

But does this range of written standards matter greatly when fine works of general and local history are published quite often (see below, Appendix 16)? My answer is 'yes', for a variety of reasons. First, highly variable standards of writing condemn local history in the eyes of too many people. This is one reason why, for example, many academics dismiss local history as hopelessly antiquarian and parochial.[9] Second, I do not believe that such standards are inevitable for all time and can never be raised. Local history need not be written obscurely or uncritically, especially if the virtues of structured research and conscientious writing are taught side-by-side. The third and last reason is the most important. Because local history is about the supposedly 'ordinary' people who form the vast majority of society at any period, and therefore has an educational and social importance, we who profess the subject should value clear, well-researched writing particularly highly. We should feel no shame in making our work accessible to the largest possible

---

[7]   For example, see Joan Dils's powerful but polite review of just such an unsatisfactory publication in *TLH* 38, 3 (Aug. 2008), 233.

[8]   Authors, quite naturally, have a possessive attitude to their own prose, but they can react very differently to changes proposed by editors. Some refuse to acknowledge their own weaknesses and resent the interference while others, equally uncritically, accept every suggestion with a cheerful lack of concern.

[9]   J. D. Marshall, 'The antiquarian heresy', *JORALS*, 15, 2 (1995), 49–54.

readership. Indeed, ours is a very special branch of history which attracts huge numbers of people, and gives rise to a voluminous literature which librarians and booksellers, in their embarrassment, usually classify as 'British Topography' or 'Local Interest'.[10] No other subject in the academic spectrum can so easily bridge the gulf between academics and non-professionals. In fact it frequently annihilates that gulf because experts turn out to have had no special training in the local approach, and lay people are able to contribute special knowledge and skills of their own. Could anything be more beneficial in an age when the study of history continues to fragment and to become ever more specialised?

[10] Biography, family history and military history are also extremely popular. However, if we include all forms of published local history (e.g. in church guides, historical trails, local newspapers, commercial county magazines, parish magazines and now online), it is probably the most widely read.

3

Choosing a subject

O NE of the most important tasks facing us as would-be writers is so elementary that it is commonly overlooked: we must carefully define a subject for research. This choice is influenced by several factors such as our existing knowledge, our family and educational background, the aspects of life which interest us most and, of course, the availability of sources. With a clearly measured objective, however large or small, we can concentrate attention more effectively and recognise the relevance and potential of evidence as it is found. Otherwise it is easy to waste time, sometimes a lifetime, vaguely enjoying the collection of facts and snippets, but not thinking about their relative value in a defined project. It should also be recognised that subjects may have to be re-defined or at least modified, as new evidence is discovered. Some topics lead to the uncovering of abundant sources, in which case the terms of reference may have to be reduced; conversely other topics reveal an embarrassing lack of evidence, and therefore the coverage may need widening.[1]

The main stimulus in choosing a subject is *not* a full appreciation of the relevant sources. We cannot possibly know all the evidence before we start, though we hope to know enough to make it seem worthwhile. The unavoidable starting-point must be a genuine interest in some aspect of life which we believe is significant. This means that we must probe our own motives with care, and ask why we are attracted to a particular slice of history. Is there a danger that our fascination with bits of evidence or with the surface glamour of certain historical events will divert us from the main task of re-creating something worthwhile from the past? Of course, in any historical project we must have sources, and the discovery of a

---

[1] But these are not invariable rules. A small body of evidence can be made, with ingenuity, to tell a fascinating human story. For example, Eileen Power's famous essay on 'Thomas Paycocke of Coggeshall' was based on no more than three pieces of evidence, Paycocke's will, house and memorial brass: *Medieval People* (Methuen, 1924).

cache of documents has frequently led to distinguished writing, but evidence is there to be used and thereby transformed into original, reasoned history.

In practice our interest should focus on a question, a problem or an area of uncertainty which nobody has tackled before. This is why professional historians constantly plead for local history to be 'question-led' and 'issue-driven'. In other words, we must try to find an historical space which we can claim as our own. Yet even here, we will always find points of contact with what other historians have already done and written before us. In that sense, no piece of research is ever divorced from existing knowledge, and history does not simply accumulate or pile up. Woe betide historians who forget this, and write as though they were in a vacuum. In the words of Keith Wrightson, 'No historian writes a book alone'.[2] Looked at more realistically, therefore, our wish may be to fill certain gaps in the record, or to show dissatisfaction with the existing state of knowledge, and thus contribute to a current debate or controversy.

On narrowing down the options, we soon find that three dimensions have to be defined and adjusted to each other. They are THEME, PLACE and TIME. In order to satisfy ourselves and exploit our evidence, we must decide on a particular theme of human history, in a particular area, over a certain length of time. Of course the number of possible variations is infinite, and we have an amazing plurality of approaches to choose from. This is why local history shades imperceptibly into many other forms of history, and why we should never waste time arguing that local history is an independent discipline. Given the difficulty of defining a topic for research, the three dimensions mentioned above are worth discussing individually. Quite deliberately, we shall begin with 'theme', even though for many local historians 'place' comes first and is totally unnegotiable!

Theme

The study of local and regional history can be seen as containing eight broadly distinct yet overlapping areas of interest.[3] Starting with our physical environment and material culture and working towards higher social and personal issues, they are:

- **Landscape history (or topography)** – rocks, soils, relief and drainage; patterns of human settlement; the built environment, both vernacular

---

2 K. Wrightson, *English Society, 1580–1680* (Hutchinson, 1982), p. 9.

3 This analysis may be worth comparing with Alan Macfarlane's more elaborate 'Potentials and Pitfalls of Local History', based on a lecture given at Homerton College in 1990 <alanmacfarlane.com>.

and élite; field-systems and land-use; natural and man-made boundaries; communications by land and water; the growth of towns, ports and conurbations; industrial landscapes, etc.

- **Population history (or demography)** – courtship and marriage; birth rates; illnesses and injury; medicine and surgery; life expectancy; mortality crises and causes of death; networks of family and kin; stability and mobility; emigration and immigration, etc.
- **Economic history** – property and landholding; agricultural trends; food and diet; retailing, crafts and industries; transport systems; prices, wages and working routines; living standards; debt, credit and banking; individual firms and entrepreneurs; consumerism, etc.
- **Social history** – gradations of income and wealth; social status and class; absolute and relative poverty; the place of women and children; ethnicity and minority groups; welfare and charity; the role of voluntary bodies; deference and defiance; suburban values, etc.
- **Political history** – governing élites; secular and ecclesiastical forms of administration; subordinate officials; popular politics and participation; law, order and policing; elections and parties; links with national government; the influence of individuals, etc.
- **Cultural history** – education and literacy; custom and customary events; informal and commercialised leisure; sport and physical recreation; scope for travel; music, dancing and drama; the applied and pure arts, etc.
- **Religious history** – public worship and liturgy; private prayer, Bible reading and devotions; doctrines and beliefs; lay and clerical relations; sectarian debate and conflict; superstition and witchcraft; religious indifference and agnosticism, etc.
- **Personal history (or biography)** – family background and education; personal character, practical and social skills; moral standards; contemporary reputation; religious or philosophical allegiances; individual achievements, etc.[4]

Writers of traditional parish and county histories touched on most of these areas, and a few brave souls still today attempt the same broad-brush approach.

---

[4] Many regard biography as concerned only with the lives of prominent people such as statesmen, military commanders and great writers. The evidence for humbler lives at the local level is usually much thinner, but the opportunities which present themselves should be all the more eagerly exploited. An excellent example is C. Dyer, 'A Suffolk farmer in the fifteenth century', *Agric. Hist. Rev.*, 55, pt 1 (2007).

Nevertheless, most of us today set ourselves far more limited objectives which seem manageable in the time available. (Even so, we normally complain that the work has turned out to be more complicated than we anticipated, and that we have been diverted into quite unforeseen directions!) In practice, we tend to concentrate on those themes of history which excite us most. For example, someone interested in religious history may choose to focus on an individual nonconformist sect like Primitive Methodism or Quakerism, or simply on the fortunes of a single chapel and congregation. Others choose subjects because of their seeming importance at a particular period, such as the formation of turnpike trusts in the eighteenth century or the spread of chain-stores in late nineteenth-century towns. The fundamental motivation is not so much a fascination with bits of evidence as the desire to answer intriguing questions. Indeed, themes may be chosen for which the evidence is relatively meagre or difficult to interpret but, even if questions remain unanswered or only partially answered, they are worth raising as a contribution to historical debate. Incidentally, it would be extremely helpful if every local historical society set about the task of identifying and substantiating the outstanding themes of its area's history, but this does not happen very often.

The range of subjects investigated by local historians has expanded greatly in the past fifty years, to cover virtually every aspect of human life. A trawl through recent journals will soon reveal this diversity. For instance the twice-yearly *Birmingham Historian*, which was started in 1987 and is almost entirely concerned with local history since 1750, has examined an extraordinary array of topics including temperance, crime, prostitution, housing, dialect, religion, local manufactures and riots. It has even carried articles on a crossing-keeper's seat beside a major road and on the installation of a urinal.[5] On a general plane, one can probably say that today's most fashionable areas of study include demography, family life, the role of women, poverty, charity, ethnic minorities, medicine, transport, entertainment and sport, crime and policing. Some of the subjects now probed by local historians are already academic specialisations in their own right with their own experts, textbooks, societies and journals. This gives us the opportunity of acquiring important background information, of reading comparative studies and thereby of appreciating where gaps wait to be exploited.[6] Amateurs now follow the lead of professionals in wanting to tackle subjects which have defined limits and are both manageable and of current interest. After all, some of the most enthusiastic

---

[5] *The Birmingham Historian*, 29 (winter, 2006), contains index of vols 1–28.

[6] Postgraduate courses often demand a 'literature review' before research into primary sources is begun. Subject indexes in major publications are a vital aid when particular themes are being explored (see p. 51).

and active students of local history have taken up the subject in retirement, and they are well aware that time has its limits.

However, as has been hinted before, a great danger lies in too much speciali-sation. Academic divisions do not reflect the past itself, but are caused by the emphasis which professionals put upon particular themes. They are what J. H. Hexter many years ago called 'tunnel history'.[7] Our task as local historians, admittedly within narrower geographical limits, is to provide a view of the past which is as broad and synoptic as we can make it. In these days of ever-increasing fragmentation, we put the emphasis on integration and synthesis (see above, p. 22). Certainly we will draw on the work of specialists, read their journals and even contribute to them, but our concern with the life of whole communities and their constituent families normally gives us a more integrative and reconciling role. For example, the study of an agricultural estate in the eighteenth century may include a discussion of local population trends, the variable distribution of wealth, the exercise of political power, the control of religious denominations and the changing tastes of the well-to-do. Whatever the chosen topic, we as local historians want to relate it to the life of the wider community in a way which does not attract specialists snuffling along contentedly in their narrow tunnels.

To develop the local dimension of history more deeply, a small number of professional writers in the 1970s attempted to write 'total history'. This was not the approach adopted in the traditional parish or town history, which usually ranged disparately over long periods. On the contrary it was an attempt to show how a community worked *as a whole*, and how its constituent parts interwove in the complex texture of local life. The aim, however impossible it sounds (and in the last resort it *is* impossible because of incomplete evidence), was to study 'life ... in its entirety'.[8] In practice such an ambitious task can only be attempted where above-average records survive. An early example published in 1974 was Margaret Spufford's *Contrasting Communities*, in which she aimed at the total history of three separate Cambridgeshire parishes during the Tudor and Stuart period. In this pioneering study the increase of breadth is clear enough yet some aspects of life, for example leisure, recreation, crime and political behaviour, are still missing. While Alan Macfarlane saw twelve categories of record as central to reconstituting a local community, including parish registers, wills and court rolls, Barry Stapleton showed that it was possible to weave together personal information from over seventy classes of record.[9]

---

[7]   J. H. Hexter, *Reappraisals in History* (Longman, 1961), pp. 194–5.

[8]   M. Spufford, 'The total history of village communities', *TLH*, 10, 8 (1973), 398.

[9]   A. Macfarlane, *Reconstructing Historical Communities* (CUP, 1977), pp. 42–80;

Not surprisingly, the quest for 'total history' was only partially successful. Striving to cover every possible dimension of local life is a herculean task and very difficult to organise, even for a short period. More importantly, this broad and detailed approach has not revolutionised the *writing* of history. Even if we achieve a thematic coverage which is close to total, and use powerful computers to analyse vast amounts of evidence, our final interpretations are still generalising and therefore selective. Perhaps the most remarkable monument to this phase of local history is 'Records of an English Village, 1375–1854' constructed for the Essex parish of Earl's Colne. Over the period 1971–83 Alan Macfarlane and a team working at Cambridge collected every source they could find for this parish, and created a massive database of 800MB which is now online and constitutes a superb teaching resource.[10] Although the objective of 'total history' is now mentioned much less often than in the 1970s, it has certainly encouraged local historians to investigate the past more holistically. Perhaps it is best regarded, not so much as an achievable goal, but as a worthwhile aspiration and attitude of mind.

Most local history is published in the form of parish and town histories, academic monographs and articles in national and local journals, but other smaller-scale opportunities present themselves. For instance, it is currently fashionable to publish collections of historical photographs and postcards from the later nineteenth-century onwards. This approach is fully justified when photographs are carefully chosen for their historical, architectural or personal significance, and when the accompanying captions or texts give adequate information about date, place, people and event. Too often, however, such publications are overloaded with images of poor quality and questionable value, or are not sufficiently explained or interpreted. Other openings exist for the writing (or rewriting) of guides to parish churches, places of nonconformist worship and other accessible historical buildings and sites.[11]

To supplement the useful work of accredited guides who lead parties of visitors around their areas, many more well-written and attractively published trails are also needed to identify routes in both town and countryside which are worth exploring – whether on foot, by bicycle or even by car. They should not only draw attention to physical features which are commonly overlooked, large and small,

---

B. Stapleton, 'Sources for the study of a local community from the sixteenth to the mid-nineteenth century', *JORALS*, 4, 2 (1984), 1–26.

[10]   <alanmacfarlane.com>. This great quarry has been recently exploited in H. R. French and R. W. Hoyle, *The Character of Rural Society: Earl's Colne, 1550–1750* (Manchester UP, 2007).

[11]   The Churches Conservation Trust (formerly the Redundant Churches Fund) has been publishing useful guides to churches since the 1970s.

but always emphasise their historical context and human significance.[12] One of the most exciting examples I have ever read is a 'walking tour' appended to one of William Fishman's books on the East End of London. In a small area around the Mile End Road, he identified fifteen points of interest including the site of the Sidney Street siege of 1911, Fulbourne Street where in 1907 the Russian Social Democratic Labour Party held meetings attended by Lenin, Trotsky and Stalin, and the spot where in 1865 William Booth started the work of the Salvation Army.[13] If we are to escape from the present over-concentration on major monuments,[14] and stop neglecting the less obvious and more vulnerable history which is always and everywhere around us, many more such aids will have to be published and kept up-to-date for the benefit of both visitors and residents (including some specifically for children). Work of this kind, which is well within the capabilities of the most energetic voluntary societies, sometimes receives the active encouragement and financial support of local authorities, voluntary societies and charitable trusts.[15]

Finally, while on the subject of themes worthy of study, we must surely recognise that excellent opportunities beckon at the expanding frontier of contemporary and very recent history. Why, for example, do not more local historians turn their attention to the relentless march of suburbanisation from the 1930s onwards and particularly after 1945? This involves far more than mapping the growth of semi-detached houses in cul-de-sacs. The suburban way of life stands for new personal, family and social ambitions which have deeply influenced our national life and are still transforming our large cities, smaller towns and, increasingly, the rural scene. Equally, ought we not to be charting the extraordinary changes which have taken place in Britain's religious life since the 1960s, with the decline of traditional denominations, the emergence of new forms of worship both Christian and non-Christian, and the spread of agnosticism and religious indifference? It

---

[12] A good example is provided by 'History Footsteps', an initiative of the Victoria County History aimed at schools; it covers 'The Slavery Trail' around Bristol, the theme of travel in a Wiltshire village (Codford), and the life of an estate village in E. Yorks (Warter). 'Walk and Explore' is a similar initiative organised by the Children's Society; it encourages children to explore towns on foot, and in its first year (2007) claimed 3,000 participants, each of whom was given an information pack and maps. The BBC's new History Trails show the potential of trails published online.

[13] W. J. Fishman, *The Streets of East London* (Duckworth, 1979), pp. 136–7.

[14] Previously this might have been called the 'English Heritage or National Trust syndrome', but that would now be unfair as both organisations are deliberately widening their social coverage.

[15] In North Kesteven (Lincs) an extensive series of trails called 'Stepping out walks' is waymarked on the ground and described online and in leaflets.

is high time that local historians staked out such massively important topics as their natural territory.[16]

Place

For generations the majority of local historians have chosen, more by instinct than reason, to study the place in which they live or were born.[17] This is not surprising because one's home parish or district is part of one's life: its houses, its hidden corners, the church or chapel which stands for something more than the earthbound, sad but evocative tombstones, the fields and their names, the river or canal which was so magnetic in childhood, the offices and factories which symbolise work and routine – all these remind us of countless people who have lived, worked and died there. The place itself is primary evidence of human endeavour, which needs interpretation as much as any written document, and which for many of us was the original spur to our historical imaginations. Therefore, many of us prefer to write about the places and communities which we know, feel part of, or genuinely love. John Walton's involvement with the history of Blackpool arose originally from family connections and 'from riding up and down the sea-front as a temporary tram conductor during the summer of 1968'.[18] At the same time a writer may have a consciously social purpose, a desire to help foster a sense of local identity and pride. When it was published, William Fishman's moving portrait of London's East End in 1888 was described as combining 'family loyalty, childhood and adolescent memory and tenderness' to the extent that it 'helps to warm the human spirit'.[19] Nobody should be ashamed of these homely characteristics, although they too carry dangers and some commentators will condemn us for being too sentimental, too desperate in our search for a stable and comfortable world that never was.

Any local or regional study which does not convey a clear sense of place is stunted. By a combination of maps, illustrations and words, local historians must give their readers a coherent impression of the landscape or townscape, and patterns of communication, which contained and influenced their human story. An acclaimed history of an Essex parish published in 1979 gave fascinating insight

[16]   See K. Tiller, 'Local history brought up to date', *TLH*, 36, 3 (Aug. 2006), 148–62; *English Local History* (2002), Ch. 6.

[17]   They have normally assumed that 'place' equals 'community', an assumption which carries its dangers (see p. 1).

[18]   J. K. Walton, *Blackpool* (Edinburgh UP, 1998), p. viii.

[19]   Richard Cobb's foreword in W. J. Fishman, *East End, 1888: A Year in a London Borough among the Labouring Poor* (Duckworth, 1988).

into the tense polarisation of a rural community in the seventeenth century, but it read as if the writers had never been there. A map of 1597 was not reproduced, and the topography of the village and farming landscape, which is well preserved, was barely mentioned.[20] As William Hoskins, Christopher Taylor and others have taught us since the 1950s, the physical setting of a local society is not only part of its uniqueness, but is important historical evidence in itself.

'Place' also incorporates the more dynamic notions of 'space' and changing physical boundaries or 'liminality'. These are related concepts which have recently become very fashionable (sometimes obsessional) in historical writing. How did the distances which former generations travelled in their working and social lives affect their view of themselves and of the outside world?[21] How did the mental horizons of different groups change over time? And how do we as historians reconstruct the spatial perceptions of earlier generations, so different from our own? Although many historical specialists overlook the importance of place and space, the local historian can never afford to do so. John Walton provides a metaphorical example of this awareness when he describes the seaside pier of Victorian and Edwardian times as:

> the essence of liminality, with more convincing credentials as phallic symbol than the tallest tower, as it points a stiff masculine technological probe into the mysterious feminine world of the sea, linking the elements to generate the special frisson of pleasure and the privileged gaze that go with occupying the bridging-point of two worlds.[22]

Another good reason for studying a particular community-cum-place can be that it is well-documented, either in a general sense or by having a single outstanding source. David Hey wrote his classic account of Myddle in Shropshire not because he lived there, but because it offered one of the most remarkable sources known to English historians – a contemporary account of its inhabitants

---

[20]   K. Wrightson and D. Levine, *Poverty and Piety in an Essex Village: Terling, 1525–1700* (OUP, 1979 and 1995).

[21]   In a WEA Summer School I once received a remarkable autobiographical essay from an elderly woman, a gamekeeper's daughter who had been brought up in a Breckland hamlet before World War I. The town of Bury St Edmunds, only six miles away, was rarely visited by her family: to the children it therefore acquired a glamorous and somewhat magical significance, like some distant Shangri-La.

[22]   J. K. Walton, *The British Seaside: Holidays and Resorts in the Twentieth Century* (Manchester UP, 2000), pp. 104–5.

by a seventeenth-century resident called Richard Gough.[23] Of course Gough's description, which was based on direct experience, conversation and memory, is quite exceptional. In general we are looking for sources relevant to the chosen subject and, preferably, sufficiently organised in layout to allow proper analysis. But, with any choice of subject, we are at the mercy of the sources which survive – good, bad and indifferent – and have to make the best of them.

While the evidence surviving for each individual parish will inevitably have its own strengths and weaknesses, many local historians miss good opportunities because they obstinately refuse to sample larger areas. For instance, parishes within a few miles of each other can show massive variations in the quantity and quality of their records, and a few outstandingly rich sources will always cry out for attention. In the rural corner of Suffolk in which I lived for twenty years, within four contiguous parishes, Stanton has over four hundred early charters, Walsham le Willows has exceptional manorial surveys and poor-law records, Bardwell has the accounts of a late medieval guild and a good town-book, and Stowlangtoft has the autobiography and correspondence of a seventeenth-century squire who was also a national figure. Equally patchy are their records from the eighteenth century to the present-day: Stowlangtoft has very few records for the nineteenth century, but Bardwell has a superb parish magazine, starting in 1892 and covering the First World War, which was the equivalent of a village newspaper. The point is that simply to investigate the life of a single parish, one needs to browse among the resources of a district. Although local historians rightly acknowledge the centuries-old significance of parish boundaries, they must never regard them as impenetrable barriers. Indeed, other important units of social and economic life quite frequently flowed over parish boundaries, as is the case with many landed estates or the organisation of particular industries. Administrative boundaries never prevented the movement of people and influences in the past, and they should not stunt our vision in the present (Fig. 2, p. 11).

So, for generations the principal unit of local historical study has been the individual parish or town. This continues to be the case for both non-professionals and academics, although it is noticeable that the latter when working in this genre tend to adopt shorter chronologies and a tighter thematic focus. Nor should we forget that since the mid-1990s leading academics have rediscovered their interest in the workings of the traditional parish, medieval and modern (see p. 20).[24] Nevertheless, it is also true that over the last fifty years growing

[23] D. G. Hey, *An English Rural Community* (Leicester UP, 1974); *Richard Gough, the History of Myddle* (London, 1981).

[24] Warwick University now has a 'Network for Parish Research' for the study of British

numbers of writers have adopted a larger geographical coverage. Thus in the early 1970s Margaret Spufford in her *Contrasting Communities* compared three widely-spaced Cambridgeshire parishes in the sixteenth to seventeenth centuries, which she saw as representative of different sub-regions within the county.[25] More recently, Margaret Shepherd has chosen to study nine parishes strung along the Upper Eden valley in Cumbria during the period 1840–95.[26] The Whittlewood Project, an archaeological-cum-documentary dissection of landscape and life from Roman times until the sixteenth century, focusses on a block of twelve parishes overlapping the boundary between Northamptonshire and Buckinghamshire.[27] Concentrating on early administrative units, David Hey charted the social and industrial history of Hallamshire which surrounded Sheffield, while Julian Whybra has reconstructed the lost Anglo-Saxon county of Winchcombeshire (now in Gloucestershire).[28] Expanding the scale still further, other studies have focussed on major industrial regions, and on particular types of rural countryside.[29]

An even more common unit of study, with a long antiquarian pedigree stretching back for centuries, is the county or shire. Older county histories such as Sir William Dugdale's *Warwickshire* (1656) or John Bridges' *Northamptonshire* (1791) were principally concerned with landowning families, their manors and estates, country houses, heraldry and genealogy, and the clergy and their churches.[30] Modern county histories are broader in scope and are, apart from the

and European parishes, *c.*1300 to 1800; it organises symposia and publishes substantial bibliographies.

[25] Her book appeared almost simultaneously with Jack Ravensdale's *Liable to Floods* which also dealt with three Cambridgeshire parishes, but adjacent ones at the southern end of the Fens; the first study concentrated on population, social structure and religion, while the second was primarily concerned with 'village landscape'. M. Spufford, *Contrasting Communities: English Villagers in the 16th and 17th Centuries* (CUP, 1974); J. R. Ravensdale, *Liable to Floods: Village Landscape on the Edge of the Fens, AD 450–1850* (CUP, 1974).

[26] M. E. Shepherd, *From Hellgill to Bridge End: Aspects of Economic and Social Change in the Upper Eden Valley, 1840–95* (Hertfordshire UP, 2003).

[27] R. Jones and M. Page, *Medieval Villages in an English Landscape* (Windgather, 2006).

[28] D. Hey, *The Fiery Blades of Hallamshire: Sheffield and its Neighbourhood, 1660–1740* (Leicester UP, 1991); Julian Whybra, *A Lost English County: Winchcombeshire in the Tenth and Eleventh Centuries* (Boydell, 1990).

[29] For example, see S. Thompson, *Unemployment, Poverty and Health in Interwar South Wales* (Univ. of Wales, 2006). Alan Everitt designated eight main types of distinctive countrysides (*pays*) ranging from fellsides to coastal marshes, and saw them as influencing not just human settlement and farming but even cultural and religious behaviour: *The Pattern of Rural Dissent: The Nineteenth Century* (Leicester UP, 1972).

[30] C. R. J. Currie and C. P. Lewis (eds), *English County Histories: a Guide* (Alan Sutton, 1994).

parochially-based *VCH*, of three main types. Some are 'popular' summaries covering huge swathes of time from prehistory to the present, like the Darwen series which devotes one slim volume to each county. Of a more substantial kind are detailed surveys like the multi-volumed *History of Lincolnshire* and the *Kent History Project* which deal separately, for example, with medieval society, the economic history of the early modern period and the twentieth century.[31] Most specialised of all are single volumes dealing with specific themes such as Hassell Smith's classic study of Norfolk's 'county community' in the reign of Elizabeth I,[32] or David Hall's detailed analysis of the field-systems of Northamptonshire before and after enclosure. For certain topics, therefore, the county may still be an appropriate unit of study, but in other contexts its choice seems a matter of convenience or quite arbitrary, and swayed more by archival and commercial considerations than historical.[33]

Surprising though it may seem, two new forms of county history have achieved some popularity in the last twenty years. First, archaeologists, landscape historians, geographers and others primarily concerned with the physical landscape have published collections of high-quality aerial photographs, vertical and more usually oblique. These images with their captions have proved a stimulating way of interpreting the evolution and meaning of local landscapes and townscapes. Second, the publication of historical atlases, which began in Suffolk in 1988, has now spread to more than a dozen counties, and is still spreading. The purpose, by means of distribution maps and short texts, is to give specialists the opportunity of summarising the existing state of knowledge on a host of topics ranging chronologically from prehistory to the twentieth century. Experience has already shown that these atlases meet a widespread educational need for brief but authoritative information, and that they genuinely stimulate new work.

For those with primarily rural interests, urban history now appears to have pulled away from the mainstream of local history. As historians such as Pamela Sharpe have demonstrated, even small market towns like Colyton (Devon) are

[31] With one exception, volumes of 'The History of Lincolnshire' (1976 to 2000) were each written by one individual, but the volume on the twentieth century involved twelve contributors. A new supplemental series was started in 2005. The *Kent History Project* has so far (in 2007) published seven volumes and several more are planned. A similar series for Suffolk, based a generous personal bequest to UEA, is making slow progress but the first volume appeared in 2007.

[32] A. Hassell Smith, *County and Court: Government and Politics in Norfolk, 1558–1603* (Clarendon, 1987); David Hall, *The Open Fields of Northamptonshire* (Northants Record Soc., 38, 1995).

[33] One reason for choosing a county scale has to do with marketing. Local people, it is argued, are more likely to buy a book on 'Borsetshire' than one on 'The West Midlands'.

much more complicated human organisms than rural parishes, and their records are often better preserved.[34] To tackle a county town or a major industrial conurbation is an even greater enterprise which may call for well-coordinated teamwork by a number of specialists, as recently shown in the cases of Dundee, Norwich and Nottingham.[35] A further problem is that British towns have been, and are, internally complicated and divided by social, economic, ethnic and religious factors.[36] Historians like Mary Prior and Frank Grace have already shown the value of studying distinctive *parts* of major towns in the quest for human community and diversity,[37] yet this is still an obviously under-exploited theme of urban history. How far did a parish, ward, quarter, 'ghetto', individual street or any other internal entity resemble the *sestieri* or *contrade* of Italian cities, generating fierce loyalty, ceremonial rivalry and even violence? A colourful example is still to be witnessed on 5 November each year in the town of Lewes (Sussex), where up to seven 'bonfire societies' representing different parts of the town have competed ritualistically and very publicly since the mid-nineteenth century. In so doing they, with their supporters and opponents, have exposed and sometimes stirred up social, political and religious differences lurking within the community.[38]

Yet in spite of increasing specialisation and the appearance of separate journals of *Rural History* and *Urban History*, historians are fast coming to realise that these two subjects can never be divorced. Every town, regardless of size or the length of its history, has around it a rural hinterland, an area of two-way economic and social influence which shows subtle and often unpredictable variations over distance and time. This outer territory is an indispensable part of urban history,

---

[34]   P. Sharpe, *Population and Society in an East Devon Parish: Reproducing Colyton, 1540–1840* (Univ. of Exeter Press, 2002). See also A. G. Crosby, 'Urban history in Lancashire and Cheshire', *Northern History*, 42, 1 (March 2005), 75–89.

[35]   L. Miskell, C. A. Whatley and B. Harris (eds), *Victorian Dundee: Image and Realities* (Tuckwell, 2000) with 10 contributors; C. Rawcliffe and R. Wilson (eds), *Medieval Norwich* and *Norwich since 1550* (Hambledon, 2004), two volumes with 20 and 14 contributors respectively; J. Beckett (ed.), *A Centenary History of Nottingham* (Manchester UP, 1997) with 22 contributors.

[36]   The significance of ethnic immigration, especially into larger cities and major ports, is brilliantly illustrated in M. Dresser and P. Fleming, *Bristol: Ethnic Minorities and the City, 1000–2001* (England's Past for Everyone: Phillimore, 2007).

[37]   M. Prior, *Fisher Row: Fishermen, Bargemen and Canal Boatmen in Oxford, 1500–1900* (Clarendon, 1982); Frank Grace, *Rags and Bones: a Social History of a Working-Class Community in Nineteenth-century Ipswich* (Unicorn, 2005).

[38]   J. E. Etherington, *The Bonfire Societies of Lewes, 1800–1913: A Study in Nominal Record Linkage* (LPSS, 1996); *Lewes Bonfire Night: A Short History of the Guy Fawkes Celebrations* (Seaford, 2001).

as demonstrated in John Goodacre's work on Lutterworth and in Maryanne Kowaleski's assessment of the region around medieval Exeter.[39] Conversely, rural and agricultural historians must always acknowledge the influence of local towns, large and small, dominant and modest, growing and failing – because a single village can simultaneously feel the pull of several towns of different rank. In other words, villages and towns do not inhabit different universes: they have always had a symbiotic and dynamic relationship which is fascinating to unravel.

Finally, we must not forget the long-running debate on 'regional history' (see p. 19). Faced with the tendency for academic history to fragment, and for much local history to focus on the single 'discrete' community, a number of professionals led by the redoubtable John Marshall have argued for the identification of historical regions larger than the parish, manor or township.[40] In practice they have postulated entities such as social neighbourhoods which may extend over six to ten miles, zones of economic dependency, genteel communities embracing whole counties, and large provinces which could incorporate several counties.[41] Such territories, it is suggested, reflect human affiliations more accurately than purely administrative units or geographical zones and farming *pays*. They are human groupings which had, at particular periods of the past, similar characteristics – whether social, economic, political, religious, or a combination of any of these. For instance, they may be traceable by marital or commercial links, the average size of farms, the prevalence of certain industrial occupations, religious affiliations, or even by rates of crime and bastardy. Some of these broader territories are mental concepts more than anything else, as they depend on the experience and contacts of groups and on well-documented individuals.[42]

Historical regions can be of very different sizes in both area and population; they may also have been short-lived and indeed overlapping. Some proponents of regional history maintain that one should *start* by trying to identify such wider groupings, however difficult the task. Others have even suggested that a larger area might be chosen *arbitrarily* in the hope that genuine affiliations will later

---

[39] J. Goodacre, *The Transformation of a Peasant Economy: Townspeople and Villagers in the Lutterworth Area, 1500–1700* (Scolar, 1994); M. Kowaleski, *Local Markets and Regional Trade in Medieval Exeter* (CUP, 1996).

[40] The main vehicle has been the Conference of Regional and Local Historians (CORAL), now merged with BALH.

[41] See C. Phythian-Adams, *Re-thinking English Local History* (Leicester UP, 1987); 'Introduction: an agenda for English local history' in Phythian-Adams (ed.), *Societies, Cultures and Kinship, 1580–1850* (Leicester UP, 1993).

[42] J. D. Marshall, 'Communities, societies, regions and local history: perceptions of locality in High and Low Furness', *TLH*, 26, 1 (Feb. 1996), 36–47.

emerge.[43] The argument goes that at a later stage one will be in a better position to understand the true character of constituent communities. Debates of this kind undoubtedly make us think much harder about the factors which united and divided previous generations, who were quite capable of viewing the same locality differently over time. Fascinatingly, such awareness can lead historians in opposite directions: towards the definition of groups *larger* than the parish or town (the main objective of Regional History), and towards the recognition of important human associations and divisions *within* parishes and *across* their boundaries.

Time

The traditional parish history always had a broad chronological canvas. It usually brought the story down to 'modern times' or the 'present day', but the starting point varied greatly. It could be 1086 because of the towering if enigmatic presence of Domesday Book, or the fifth to seventh centuries AD when Anglo-Saxon immigrants supposedly took over an abandoned wilderness, or deep in prehistory on the basis of a few cinerary urns or axe-heads. This kind of general history has always been a difficult undertaking, not least because of the challenges of medieval palaeography and Latin. Now the Anglo-Saxon and medieval periods are even more difficult to penetrate because of the volume of new research and the staggering proliferation of sources and techniques. For example, it would be very unwise for a modern writer to ignore recent archaeological research into the origins of villages, scattered settlements, field-systems and market towns.[44] In spite of the difficulties, however, a significant number of individuals are still brave enough to attempt local history from A to Z and some, it must be admitted, produce books which are instructive and stimulating.[45]

A parish or town history need not always be a fat tome like Sir Matthew

---

[43] Phythian-Adams, *Re-thinking English Local History*, p. 43; Marshall, *Tyranny of the Discrete*, pp. 83–4. Some so-called regions have been chosen for purely publishing and personal reasons: the English Heritage Regional Series and the aborted Longman Regional Series were both based on unconvincing carve-ups of the map of England. The second was equally cavalier chronologically, dividing volumes at the arbitrary date of 1000 AD.

[44] In this connection the most important national journals are *Medieval Archaeology, Post-Medieval Archaeology, Landscape History* and the *Annual Report of the Medieval Settlement Research Group*.

[45] For example, J. V. Beckett, *A History of Laxton: England's Last Open-Field Village* (Blackwell, 1989); M. and F. Heywood, and B. Jennings, *A History of Todmorden* (Smith Settle, 1996); C. P. Lewis, *History of Kirtling and Upend: Landowners and People in a Cambridgeshire Parish* (Wallasey, 2000).

Nathan's *West Coker* with its 521 pages,[46] but may be a relatively slight volume or a brief article. The shorter the treatment, the greater the need for careful selection and judgement. For example, in the 1960s–70s the historian of a Fen-Breckland parish in Suffolk had the courage to say that the three main events in its history were the drainage of the fen in the seventeenth century, parliamentary enclosure in the early nineteenth century, and rapid expansion and suburbanisation since World War II. Whether or not he was right, this is the kind of judgement and debate which local history should contain.[47]

Because of the increasing sophistication of research and the sheer number of sources now available, most of today's local historians deliberately work within much narrower chronological limits. They are not tempted by the full span of history, and they have mostly abandoned the old temporal straitjackets of centuries, dynasties and reigns. Like other specialists they find it more satisfying to seek out relatively 'short' topics: teasing out their significance, discussing their origins and consequences, and putting them into wider context. In 2006, for example, *The Local Historian* carried articles on the life of a Catholic Apostolic church in Bradford in 1872–82, the policing of Keighley (Yorks) in 1856–7, the war-time evacuation of a Scottish peninsula in 1943–4, an outbreak of typhoid in Worthing (Sussex) in 1893, and a very rare local census taken in Barford (Oxon) in 1942. Other historians would undoubtedly contribute more to knowledge and keep in better touch with specialists, if they attempted less ambitious and more manageable chronologies. On the other hand, we should not go too far in squeezing our chronological perspectives: another of the distinguishing strengths of local history is a willingness to survey periods longer than those commonly used by other historians, and to make comparisons over broader swathes of time.[48] Of course the final choice of time-span must be determined by the quantity and quality of sources and by the variable character of individual communities.

While on the subject of time, we should remember the value of recording the present for future generations. No better example can be found than the multi-volumed *Statistical Accounts of Scotland* published in 1791–9, 1845 and 1951–92, which are all contemporary descriptions of life at the local level (see Appendix 2, p. 132). On similar lines, many communities in Britain celebrated the millennium

---

[46] M. Nathan, *The Annals of West Coker* (CUP, 1957).

[47] In the 1960s and 1970s, John Munday, one of a dying breed of scholar-parsons, wrote and published a large number of pamphlets on the parishes of Eriswell and Lakenheath (Suffolk).

[48] Phythian-Adams argues that students should be made to experience the sheer length of history, while Marshall stresses the value of teaching history backwards (*Tyranny of the Discrete*, p. 123).

of 2000 by writing contemporary histories, recording personal interviews, drawing up parish maps, compiling videos and photographing the local population outside their homes. Because of the pace of change, the need for work of this kind increases with the passage of time. At the beginning of the twenty-first century we as a society produce vast quantities of paper, film, tape and disks, much of which is invaluably personal in character, but we also destroy evidence on an unprecedented scale (or neglect to record it). Text-messages and e-mails are deleted; the internet is in constant flux; shredders are constantly whirring; and discussions on the telephone leave no trace. Meanwhile, the art of letter-writing is fast dying and today's local newspapers, which successfully combine triviality and sensationalism, are no more than juvenile comics when compared to their sober predecessors in the nineteenth century. On top of all this, archivists are given the awesome responsibility of 'weeding' the records of modern government, business and society as they become available.

While some elderly people write their own reminiscences, usually for the benefit of family and friends, more of us surely ought to grasp the opportunity of writing the first historical accounts of local life and events as we have actually witnessed them – such as planning controversies, industrial disputes and cultural trends.[49] Of course we may not be able to create a full and balanced picture of our own times because we are too closely connected, and sensitivities have to be observed. If that kind of instant history is too daunting, we can certainly amplify the evidence to be left behind in both oral and documentary forms, ensuring that journalists, politicians and bureaucrats will not be the only sources of information in the future. Happily, some county organisations encourage volunteers to make notes, collect ephemera and take photographs in their own communities.[50] This approach can have great personal benefit. From the contemporary world of which we form part, we as historians derive not only our curiosity about the human condition, but also our awareness of how truth gets clouded and evidence lost.[51]

Group-work

Although most local history is researched and written by individuals, and always will be, it can also be pursued rewardingly by groups. The justification for this

[49]   A good example is work done on events surrounding the death and funeral of Diana Princess of Wales in 1997: *Folklore*, 109 (1998). No doubt the Olympic Games of 2012 will provide similar opportunities.

[50]   See V. Norrington, *Recording the Present* (BALH, 1989).

[51]   A related phenomenon is the 'Black Book', which for legal reasons is not published in the author's lifetime but left in a safe place to await the verdict of posterity!

approach, which has become far more commonplace in recent decades, is two-fold.[52] First, it helps to overcome the isolation of much historical endeavour, and second it encourages and harnesses the energy, varied skills and expertise of people who may not have embarked on such work by themselves. After a subject has been agreed, methods of analysis can be established, basic tasks shared out, and difficulties of interpretation discussed by the whole group. Careful planning and supervision are essential to ensure consistent standards of transcription and analysis, and it is always advisable that people with academic training should co-ordinate the work and be in editorial control. As Nigel Goose has argued, 'one of the most constructive ways forward is for the amateur and the professional to work together, forming an alliance that combines their respective talents'.[53]

With group-work a difficulty which should not be overlooked is deciding who shall do the final write-up. Indeed this is a problem which arises whenever a book, article or research report has more than one author. The best solution is for one experienced person to take on the final responsibility as 'general editor'. If this is not practically or diplomatically possible, different individuals are often given responsibility for particular sections or chapters. Where, by contrast, several writers tinker with drafts in a desultory fashion, throwing in their own contributions and giving nobody the final word, the result can be very inflated and uninspired.

Group-work has been a marked feature of adult and continuing education, especially in the 1960s–80s when many classes and their tutors embarked on participatory history. An impressive example published in 1980 was an extensive study of the Telford area in Shropshire, based on an analysis of probate inventories in the period 1660 to 1750.[54] More recently an Historical Research Group at Thame (Oxfordshire) has illustrated how some adult classes can transform themselves into semi-permanent research groups. With academic leadership it has generated computerised records and analyses, and is publishing articles in the relevant county journal. At York adult students from a WEA class have formed 'The Latin Project'; under the guidance of a tutor they transcribed the wills of an important fifteenth-century merchant family and the accounts of a local fraternity, and published

---

[52] A. J. H. Jackson, 'Opinion: Published Parish and Community Histories ...', *TLH*, 36,1 (Feb. 2006), 46.

[53] N. Goose, *Hertfordshire Archaeology and History*, 14 (2004–5), 167; *Archives*, xxii, 97 (Oct. 1997), 98–110. Scores of local and family historians in Hertfordshire are working with academics, archivists and librarians to establish a computerised resource base for the county's history including documents such as parish registers, the census enumerations of 1851 and registers of union workhouses.

[54] B. Trinder and Jeff Cox, *Yeomen and Colliers in Telford* (Chichester, 1980). See also A. Rogers (ed.), *Group Projects in Local History* (Dawson, 1977).

their transcripts with explanatory notes and introduction under the aegis of the Centre for Medieval Studies of the University of York. Along similar lines, a whole array of impressive projects is promoted by the Ranulph Higden Society in the north-west of England, and is supported by the universities of Keele, Liverpool and Manchester: among the sources being worked on are poll-tax returns, assize rolls and manorial court rolls.[55] These are heartening examples of how group-work can, with planning and proper supervision, contribute to the study of the early modern and medieval periods.

In a similar way some local history societies, wishing to go beyond the normal routine of lectures and excursions, have organised their own projects and publications. For instance, since 1964 the Faversham Society in Kent have produced nearly a hundred 'Faversham Papers' on the town and district, which include transcribed records and thematic studies.[56] In 2003 a ground-breaking study of seventeenth-century St Albans was published by an amateur research group working under the aegis of the local Architectural and Archaeological Society. Sixty-one individuals took part, of whom at least ten were responsible for the writing of individual chapters.[57] Such enterprises are not so different from 'Community history', already mentioned on p. 4, which is a collaborative form of research with a strong social and civic purpose. In contexts which are usually urban, suburban and industrial, local residents collect, study and publicise documentary, photographic and oral evidence (with a heavy and perhaps inevitable emphasis on recent history), and use it to awaken some sense of pride and belonging in their neighbourhoods.[58]

Successful group-work has also proved possible at a county level. For example, in 1987–95 under the aegis of the Woolhope Naturalists Field Club, the 'Herefordshire Field-Name Survey' attracted 118 volunteers who recorded, analysed and mapped

---

[55]   Thame Historical Research group, www.thamehistory.net; The Latin Project, *The Blackburns in York: Testaments of a Merchant Family in the Later Middle Ages* (York, 2006) and *Before the Merchant Adventurers: the Accounts of the Fraternity of Jesus and Mary* (York, 2007); Ranulph Higden Society, www.dragonslair.eclipse.co.uk; also J. D. Marshall, 'A co-operative local history project and some lessons learnt from it', *TLH*, 31 (2001), 66–82. For a Scandinavian dimension and the concept of the 'Sunday historian', see R. Rodger, 'Review Essay: Historiens du Dimanche', *Urban Hist.*, 23, pt 1 (May 1996), 86–9.

[56]   See J. H. McKay, 'Community historians and their work around the millenium' in R. Finnegan (ed.), *Participating in the Knowledge Society: Researchers Beyond the University Walls* (Palgrave Macmillan, 2005), 125–27.

[57]   J. T. Smith and M. A. North (eds), *St Albans 1650–1700: A Thoroughfare Town and its People* (Herts Publications, 2003).

[58]   K. Tiller, 'Local history brought up to date', *TLH* (2006), 150–54.

more than 125,000 field-names in 260 parishes (based on the tithe-maps of *c.*1840). They won a national prize for their efforts, and their data are now available online. Since 2005, in a totally different field of research, local historians and societies have embarked, under professional guidance over two years, on a project entitled 'Eighteenth-Century Devon: People and Communities'; the purpose was to transcribe major sources such as oath rolls and diocesan visitation returns, and to publish them electronically. While the voluntary contribution was of absolutely fundamental importance, it should be noted that this work was also supported by the county council, record office and University of Exeter, and was awarded £50,000 from the 'Your Heritage' programme of the Heritage Lottery Fund.

On a national scale, too, group-work is making its mark. One of the earliest examples occurred in the 1970s when the Cambridge Group for the History of Population and Social Structure enlisted local historians from all over the country to analyse baptisms, marriages and burials recorded in parish registers.[59] In those pre-computer days, the whole exercise was carried out on paper. The Victoria County History, as well as continuing to produce its 'big red books' on individual counties, has recently undertaken more limited studies in over a dozen different parts of England under the title 'England's Past for Everyone'. Professionals lead teams of volunteers to transcribe and analyse sources, and where possible local schools are involved; the results of their research are published both online and in attractively produced softbacks.[60] Meanwhile, the Family and Community Historical Research Society organises group-work on nationally significant topics such as the Swing Riots, allotments, almshouses and pauper emigration. For each project, which runs for a limited period, co-ordinators and academic advisers are appointed and volunteers sought from all parts of the country. Again the final aim is some form of publication.[61] Perhaps the most ambitious proposal to date

[59] E. A. Wrigley and R. S. Schofield, *The Population History of England, 1541–1871* (Edward Arnold, 1981), pp. 5–6. This book was dedicated 'To the local population historians of England'.

[60] For news of these *VCH* studies, see www.englandspast.net; the first four volumes appeared in 2007. C. Smith, 'Continuity and change: the future of the Victoria County History of the counties of England', *TLH*, 32, 2 (2002), 84–9. The Derbyshire Trust of the VCH is 'keen to harness the energy, enthusiasm and expertise of local historians throughout the county' and has produced a '60-page research handbook'.

[61] M. Holland (ed.), *Swing Unmasked: the Agricultural Riots of 1830 to 1832 and their Wider Implications* (with CD-ROM; FACHRS Publications, 2005). Another project being run from Liverpool University is concerned with the cholera outbreaks of 1832 and 1849. For the concept and mechanics of such 'participatory history' involving universities and external students, see M. Drake, 'Inside out or outside in? The case of family and local history' in Finnegan (ed.), *Participating in the Knowledge Society* (2005).

came from The National Archives. On top of its already successful creation of a Local History Research Group, which draws members from local and family history societies to calendar particular documentary sources,[62] the TNA in 2007 announced a plan to catalogue the vast amount of correspondence between the Poor Law Commissioners and local Unions after the Poor Law Reform Act of 1834. It was hoped that the work could be done by trained volunteers drawn from local history societies across England and Wales, and that the results would appear online. Unfortunately the project failed to obtain funding from the Heritage Lottery Fund, though it is hoped to substitute a scaled-down version of the scheme in due course.[63]

In spite of these and many other initiatives, some critics regard this kind of work as unscrupulous exploitation: professionals using the goodwill of amateurs to get donkey-work done. Others, with more justification, point to the difficulty of ensuring consistently high standards when research is done by volunteers, however well motivated. That this problem can be successfully combated has been proved conclusively in the pages of two journals, *Local Population Studies* (founded 1968) and *Family and Community History* (founded 1998 and available online), which have become worthy monuments to fruitful co-operation between professional and lay historians, inside and outside the walls of universities. Indeed they have helped to blur that distinction by showing that non-professionals not only have their own special skills to offer, but by adjusting to the demands of critical research can genuinely contribute to knowledge and academic debate.[64] It could be said that voluntarism is now aiding the historical profession and its institutions at a time when public money is in chronically short supply, and in return newer forms of adult education are available to those non-professionals who offer their time and services. All the schemes mentioned above enable teams to survey large numbers of sources, sometimes over considerable geographical areas, assembling much more evidence than could ever be achieved by individuals working alone. Where groups are scattered geographically and cannot on a regular basis meet face-to-face, it becomes important to establish a strong central organisation and

[62]   See, for example, *Pardons and Punishments: Judges' Reports on Criminals, 1783 to 1830* (List and Index Soc., 2006).

[63]   So far this project has failed to obtain funding from the Heritage Lottery Fund, but it is hoped to substitute a scaled-down version: *Local History News*, 88 (Summer 2008), 13.

[64]   These two journals often reveal that their contributors, though technically 'amateur', are experienced and well qualified in other ways. For example, in *Family and Cammunity History*, 10, 1 (May 2007) authors included a local government officer currently enjoying motherhood and the OU; a PhD student who had had a long career in banking; and a retired professional engineer studying with the OU.

to maintain good communications – now made so much easier by the use of e-mail and the internet.

Aids to research and teaching

Original reconstructions of the past are not the only forms of writing to be considered. The value of gathering contemporary evidence for the benefit of future generations has already been mentioned (see pp. 45–6). Another important task is the compiling of indexes. In every part of Britain, the usefulness of many books, journals, newspapers, photographic collections and record publications is reduced by their having no indexes, or only poor ones. But the situation is improving: for example *The Local Historian* is now indexed and abstracted, and in 2002–3 alone three other indexes to local history journals were made available. New indexes, preferably divided into People, Places and Subjects (see below, pp. 117–18), can be easily duplicated, printed or put online, and hard copies deposited in relevant record offices and major libraries.

A related problem is that we often lack bibliographical information. Only a few counties, such as Kent and Oxfordshire, possess full-scale printed bibliographies listing all kinds of published material. This is an enormous task to undertake, and it still leaves the problem of updating as new publications thump from the press.[65] A bibliography for Staffordshire appeared in 2004 and another for Rutland in 2005,[66] but in future this work will undoubtedly be done online, a medium which allows easy revision and updating. In fact, the Bedfordshire Historical Record Society is already preparing an 'interactive online index' of published sources. An impressive model for work of this kind is the bibliography of British and Irish history made available online by the Royal Historical Society. On it local historians can search by subject, place-name and surname (of writers and historical figures), drawn from over 427,000 books, articles in journals, articles in collective volumes and review articles, all published since 1900.[67]

Lastly, we come to the vital task of preparing record publications. This of course entails the transcribing or abstracting (and sometimes translating) of original documents for the benefit of students, academics and general readers. At one end of the scale are volumes published by record societies serving individual

---

[65] This is normally done by producing supplements, as the Oxford Historical Society has done.

[66] C. J. Harrison, *A Bibliography of the History of Staffordshire* (Keele, 2004); J. D. Bennett, *Rutland in Print: a Bibliography of England's Smallest County*, Rutland Record, 25 (2005).

[67] <www.rhs.ac.uk/bibwel.html>.

counties, regions or the whole country. This admirable work continues though it is often supported by perilously small numbers of subscribers.[68] At the other end, transcriptions and translations of records frequently appear in journals, newsletters, archive packs, teaching-aids and on CDs. Whatever the form of publication, the addition of critical comments helps a reader to appreciate the character of the original, its provenance, the nature of its contents and problems of interpretation.

Although the publishing of historical records is normally done at national or county level, the task has also been undertaken by local societies (other than specifically record societies). For example, since its foundation in 1957 the enterprising Banbury Historical Society in Oxfordshire has not only produced well over a hundred issues of its magazine *Cake and Cockhorse*, but up to 2007 had published thirty volumes of local records including parish registers, corporation books, churchwardens' accounts and chapbooks.[69] Transcriptions and translations have also been published by family historians, mainly of sources containing abundant personal names.[70] Finally, documents have been put into print by individuals, entirely on their own initiative and sometimes at their own expense.[71] It is undeniable that at present the standards of transcription, translation, abstracting and editing vary from excellent to distinctly weak, while the volume of record publishing, particularly online, is expanding sharply. In future we must hope that this work is taken up increasingly by well-led and properly organised voluntary societies, research groups and adult classes, who will devote time to the choice of the most significant documents for their areas and then publish them to the highest possible standards.

---

[68] One of the most public-spirited things any historically-minded person can do is to subscribe to a record society. Most counties have such a voluntary organisation.

[69] J. Gibson, 'Fifty Years of "Banburyshire" Publication', *TLH*, 37, 4 (Nov. 2007), 228–32.

[70] For instance, a local team of volunteers is currently tabulating data drawn from the gaol registers of Bodmin (Cornwall) in the nineteenth century, and are publishing them as CDs.

[71] For example, R. L. Sawyer, *The Bowerchalke Parish Papers: Collett's Village Newspaper, 1878–1924* (Wilts Library, 1989) gives extracts from a remarkable parish magazine from Wiltshire. In the period 1894–1915 Sydenham Hervey edited no fewer than twenty-two volumes of original records known as the 'Suffolk Green Books'.

4

The search for sources

The task is fraught with immense difficulty, for the historian is never allowed to invent; he must always find evidence for his statements.

(Joan Thirsk, in M. K. Ashby, *The Changing English Village*, Roundwood, 1974, xv)

P UBLIC ACCESS to original documents has been revolutionised in the last half-century. Indeed, searchers of all kinds, including total beginners, are now positively welcomed at record offices and local-studies libraries.[1] Some cynics have argued that 'never have so many historically untrained people come into contact with so many documents',[2] but it is surely true that these post-war developments have had mostly good effects. Contact with real historical sources has been hugely valuable in personal and educational terms: it has given searchers direct experience of the past, taught them the rudiments of historical method and stimulated practical research. Less desirably, however, it has deluded some people into thinking that history is simply the study of original documents: we have only to look at manuscripts, get them photocopied, stitch them together and the job is done.

Not only can documents be dull, repetitive and comparatively unrevealing, but they are inevitably patchy and unpredictable in their survival. From these charac-teristics, important consequences follow. On the one hand, we must certainly seek out and weigh every scrap of evidence relevant to our chosen subjects, observing Kate Tiller's universal rule 'never to use a single source in isolation'.[3] On the other hand, we cannot escape the fact that archival collections, even the very best ones,

---

[1] In 1980 few searchers would have guessed that, before the end of the century, the PRO (now TNA) might have a series of popularly written readers' guides, with titles like *Never Been Here Before?* and *New to Kew?* Some county record offices and local-studies libraries have been brought together in the same building, which is a great boon to the researcher.

[2] Marshall, *Tyranny of the Discrete*, p. 47.

[3] Tiller, *English Local History*, p. 160.

are incomplete. This means that our work is, in the words of French and Hoyle, 'also shaped by what does not survive'.[4] (See Pl. 4.)

In practice, the sources which *are* available to us become meaningful only when seen in two contexts. First, we have to appreciate the different public or private backgrounds from which they come. For example, many primary sources stem from administrative bodies such as parishes, boroughs and counties; from economic organisations such as landed estates and commercial firms; or from voluntary associations such as guilds and friendly societies. Yet others are essentially private and personal in origin. An awareness of these differing origins is essential if we are to understand any documents which happen to survive. Second, we need a clear sense of direction based on what other historians have written in the relevant field. In public searchrooms, it is noticeable that trained historians skim through large numbers of documents, often for wide geographical areas, searching for evidence which is strictly relevant to their purposes. In doing so, they reject far more than they use. By contrast, many beginners doggedly plough through (and transcribe or xerox) everything they can find relating to their 'place', sturdily refusing to look at anything outside the magic boundary. Sadly, such shortsightedness frequently leads to writing which is unrelated to existing knowledge and current historical debates.

The search for new evidence, and for new uses of old evidence, never ends. For over forty years books, articles and pamphlets have been written on this aspect of research. Some of the older books of a general kind are still worth consulting such as W. G. Hoskins, *Local History in England* (3rd edn, 1984), W. B. Stephens, *Sources for English Local History* (2nd edn, 1981) and Alan Macfarlane, *A Guide to English Historical Records* (1983). Especially helpful are Philip Riden's *Record Sources for Local History* (2nd edn, 1998), Paul Carter's and Kate Thompson's *Sources for Local Historians* (2005) and Evelyn Lord's *Investigating the Twentieth Century* (1999). This broad approach has been kept alive by the Historical Association's re-issued *Short Guides to Records*, edited by Lionel Munby and Kate Thompson (1994 and 1998). In parallel with these introductory works are more specialised guides dealing either with with particular groups of sources such as P. D. A. Harvey, *Manorial Records* (1984), or with major historical themes such as A. Morton, *Education and the State from 1833* (1997).[5] Nor should we forget that county record offices still

<hr>

[4]   French and Hoyle, *The Character of Rural Society*, p. xxiii.
[5]   Guides to subjects and sources were regularly published by TNA (Research Guides), the British Records Association (Archives and the User), the Historical Manuscripts Commission (Guides to Sources in British History) and the Historical Geography Research Group (Research Series).

produce guides and pamphlets to their own collections,[6] that journals like *The Local Historian* and *Family and Community History* regularly publish articles about particular kinds of evidence, and that important leads can be found in *VCH* volumes, especially through their numerous footnotes.

Nevertheless, a major shift has occurred in recent years. The spate of printed guides to sources, which was such a feature of the 1980s and '90s, is fast drying up. It is now accepted that advice of this kind is better conveyed through the internet, where sites can be much more easily updated. Thus the 'Research Guides' which for many years have been produced by TNA as paper handouts can now be consulted online. Completely electronic is 'Access to Archives' (A2A) which was founded in 2000 and by December 2007 contained over 10 million searchable records held in 414 record offices and other repositories.[7] Other initiatives using the internet are county-based or regional. Thus, in 'Access Hampshire Heritage' the county record office, museum service and other local groups provide examples of typical sources available in that county, and the 'Cumbrian Manorial Records Project' run from Lancaster University aims to encourage the use of this important class of record, especially for the period from the fifteenth to eighteenth centuries.

It is not the purpose of this book to discuss the potentialities of particular manuscript or published sources, but five general points about the search for evidence ought to be mentioned, because they inevitably affect the quality of our research and writing.

Published primary sources

Transcribed sources and edited texts must be approached with the same caution as raw manuscripts. It has to be remembered that transcription and editing have not always been of a consistently high standard. Editors have been known not only to make mistakes but also to select, omit, alter, add and transcribe freely – all without proper acknowledgement.[8] The problem continues into the electronic era because online publications are often flawed and inadequately checked. Even with a scrupulously accurate transcription or abstract, an editor always stands between us and the original manuscript. For example, we rely on that person for

---

[6] For example, Derbyshire in 1994 and West Glamorgan in 1998.

[7] <www.nationalarchives.gov.uk/a2a>.

[8] Though their achievements were monumental, the publications of the Record Commissioners contain some interesting flaws. In their version of the Hundred Rolls (*Rotuli Hundredorum*, ii, 499) published in 1818, the nunnery of Chateris (Cambs) appears as OKACERIF: L. Munby, S. Hobbs and A. Crosby, *Reading Tudor and Stuart Handwriting* (2005), 6.

our appreciation of the 'archaeology' of the document – the material of which it is made, its state of preservation, the character of the handwriting, the layout, and the physical background from which it comes.

It is regrettable that although local historians can be very knowledgeable about manuscript sources, they can be comparatively ignorant about those in print. If they were more willing to comb the latter, particularly those with good indexes, they would find not only new evidence for their own research, but also highly instructive parallels from other places and periods. Most major libraries and record offices contain printed transcripts and abstracts which can yield valuable evidence for every local historian. Obvious examples include the large folio volumes of the old Record Commissioners, official calendars produced by The National Archives (TNA, formerly PRO) and the Historical Manuscripts Commission (HMC, now part of TNA), and volumes issued by record societies both nationwide and for individual regions and counties (Appendix 1, pp. 127–31).

In this field, the effects of today's digital revolution are unavoidable for both professionals and non-professionals. The growth of electronic transcriptions, facsimiles, databases, calendars and indexes of a wide variety of primary sources is exponential and can be baffling to the inexperienced. Fortunately, specific guidance for local historians is now available through the work of people such as Jacquie Fillmore.[9] Examples of digitised sources which could be of value in many different contexts include the complete CD version of the 1881 census published by the Church of Latter Day Saints; the Historical Population Reports which reproduce abstracts of censuses from 1801 into the twentieth century (over 185,000 printed pages); the 'Old Bailey Online' website with its fully searchable accounts of over 100,000 criminal trials; the 'Clergy of the Church of England Database' which aims to document all clerical careers between 1540 and 1835; and the official calendars of state papers, including the *Letters and Papers of the Reign of Henry VIII*.

Meanwhile, sources for individual places (yet with potential for more general application) are also proliferating online or on CDs. Typical examples are a summary of York's medieval deeds from 1080 to 1530; a calendar of the court rolls of Dyffryn Clwyd from 1294 to 1422; the port books of Gloucester 1575–1765; and a collection of nineteenth-century records belonging to the Hampshire village of Sparsholt.[10] A ground-breaking project in Cheshire has resulted in the placing

---

[9]   J. Fillmore, 'Local History Internet Sites: A Handlist', *TLH*, 37, 3 (Aug. 2007), 193–203; *TLH*, 38, 3 (Aug. 2008), 216–23; these lists appear annually in August, with a website review article in the February issue of *TLH*.

[10]   Church of Latter Day Saints, *1881 British Census and National Index*, CD-ROM, Salt Lake City (1996); Historical Population Reports, <www.histpop.org>; official calendars,

online of all the county's tithe maps (nearly 500 of them), with direct electronic comparison to Ordnance Survey maps and aerial photographs.[11]

The electronic publication of facsimiles has the happy effect of reducing wear on originals, and at the same time reducing the chances of being misled by an editor. Further consequences follow. The digital revolution is already thought by some to be causing a decline in the numbers of searchers visiting record offices (particularly family historians from home and abroad), because they are now able to find evidence online in their own homes. Others have argued that the changes are creating a more educated and demanding type of searcher. Either way, we cannot dodge the fact that many contemporary documents exist *only* in digital form (the so-called 'born digital' sources). They will have to be conserved, catalogued and accessed in a totally different way from traditional parchment and paper. As Margaret Procter has warned, the record office of the future will undoubtedly be quite different from that of today.[12]

Secondary sources: published work of other historians

This aspect, though it may seem merely an extension of the last, cannot be over-emphasised. We must never forget the value of wide reading in and around our chosen subject and period. Indeed we should start with such reading, and continue it for as long as the project lasts.[13] A reading of the published work of other historians (usually referred to as 'secondary sources' or 'historiography') yields several substantial benefits. It helps us to avoid unnecessary duplication, leads to the discovery of other comparative studies, and gives background knowledge which powerfully influences our own reconstruction of the past. This is how, for example, we judge how far local events were reflections of national life, how far they were part of regional trends, and how far they were uniquely local. An

<www.british-history.ac.uk>; Old Bailey trials, <www.oldbaileyonline.org>/; clergy of C of E, <www.theclergydatabase.org.uk>; Arts and Humanities Data Service, <http://ahds.ac.uk>; Gloucester Port Books purchasable as CDs from Adam Matthew Publications; R. Young (ed.), *Sparsholt, 1841–1901: a Hampshire Village Microhistory*, CD, Wessex Historical Databases, Univ. of Winchester (2007).

[11] 'e-mapping Victorian Cheshire: Cheshire's tithe maps online', <http://maps.cheshire.gov.uk/tithemaps/>. Worcestershire's tithe and enclosure maps are also available online and by CD; see *Landscape History*, 29 (2007), 89–92.

[12] See Margaret Procter, 'The end of [Local] History: Will twenty-first century sources survive?', *TLH*, 36, 4 (Nov. 2006), 249–51; also Steve Bailey, 'Taking the road less travelled by: the future of the archive and records management profession in the digital age', *Jour. of the Soc. of Archivists*, 28, 2 (Oct. 2007), 117–24.

[13] A. Rogers, 'Reading about Local History', *LHM*, 36 (Nov.–Dec. 1992), 19.

obvious example lies in the effect of parliamentary legislation. When a parish is found to have built a workhouse in the early eighteenth century, it should be seen in the light of the Workhouse Test Act of 1723 which positively encouraged such initiatives. Similarly, when we read in sixteenth-century churchwardens' accounts of the destruction of images, stone altars, relics and vestments, we have to be aware of the acts, ordinances and injunctions which drove the English Reformation.

We cannot assume that if something is in print it is 'right'. In fact, we should approach the secondary literature as we would grandfather's diary or tomorrow's *Guardian*. They are someone else's version of the past, never entirely correct or complete, and not in any sense holy writ. Nor can historians ever start with a blank sheet, but are inevitably influenced by their own preconceptions, impressions and snippets of knowledge. Moreover, because they have a duty to interpret and to use their evidence with controlled imagination, they often disagree. At first this may seem an embarrassment, but disagreements and historical controversies frequently lead to significant advances in knowledge – because scholars stimulate each other to think again, to ask new questions, to analyse sources more deeply, or to seek entirely new evidence. An awareness of the background historiography constantly reminds us that we are not working on our own, and that history is a cooperative and cumulative search for the truth. Furthermore, it never ends.

It is no accident that most academic articles and books begin by reviewing the publications of other historians. This means concentrating on the latest available research, and not remaining content with material published, for example, in the 1960s or '70s. In truth, a well-researched project does not merely touch the published work of others, but grows organically out of it. By weighing the interpretations and opinions of our predecessors, in and around a particular subject, we gain two priceless advantages. First, we find cracks in their arguments for us to prise open and insert our own contributions and, second, we better appreciate the relevance and potential of our primary evidence. In that way, we avoid the aimless accumulation of information for its own sake, and begin to work more logically and cumulatively. Indeed, this interaction does not only happen when embarking on a project; it commonly recurs in the course of research and writing, and becomes almost cyclical. As we write, we return to what others have written, bouncing our thoughts off theirs, articulating our own interpretations with more precision, and simultaneously trying to fit them into a web of existing research.[14]

The amount of history now being published in books and journals is truly

---

[14]   Essays and dissertations often receive lower marks than their writers expect, because of insufficient background and general reading.

daunting, not to speak of newsletters, bulletins, CDs, DVDs and the internet. For local historians, the problem is compounded by the width of their interests, for they rightly try to keep in touch with a wide range of specialisations. In practice, the best chance of coping and using time productively lies in the regular scanning of references, bibliographies, reviews and abstracts.

Most national and local journals contain book reviews (although delays of several years after publication are not uncommon). Among the most obvious periodicals for local historians to comb are *English Historical Review, History, The Local Historian, Archives, Scottish Historical Review* and *Welsh History Review*, and regional journals such as *Northern History, Midland History* and *Southern History*. Most of us, according to our interests, will also want to consult journals of a thematically specialised kind, for example *Local Population Studies, Family and Community History, Economic History Review, Rural History, Agricultural History Review, Urban History* and *The Journal of Ecclesiastical History*. In addition to formal book reviews, some journals publish useful lists of recent publications. For instance the *Economic History Review* in its November issue has an annual 'List of publications on the economic and social history of Gt Britain and Ireland', divided according to themes such as social structure, religion, education *and* 'local history'. *Urban History* is particularly noteworthy for its bibliographical aids which include 'review essays', a review of articles in periodicals (written by leading authorities and divided chronologically), a review of recent academic theses, and an annual bibliography of urban history divided thematically. Every quarterly issue of *The Local Historian* has an invaluable section entitled 'Recent publications in local history' which details not only all books, pamphlets and CDs sent to the reviews editor, but also a very wide range of local and regional journals, many published by local history societies. No such listing can ever be complete, but this is certainly the most comprehensive available coverage of locally-published material.

Especially stimulating are articles which 'round up' and critically assess the latest and most significant work on a particular subject. In recent issues *The Local Historian* has carried 'review articles' on the local political history of inter-war Britain, the role of record societies, and recent research on Wales and on the London area. In a similar way, *Archives* and *Agricultural History Review* publish annual reviews of work in progress, while the *Annual Bulletin of Historical Literature: a Critical Review of New Publications*, published by the Historical Association, divides British history by period and subject.

Another useful guide and time-saver is provided by abstracts (brief summaries) of articles within periodicals. Increasing numbers of academic journals are printing these summaries, usually at the head of individual articles and sometimes gathered together at the beginning of an issue.[15] This extra editorial requirement puts pressure on contributors to think hard about the essence of their research. While some abstracts are undeniably weak and unrevealing (often ending with the words '… are discussed' or 'will be considered'), the better ones are a great boon to readers who want to know quickly whether a particular article is likely to be of interest and relevance to them.

Appendix 1 on pp. 127–31 gives more information on printed sources, both primary and secondary. Here it is enough to say that they include books and journals of general and national history; histories of parishes, towns, counties and regions; biographies, diaries and journals; official calendars or summaries of original documents; lists and indexes of national archives; the publications of record societies; county historical and archaeological journals; newspapers and advertisements; maps, engravings and photographs.

Making human contacts

Anyone committed to research and writing must seek contact with people who may be able to help, whether in the finding of evidence, in its interpretation, in suggesting relevant reading, or in commenting helpfully on drafts. Of course students writing dissertations and theses automatically receive the critical appraisal of supervisors. Those outside formal courses, however, must seek advice from archivists and librarians,[16] and where necessary make contact with other specialists such as place-name experts, archaeologists, ecologists and art historians. It may also help to gain the confidence of any person who can get admission to places normally inaccessible, open up private collections, or recall useful memories. But the most valuable links are undoubtedly with other working historians. For example, much information and many sources are found by accident, and if we

---

[15]   For example, in *Urban History* and *Economic History Review* the abstract appears at the head of each article, while in *Northern History* abstracts are gathered at the beginning of each issue. The *Welsh History Review* has an excellent series of short abstracts collected on an annual basis. The *British and Irish Archaeological Bibliography*, published twice a year, contains abstracts relating to local history. Useful information can also be obtained from wider-ranging abstracts. The *British Humanities Index* is a quarterly guide to articles in British journals and newspapers; it surveys most national and regional (not county) journals of history and archaeology. *Historical Abstracts* is a quarterly which surveys 'the world's historical literature' in two main series, A (1450–1914) and B (1914 to present), each with a good index. Abstracts of each article published in *The Local Historian* appear on the website of the British Association for Local History.

[16]   See Diana Winterbotham and A. Crosby, *The Local Studies Library: a Handbook for Local Historians* (BALH, 1998).

hope that others will note references which may be useful to us, we must be prepared to do the same for them.

Such help clearly depends on good personal relations, and on the regular exchange of news and views. Both have been promoted in recent years by the widespread use of e-mail and the internet. On the other hand, it still remains important for historians to meet and talk face-to-face, especially at county and regional levels. Good examples can be seen in lectures and seminars organised by universities, in their centres of local and regional history, which enable professionals and amateurs to discuss current or recently completed research. Another source of inspiration can be major national conferences organised by universities, societies and research groups. The essential point is that individuals who are isolated inevitably restrict their own development as historians, and anyone intending to write cannot afford to be without such help and support. Naturally, whenever significant help of any kind is received, it should be acknowledged as a matter of courtesy and honesty.

Physical evidence

By definition, an historian's basic task is to interpret verbal evidence. This he or she will find in primary sources produced for many purposes in the course of everyday life, in sources which have been edited and published, in oral evidence which is now firmly within the historian's domain for the study of the twentieth century,[17] in the rapidly growing mountain of secondary literature in which generations of historians have attempted to reconstruct the past, and of course on websites. Nevertheless, sensitive local historians will also be very conscious of the physical landscape or townscape around them, which was created and minutely named by successive generations as they adapted their environment according to their economic resources and technical abilities. For example, how can anyone writing about religious beliefs neglect the fabric and furnishings of local churches and chapels?[18] Is it possible for a student of farming to ignore basic soils, relief and drainage, the changing shapes and sizes of fields, earthworks like ridge-and-furrow and wood-banks, and the patterns revealed by aerial photography? All these features are not merely of antiquarian interest, but are serious historical evidence of how previous generations thought and made decisions. In spite of the documentary-cum-archaeological work of modern scholars such as Chris Dyer

---

[17] See <http://oralhistory.org.uk> for advice on this approach.

[18] The argument cuts both ways. How is it possible for someone studying ecclesiastical architecture to neglect liturgical practices and religious beliefs?

and Oliver Rackham, some historians are still very distrustful of fieldwork and archaeological evidence. It is amazing how often, for instance, economic historians writing about urban markets have ignored the market-places themselves with their special internal buildings, zoned stalls, encroachments, inns, weights and measures, and instruments of punishment. In doing so, they have stubbornly omitted evidence relevant to their subjects. Incidentally, certain kinds of visual document such as maps, paintings, engravings and early photographs may prove vital in linking the material world to standard written sources.[19]

Nobody expects the local historian to become expert in other, fundamentally different disciplines. Without adequate training it is dangerous to blunder into highly specialised fields like the study of place-names. Nevertheless, with our more catholic approach to the past we should consider other forms of evidence and draw on the knowledge and publications of other specialists – where they are relevant to our own interests and where two or more kinds of evidence can be usefully cited and combined. While recognising the perils of stepping into unfamiliar territory, we must be flexible enough to follow where our subject leads. Above all, this means having the confidence to approach recognised authorities in other fields of study.

The storage of information

Local historians ought to acquire the elementary techniques for finding and storing information. For example, without reading every word, they must 'gut' books and articles to assess their value, by skimming contents-pages, conclusions and indexes. They need to become familiar with the conventions behind transcripts, translations, abstracts, calendars and bibliographies; and must know how to use indexes and catalogues in libraries and record offices whether they be in the form of card-indexes, files, microfilm, fiche, disks or online. These are skills which we should all have been taught at school but, alas, seldom were until quite recently. Fortunately, librarians, archivists and searchroom assistants are usually prepared to explain how their reference-systems work – if asked at a convenient moment – or they can provide introductory leaflets. It is significant that most postgraduates beginning research today need an introduction to 'study-skills' of this kind.

---

[19] See N. W. Alcock, *People at Home: Living in a Warwickshire Village, 1500–1800* (Phillimore, 1993), pp. 12–19. A catalogue of prints and drawings in the British Museum is available online: <http://tinyurl.com/3ah3og>. For a stimulating local selection of images, see J. H. Farrant (ed.), *Sussex Depicted: Views and Descriptions, 1600–1800*, Sussex Record Soc., 85 (2001).

The next step is to develop an efficient system of note-taking. Many able people never write because their information is badly recorded and stored. It is asking for trouble to scribble on odd bits of paper or the fabled 'backs of envelopes'. Similarly, if one fills up bound notebooks with hundreds of miscellaneous facts and references, one simply buries the information yet again, and complicates the business of retrieval at a later stage. Admittedly time should not be spent on unnecessary organisation, and in practice most of us improvise rather reluctantly as the raw materials, in whatever form, threaten to engulf us. In the last three decades, however, historical research has been revolutionised by the adoption of personal computers and portable laptops with their ever-increasing speed and memory. This modern technology is proving especially valuable for the storage, retrieval and analysis of historical information, principally in the form of spreadsheets and databases. In record offices and libraries, the laptop is now a common sight (and less than welcome sound). With this machine, researchers can cut out intermediate tasks and dispense with traditional pencils, rubbers and notepads. They can, for example, type transcripts of original documents straight into the machine and print-out any number of copies; or they can immediately transfer data from manuscripts to a previously prepared scheme of analysis with many different categories or 'fields'. Thus, details from tithe apportionments can be directly allotted to an unlimited number of headed columns in a spreadsheet (containing either numbers or words, or both), such as number, name, acreage, land-use, owner, occupier and tithe-rent.[20] Most of us, at any age, would benefit from courses introducing such helpful programs as Excel and Access (see p. 147).

However, for reasons of finance, temperament or age, some historians will always prefer to work in traditional ways. A good manual method, developed long ago by the staff of the *VCH*, can still be adapted to most circumstances. Basically, each discovered 'fact' with its reference and a short heading is put on a separate slip of paper.[21] Slips need to be of a standard size, stored in a filing cabinet (or cheap substitutes such as shoe-boxes or stout envelopes), and divided into obvious categories by means of index-cards: Church, Market, Public health, Disorder, etc. When it comes to writing on a particular topic, the relevant slips can be pulled out, perhaps from several subdivisions, re-read and arranged in logical order.[22]

---

[20]   Software manuals are notoriously difficult to follow. Nevertheless, helpful introductions to the mysteries of word-processing and computing can be found in some recently published books such as S. Cameron and S. Richardson, *Using Computers for History* (Palgrave Macmillan, 2005). See Bibliography on p. 124 below.

[21]   See 'Notetaking for VCH' on the Derbyshire VCH website.

[22]   R. B. Pugh, *How to Write a Parish History* (Geo. Allen and Unwin, 1954), pp. 136–9. Of course the logical order of slips will not necessarily be chronological (see above, pp. 90–1).

An advantage of slips is that they can be run through quickly, like bank-notes. On the other hand, cards are more hard-wearing and stand better in a box. As a further refinement, some researchers use slips or cards of different colours: to facilitate sorting each colour is devoted to a major aspect of the subject. Other frequently chosen methods include loose-leaf files, box-files, large envelopes, wallets, heaps on the floor and heaps going up the stairs. Needless to say, all quotations, transcripts and appropriate references must be made accurately, so that one does not in any way misrepresent a source. Finally, because the progress of research is not predictable, one has to be ready to incorporate new and unexpected developments. This means that, whatever system of recording is adopted, manual or computerised, it must be flexible, easy to sort and capable of both expansion and subdivision.

As one's work proceeds, one should always make separate records of primary and secondary sources. For example, a careful list should be made of all manuscript sources consulted, under their respective repositories. Similarly, every time a useful book is found, its bibliographical details should be fully noted (including a library reference for anything rare or early). Thereafter, any information derived from that source need only be abbreviated.[23] Another major aspect of modern research is that one frequently photocopies articles in journals, wholly or partly,[24] or makes notes from them. Again, one needs to keep these secondary sources in an orderly way (box-files are highly suitable, with marked spines). It also pays to maintain a special computerised file or 'article bank' recording all those articles which one has found useful, with their full bibliographical references.[25]

---

[23] Thus, one's index of sources might contain: J. Thirsk (ed.), *Hadlow: Life, Land and People in a Wealden Parish, 1460–1600* (Kent Archaeological Soc., 2007). Individual references from the same book need only carry an abbreviation such as: Thirsk, *Hadlow*, p. 55 *or* Thirsk (2007), p. 55.

[24] It is amazing how often in photocopying one accidentally cuts out the page-numbers.

[25] I am grateful to Heather Falvey for this point.

5

Transcribing

F ACED WITH original documents, the first task of historians is to transcribe the written message or that part of it which they want to use. In many cases this means no more than careful reading and accurate copying. The earlier the document, however, and the less familiar the handwriting, the more necessary it is to deploy the skills of the palaeographer. For many researchers this in practice means becoming familiar with the Secretary Hand of the Tudor and Stuart periods, but for a smaller and braver number it means tackling the double problem of medieval palaeography and Latin. Yet even with quite modern documents, a measure of palaeography is always needed: for example the long 's' was still being used in the nineteenth century, and most local historians have been baffled by certain words written in the tight copperplate of Victorian census enumerators. Moreover, in every generation individuals have had their own idiosyncracies of style, and some have always written hurriedly and badly. And, to be honest, most of us at times have been unable to read our own handwriting! This is a reminder that palaeography always involves two styles: that of the period and that of the individual writer.

This book is no place for a detailed discussion of handwriting and its elucidation. Fortunately good manuals are available, covering both the medieval and early modern periods, and courses in palaeography can now be found online.[1] Not only do they explain the normal forms of capital and lower-case letters, but also deal with related problems such as joined letters (ligatures: ff, st), the survival of Anglo-Saxon characters (the 'thorn' (Þ, þ) and 'yogh' (ȝ, ȝ), or the tironian et (7) which is an early form of ampersand), Roman and Arabic numerals, and the vexing habit of abbreviation (see pp. 135–6). Even the simplest manuals, which usually provide

---

[1] The courses on medieval and early modern palaeography constructed by Dave Postles of Leicester University are amazingly detailed. Other good aids are provided online by TNA and The National Archives of Scotland.

facsimiles on one page with a full transcript opposite, are sufficient to motivate the novice who is willing to practise.[2]

In the last resort, palaeography is not so much taught as learnt by sustained practice. One must try to explain every stroke of the pen and mark on the document, even if they turn out to be unimportant – like a space-filler, the 'pip' on the end of a bracket, an ink-blot or an imperfection in the paper or parchment. The modern photocopier, scanner and digital camera are blessings which enable us to practise at home on documents which we positively want to crack.[3] We can begin with relatively easy examples and then, motivated by success, tackle more demanding ones. Students can often, after a few months' persistence and hard work, acquire the expertise to read documents back to the early sixteenth century. A few go much further and in time become competent readers of medieval palaeography.[4]

In reading and transcribing historical documents, it is vital to develop good habits from the start. (Let us take for granted good light, the right pair of spectacles, a magnifying glass, a copy of an 'alphabet' showing the different forms of each letter,[5] and perhaps access to an ultra-violet lamp.) A fundamental principle is that we must not guess or muddle through, but read slowly, deliberately and comparatively. If a word is difficult to interpret, look for it elsewhere in the same document where it may be clearer. In reading historical documents one frequently asks oneself questions such as: how does this scribe normally write his lower-case 'r' or his capital 'S'?

Transcriptions of documents are normally made in one of three ways. Although an increasing number of people type directly into laptop computers, the majority of searchers in record offices still (in 2009!) make a copy in long-hand using the required pencil.[6] A few, at the risk of disturbing other searchers, dictate their

---

[2] L. C. Hector, *The Handwriting of English Documents* (E. Arnold, 1958); G. E. Dawson and L. Kennedy-Skipton, *Elizabethan Handwriting, 1500–1650* (Faber, 1968); P. M. Hoskin, S. L. Slinn and C. C. Webb, *Reading the Past: Sixteenth and Seventeenth Century English Writing* (Univ. of York, 2001); L. Munby, S. Hobbs and Alan Crosby, *Reading Tudor and Stuart Handwriting* (BALH, 2002). Particularly helpful and well illustrated is Hilary Marshall, *Palaeography for Family and Local Historians* (Phillimore, 2004). For abbreviations, see C. Trice Martin, *The Record Interpreter* (Phillimore reprint, 1994).

[3] Permission has to be sought for photographing documents in record offices, and a fee may be payable.

[4] Courses are available in palaeography and medieval Latin, residential, non-residential and online. For example, the Latin and Palaeography Summer School at Keele University has been running for over 30 years.

[5] As in H. Grieve, *Examples of English Handwriting, 1150–1750* (Essex Record Office, 1954), fig.1, and Munby, Hobbs and Crosby (BALH, 2002), pp. 4, 7–10.

[6] By far the best tool is a propelling pencil, which eliminates the use of pencil-sharpeners.

reading into tape-recorders and later transcribe their tapes.[7] If, like me, you still transcribe in long-hand, remember to write in a large, clear and well-spaced hand. Otherwise, at a later stage, details may be easily misconstrued. For example, a hastily scrawled transcript may fail to distinguish 'c' from 't', '3' from '5', and capitals from lower-case letters.

If you are stuck over a particular word, leave a space in your transcription and read on. Sometimes a later line will give you the same word in a clearer form, or the context will suggest a meaning. If neither happens, the mere act of leaving and later returning with a fresh eye often leads to success: what had been a shapeless squiggle suddenly becomes understandable. But even the most skilled palaeographer will sometimes be defeated, and must honestly admit failure by leaving a gap or writing 'illeg.'. Sometimes we may provide a reading but are not entirely sure of it. Here, in the interests of honesty and accuracy, a question-mark should be inserted immediately before the word or number. All such editorial insertions should be placed within square brackets and, if later published, in italics: thus [?], [sic], [damaged] or [illeg.]. One final point of great importance. Having transcribed a document, re-check your transcript against the original at least once, because errors can easily creep in. And check it again if you go on to publish it, or quote from it. For the basic rules and conventions in transcribing original documents, see Appendix 3 on pp. 135–41.[8]

Translating

Where documents are written in a language other than English, historians also have to translate. They certainly do this mentally as they read and transcribe their sources, but at a later stage they may also need to write a formal translation – especially if it brings a significant document to the attention of a wider audience. While the palaeographer is concerned with symbols or characters, the translator

---

Another useful piece of equipment is a rubber, preferably pen-shaped because it can be used quite delicately. Note, however, that some record repositories including TNA ban the use of rubbers.

[7] Technologically it is possible that scanners will in the future be able to produce transcripts of manuscripts, as they already do for printed materials. Will they ever be capable of producing reliable translations?

[8] Every teacher of palaeography remembers spectacular howlers. Instead of the familiar phrase in early wills, 'for tithes forgotten', I was once offered 'for tips for Satan'. An interesting trap is presented by the English word 'eme' or 'eam' meaning 'uncle', which is sometimes interpreted as a woman's forename: 'myn *Emma* and myn awnte' (see J. O. Halliwell, *Dictionary of Archaisms and Provincialisms*, I (London, 1852)).

focuses on meanings. At this point, the complexities of historical interpretation begin to appear: our understanding of what the writer meant to convey starts with his or her choice of words. In practice the foreign language which the local historian is most likely to meet is Latin, which continued to be used in legal documents until 1733. We are fortunate to have good aids in R. E. Latham's *Revised Medieval Latin Word-List* (reprinted in 2004) and the *Dictionary of Medieval Latin from British Sources* (up to 'Pel' in 2007), backed up by that old faithful, B. H. Kennedy's *Revised Latin Primer* (reprinted in 1993). It is also advisable to have access to classical dictionaries such as C. T. Lewis and C. Short, *A Latin Dictionary* (last impression 1991) and the *Oxford Latin Dictionary* (2 vols, 1968 and 1982). For those with no knowledge of Latin, or who need to revise the Latin of their schooldays, the best printed helps are Eileen Gooder's *Latin for Local Historians* (1961) and Denis Stuart's *Latin for Local and Family Historians* (1995), while online the TNA offers a practical tutorial called 'Beginner's Latin, 1086–1733'.

An element of translation is necessary in the reading of any document, even relatively modern ones written in English. This is because words are constantly changing in meaning and emphasis. Just think of the traps waiting for the unwary in the following:

- 'prevent' which formerly meant 'go before'
- 'honest' meant 'competent'
- 'impotent' meant 'frail' or 'aged'
- 'steeple' meant 'tower'
- 'carpet' meant 'table cloth' or 'covering'
- 'indifferent' meant 'impartial'
- 'incontinently' which in the Middle Ages meant 'without delay', later meant 'unlawfully' or 'sinfully', and finally became associated with bodily malfunctions.[9]

In addition, documents often contain dialect words and technical language which need to be recognised. Here again, help can be found in key reference books. If the full *Oxford English Dictionary* does not provide the answer, then turn to the valuable *Middle English Dictionary* (completed in 2001 and available online), or Joseph Wright's *English Dialect Dictionary* (6 vols, 1898–1905), J. O. Halliwell's *Dictionary of Archaisms and Regionalisms* (2 vols, 1852), and *A Medieval Farming*

---

[9]   A dramatic modern example is the fate of the word 'gay' which, in a few years, acquired a completely new meaning and lost its traditional one. It may now be undergoing another change of meaning, known only to the young.

Glossary of Latin and English Words (revised by A. and R. Powell, Essex Record Office, 1998). Further help can be found in, for example, Joy Bristow's *Local Historian's Glossary* (1994) and David Hey's *Oxford Companion to Local and Family History* (1996, revised 2008) which is in effect a dictionary.

Historians who compile glossaries of regional or technical words perform a valuable service. Two impressive recent examples are David Yaxley's *Researcher's Glossary of Words found in Historical Documents of East Anglia* (2003) and David Butcher's *Rigged for River and Sea: A Researcher's Guide to Late Medieval and Early Modern Terms relating to Fishing*.[10] Fortunately this practice seems to be spreading in record publications and elsewhere.[11] When words are rare or important historically, glossaries are particularly useful if they contain cross-references to: 1) the published dictionaries which help to explain them, and 2) the folios or pages where they occur in the original document or record publication (see Appendix 19, pp. 194–5).

It should be noted that through its Historical Reading Programme the *Oxford English Dictionary* now incorporates information from modern editions of original documents. These can sometimes reveal forms of words earlier than those in literary texts, and even totally new words. The *OED* is interested in hearing from local historians on such matters, and already receives a steady trickle of information as well as queries about unidentified words. Contact can be made through the *OED Online* website. Here, once again, local history is contributing to a different specialisation.[12]

Abstracting and extracting

Frequently, however, working historians do not transcribe or translate every word in the manuscripts they study. They choose to create an 'abstract', which

[10] David Yaxley, *A Researcher's Glossary of Words found in Historical Documents of East Anglia* (Larks Press, 2003); David Butcher, *Rigged for River and Sea: A Researcher's Guide to Late Medieval and Early Modern Terms, relating to Fishing ... mainly from English Sources* (North Atlantic Fisheries History Assocn, Maritime Historical Studies Centre, University of Hull, 2008).

[11] For example, A. J. L. Winchester (ed.), *The Diary of Isaac Fletcher of Underwood, Cumberland, 1756–81*, Cumberland and Westmorland Antiq. and Archaeol. Soc., extra ser. xxv (1994), 453–7; D. Levine and K. Wrightson, *The Making of an Industrial Society: Whickham, 1560–1765* (Oxford, 1991), pp. 447–9; French and Hoyle, *The Character of Rural Society*, pp. xiv–xviii.

[12] *ex inf.* Kate Tiller and Edmund Weiner.

is a careful summary in modern English.[13] In this way they record all significant statements in a more compact form. For example, wills contain a great deal of repetitive verbiage such as 'Item, I leave and bequeath ...' and 'The residue of all my goods and chattels', which are easy to summarise (Appendix 4, pp. 142–3). The danger of this approach is that one might omit detail which later turns out to be important, for example the opening religious clauses of mid sixteenth-century wills which have recently been the subject of vigorous controversy. This surely suggests that abstracts should be made only when one is thoroughly familiar with a particular class of record. Within an abstract most historians choose to transcribe certain words and phrases exactly, within inverted commas, because they could be worthy of later quotation.

Even more commonly, we find it sufficient to 'extract' those parts of documents which are relevant to our interests. For example, some historians comb church-wardens' accounts for references to poor-relief, while others hunt for drama and festivities. The technique is the same as for making notes from printed sources. Again, it is usually important to transcribe particular words and phrases exactly, because they may be useful quotations, and one should always be careful to note the source of each extract (including page or folio, and date). It is very easy to extract carelessly, failing to distinguish genuine quotations and omitting references. This either wastes time because one has to go back a second time to check detail or, worse still, introduces error into one's writing.

Handling the results

By all such methods – transcribing, translating, abstracting and extracting – one accumulates great quantities of handwritten notes or print-outs which have to be kept under control. Certainly it is advisable that paper should be of standard size, and properly filed so that items can be easily recovered when needed. One may choose to transfer salient details with appropriate references into a computerised database, or into a separate card- or slip-index.[14] Alternatively, transcriptions can be given various underlinings, highlighting, asterisks, marginal headings and notes, so that useful information can be more easily retrieved when one comes to writing. Such additions should be distinguished from the original transcript

---

[13]   In this book, the word 'abstract' is used in two related senses: a) a summary or calendar of the contents of original documents, some more 'full' than others, and b) a brief summary of published articles and books (see above, pp. 59–60).

[14]   Every time one copies information or references, one increases the chance of making errors. All the more reason, therefore, to check carefully.

by, for example, using a different writing material or colour. The same treatment can be given to photocopies and other types of facsimile. (For group-work in palaeography, see pp. 47–8.)

A note on dating

When transcribing a document, one must be careful to note any kind of dating. To avoid confusion, the best policy is to transcribe the date *as given* and then, if necessary, to give its modern equivalent in square brackets. Such conversions depend on knowing when the year began in the past. For example, in England from the late twelfth century until 1752, the New Year began on 25 March ('Lady Day', the Annunciation of the Blessed Virgin Mary). Also relevant to dating across the centuries is knowledge of the regnal years of kings and queens, the official years of popes, bishops and abbots, and above all the liturgical feasts of the Christian church. As a guide through this maze, we have C. R. Cheney's classic *Handbook of Dates for Students of British History* which first appeared in 1945 and is still kept in print by the Royal Historical Society (last revised, 2000). For its detailed use, see Appendix 5, pp. 144–5, 196.[15]

---

[15] For the official years of bishops, archbishops and holders of major offices of state, see E. B. Fryde *et al.* (eds), *Handbook of British Chronology* (CUP, 1996). Relevant volumes of the *VCH* give the official years of local abbots and other heads of monastic communities under 'Religious houses'. For popes, see Cheney, *Handbook of Dates* (CUP, 2000), pp. 48–58. For a general discussion of dating and useful lists and tables, see L. M. Munby, *Dates and Time: a Handbook for Local Historians* (BALH, 1997).

6

Analysing and
assembling evidence

No document and no statement, official or non-official, is beyond question.
(G. Kitson Clark, *The Critical Historian*, 1967, p. 80)

A historian is always concerned with not one but two distinct events – the historical event which he is studying and the event of communication which has produced his evidence.
(D. Vincent, *Bread, Knowledge and Freedom*, 1981, p. 5)

D ocuments do not present the historian with established 'facts' or straight-forward, reproducible 'truth'. Indeed we are doomed to failure if we merely collect pieces of information, and attempt to write history by stitching them together. An historical document can only convey someone's version of what happened in the past, and it will assuredly mislead anyone who approaches it uncritically and with no sense of historical context. Historians have a duty to interpret, and must read and re-read, always pondering on the significance of the text before them. The main method of analysis is, first, to ask relevant and probing questions; and second, because the original writers cannot normally be re-interviewed, to work out as many answers as are possible. Questions will be concerned with both the general character of sources and the detail which they contain. As Gordon Forster wisely remarked, 'In the use of archives, he finds the most who has some idea of what he is looking for.'[1]

Practical researchers, whatever their period of study, cannot remain entirely

---

[1] G. C. F. Foster in an unpublished paper read in October 1980 at a meeting of CORAL, to discuss methods and problems in the teaching of local history in higher education.

unaware of the historical science of Diplomatic. This set of critical techniques was developed in the nineteenth century for investigating the origins, character and legitimacy of documents – particularly, as the word implies, the official diplomas and charters of the medieval period. The essential point is that the questions which a diplomatic historian might ask about a medieval charter should pass through the mind of any historian faced with original evidence. Who wrote it, or at least what kind of person? When, if only approximately, was it written? Does its physical character, say the handwriting, fit the alleged date? Is it a copy? Could it be a forgery?[2] This is not necessarily a process of rejecting some sources and accepting others. For example, forgeries may contain useful information; by contrast genuine documents do not necessarily tell the whole truth and are most revealing of writers' priorities, assumptions, guesses and prejudices, and of the system within which they were working.

Pressing deeper into the character of a document, we as critical historians try to enter the writer's mind and assess his or her purpose. As before, we consider a range of pertinent questions. For example:

- For whom was the document written?
- What parts of the document reflect the personality of the writer (temperament, knowledge, ignorance, interests, emotions or prejudices)?
- How far is the document based on first-hand experience; or derived at second or third hand? What parts appear to be opinion or guesswork?
- What parts, if any, are determined by administrative procedures or by the conventions of the period?
- Does the document contain information which can be corroborated in other sources? Conversely, to what extent are its contents unique?
- What does the document not say? Does silence mean that something did not happen, or that it was consciously omitted? (This is the vexing dilemma of negative evidence.)

The whole purpose of this critical exercise is to assess the document's strengths, weaknesses and real historical significance (as opposed to its stated meaning). In other words, how far can it be assessed in terms of truth, ambiguity, omission, distortion and falsehood? In a single document, any or all of these qualities

---

[2] A valuable application of diplomatic technique is in identifying the work of early writers and antiquaries. The manuscripts of such people are often unsigned, undated and at a later date frequently dispersed, re-arranged and copied. See A. Hassell Smith, *The Papers of Nathaniel Bacon of Stiffkey* (4 vols, 1979 to 2001).

can appear. Such enquiries do not constitute an arcane method known only to professionals. They are the kinds of question which will occur to any thoughtful reader, or which any good teacher will try to stimulate in the minds of students faced with a literary text, a piece of music or a work of art. It should be noted that the questions themselves will not normally feature in our writing. The answers, however, will inevitably colour the way in which we construct our argument.

The vast majority of historical documents were written either for contemporary purposes or as a record for personal, legal and administrative reasons. They were certainly not composed to supply evidence for future historians. When we first deal with a new class of record, the special procedures of the originating system may not be immediately obvious. With experience, however, we learn what kind of information to expect and the kind of language normally employed. Among other things, we come to appreciate 'common form', the recurrent words and phrases which say more about the administrative system than about the individual case. When, for example, a pre-Reformation will mentions money bequeathed to the high altar of a parish church 'for tithes and offerings negligently paid and forgotten', it is not commenting on the shameful life of that particular testator, but using a time-honoured formula whereby the laity of this period compensated the clergy for inevitable lapses and carelessness. So in practice the answers to many critical questions will depend on the width of our experience and the depth of our background knowledge. Alternatively, for the beginner, it will depend on getting the right kind of advice from suitable reading and from more experienced historians.

Methods of analysis

To wrestle with the details within documents, we must again adopt a questioning approach. For instance, in the case of probate inventories, we may ask how many rooms are noted in local houses (remembering that some, especially if empty, may not have been mentioned at all)? How were rooms named? How many rooms were heated? Is it possible to reconstruct the plans of ground-floors and first floors? Do furnishings reveal how rooms were used (e.g. for cooking, eating, sleeping, receiving guests, storage, etc.)? What were the dominant colours and textures in rooms? Our questions are not necessarily purely 'factual'. They often contain assumptions and judgements based on previous reading. For instance, we presume that the presence of fire-irons in a room implies a fireplace; we are not told as much and could sometimes be wrong.

When dealing with a mass of documents, historians inevitably produce large quantities of notes, transcripts, photocopies or printouts. We are therefore forced by the sheer mass of information not only to store it efficiently but also to process it in a systematic way. Many different methods are possible, ranging from elementary to computerised, but they are all intended to sift, sort and re-assemble so that helpful distinctions can be made, and comparisons and generalisations built up. When all the information on a particular theme has been gathered, we are in a much better position to make our own judgements and calculations, and thus turn the corner from mere analysis to creative interpretation.

How, therefore, do we handle all the verbal and numerical information in our documents? A common method is to draw up forms or databases where details can be noted or counted in appropriate boxes or columns. Well-known examples of a traditional kind are the paper forms for the analysis of parish registers designed by the Cambridge Group for the History of Population and Social Structure. They provided standardised ways of discovering overall trends in baptisms, marriages and burials, of identifying crises such as plague and dearth, of reconstituting families over generations, and of uncovering factors such as age at first marriage, fertility, family size, illegitimacy and life expectancy. To return to probate inventories, forms of analysis have been compiled for household furniture such as beds, tables and chairs, for stock-in-trade such as the contents of shops and craftsmen's tools, for various kinds of crops and animals owned by farmers, and for highly-priced goods such as glassware, silverware, clocks and maps.

Of all forms of analysis, the most valuable are those which conflate information from two or more documents. Some historians, for instance, regularly devise databases which bring together, for named individuals, evidence from wills, inventories, parish registers, hearth-tax returns, rate-books, poor-law examinations and so on (Appendix 6, pp. 146–50). It should also be remembered that well-designed analyses lead directly to the creation of figures, tables and graphs which are an important part of modern historical writing.

Historical analysis has been revolutionised by the use of fast and powerful computers, allied to highly sophisticated software. The spread of scanners, moreover, ensures that documents can now be transferred directly into computers in their original printed or manuscript forms. Many still need to be transcribed and/or translated, but scanners in the future will probably do that too! Of course, it must be recognised that digitisation, now so beloved of archivists, is only an interim stage in making sources accessible: much remains to be done educationally to help users extract the true meanings and historical significance of what they are reading. But given both factors, the present generation of historians can handle much larger quantities of data, and question and process them much faster and are expected to do so. At Sowerby and Calverley in Yorkshire, for example, detailed computerised work on a wide variety of familiar sources helped to reconstruct the lives of poor landless cottagers:

> We can now see how often and at what points in the life cycle they received poor relief; discover from whom they rented accommodation or land; identify the ways in which their occupations changed over time; and study the constant short-distance movement which appears to have been characteristic of weavers and labourers in the townships. We can see who they married, how many children they had, how many died in childhood or became pauper apprentices …[3]

Across the whole of Britain an impressive list of documents is now being computerised including parish registers, port books, hearth-tax and land-tax returns, wills and inventories, probate accounts, census enumerators' books, admission books for workhouses and prisons, urban rate-books and trade directories – all of which are familiar to local historians. A good example of local enterprise is a project called Bristol Historical Databases, which has amassed many original sources for the city, including poll books, local obituaries and historical statistics, and makes them available cheaply on disk.[4]

This technological revolution works for the local historian at several different levels. For example the computerised cataloguing of archives is opening up new areas for exploration. Already from our own homes we can consult the detailed catalogues of some libraries and record offices. Once complete sources or extracts have been fed into a word-processor, details can be retrieved, re-arranged, linked to produce new knowledge and also mapped. Of course the largest projects involve groups of academics and special funding, but some lay historians are as committed to this powerful new technology as their professional colleagues.

No two people will draw up identical spreadsheets or forms of analysis, and there is no reason why they should. Documents are infinitely variable, and historians themselves have different priorities. A method has to be found which is appropriate to each task. In scale it must be large enough to wring useful generalisation from all relevant detail, but not so elaborate as to have almost as many headings as the document has details. The easiest documents to process are those which have standardised layouts like poll-books and census enumerations.

---

[3]   P. Hudson, 'A new history from below: computers and the maturing of local and regional history', *TLH*, 25, 4 (Nov. 1995), 219.

[4]   Bristol Historical Databases Project, <www.uwe.ac.uk/hlss/history/staff-pwardley_bhdp. htm>.

The most difficult are those which have variable and unpredictable contents such as letters and personal journals.

Systematic analysis conveys another important advantage: it encourages us to make mathematical calculations. Certain classes of document contain many numbers, such as acreages in surveys or sums of money in accounts, while others present verbal information in such a repetitive way that it too can be quantified, as with different types of offence brought before magistrates in quarter sessions. The word 'cliometrics' is sometimes used to describe the mathematical revolution within history, and manuals are regularly written to encourage greater numeracy among historians.[5] Numbers and statistics must not be allowed to obscure the essential humanity of the subject, but at the same time we must not neglect any opportunity of giving our work greater precision.

Another major benefit to flow from documentary analysis is the discovery of entirely new historical 'facts'. For example, in a classic article published in 1966 E. A. Wrigley showed that an outbreak of plague between November 1645 and October 1646 had killed 392 people in the east Devon town of Colyton. He did not read that figure in any document, but calculated it by counting hundreds of entries in a parish register. Then, by making certain assumptions about the birth-rate at that time, he estimated that those deaths represented about one-fifth of the whole population.[6] So, by re-arranging and re-assembling information, the historian is able to create broader, more generalised and integrative pieces of information. These usually prove valuable in writing because they 'boil down' detail which could never be presented in its original cumbersome form.

Relating varied sources

Historical research normally involves 'record linkage', that is, the simultaneous use of several kinds of evidence to discover how they interact. Thus as a way of giving width and depth to our work, we regularly survey clusters of documents, although individually they were written for different purposes and from different points of view. Take for example the census returns, tithe apportionments and commercial directories which are widely used by students of the nineteenth century. Censuses were organised by central government to provide standardised statistics on population; tithe apportionments were part of a national movement

---

[5]   P. Hudson, *History by Numbers: an Introduction to Quantitative Approaches* (Arnold, 2000).

[6]   E. A. Wrigley, 'Family limitation in pre-industrial England', *Econ. Hist. Rev.*, 2nd ser., xix (1966), 82–109.

to rationalise clerical incomes, by ensuring that money-rents replaced payments in kind; directories were commercial surveys aimed at selling useful information to the principal inhabitants of local towns and villages. Therefore evidence drawn from these sources varies in range, depth, reliability and levels of involvement with the subjects described. Yet out of this puzzling mixture of statements and statistics historians have to reconstruct, as best they can, what local communities were like. This linking of different sources is a way 'of controlling vast quantities of information and enabling the historian to see patterns and make hypotheses that would otherwise be impossible'.[7]

Where points of contact exist, we are naturally keen to discover how far sources seem compatible and mutually supporting, and how far they are discordant. This is not to isolate some documents as true and others as false: we are embarked on a far more hazardous and subtle process than that. Our interpretation will certainly be more complicated than if we had used only one source, but at the same time it will be a more realistic reflection of the convoluted truth. In our minds we allow documents to adjust to each other, so that we become increasingly conscious of their relative strengths and weaknesses, and can begin to construct an overall picture. Census enumerations, for example, give us information about every man, woman and child in a given locality (names, relationships, ages, occupations and birthplaces), but they can be misleading about certain family relationships and the occupations of wives and children. They will describe some individuals as farmers, and even mention their total acreages and the number of men and boys employed, but they will not reveal where each person's land lay. By contrast, a tithe apportionment with its map can show who owned and who tenanted every field and plot in the parish. In its turn, however, it may be vague about the number of tenants in a tightly built-up area, and which cottages or tenements they actually occupied.

In spite of such difficulties, these two kinds of source are often compared and interwoven, especially when they are close in date. They underpin the technique of 'house repopulation' which is used to discover where individuals and families lived in nineteenth-century settlements. In other words, the strongly topographical evidence of tithe apportionments is deliberately put against the much more personal detail of census returns.[8] The normal point of contact between the sources lies in personal names: the head of the family mentioned by the census

---

7   A. Tanner, 'The Great Ormond Street historical patient database project', *Archives*, xxviii, 109 (Oct. 2003), 141.

8   A. Henstock, 'House repopulation from the census returns of 1841 and 1851', *LPS*, 10 (Spring 1973), 37–52.

enumerator may be repeated, or is at least recognisable, in a list of owners or tenants in the apportionment. Once links have been recognised, it may be possible to see not only where families lived and where they held land, but where particular classes, occupations and even ethnic groups tended to congregate, and what living conditions were like in particular streets and houses.

One of the fascinations of local history is that it usually gives the opportunity of using non-verbal, physical evidence – such as domestic buildings, churches, funerary monuments, tools and implements, archaeological sites, field-systems, industrial remains and a host of other artefacts and landscape features. For example, many years ago I was thrilled to discover that an attractive green lane along our parish boundary, now merely a farm-track noted for prolific cowslips, was described in a sixteenth-century manorial survey as 'The Quene's High Waye' leading to a market town ten miles away. It is in fact part of a broad drove-road which for centuries linked two different but interdependent agricultural regions. But exciting though this kind of coordination can be, it often raises new problems.

Words and physical remains are very different kinds of historical evidence, and sometimes they appear to conflict. They therefore have to be carefully studied, each in its own terms, before they can be convincingly associated. Apparent contradictions invariably disappear when we realise that we have wrongly or inadequately interpreted one or both kinds of evidence. Let me give two very different illustrations. In 1860 a Suffolk clergyman named Richard Cobbold wrote of his rectory, 'I built this house in the year 1827'. A superficial inspection of the surviving building soon reveals a substantial timber-framed structure probably dating from the sixteenth century, to which a large 'Regency' wing of brick had been added in the early nineteenth century. The building therefore has a more complicated structural history than Cobbold's loose language suggests. The written statement, however, does reveal his personal attitude to the old-fashioned parsonage which he had inherited and thought beneath his dignity. The second example, more complex, comes from a late-medieval burial found in 1987 under the crossing of Worcester cathedral; it belonged to a well-nourished layman aged about 60 whose skeleton was clothed in woollen garments and long boots. He wore a pierced cockleshell and beside him lay a long ash-staff stained deep purple from an expensive and exotic dye called 'kermes'. When discovered in 1987 this 'Worcester Pilgrim' was already thought to be Robert Sutton, the wealthiest dyer of Worcester in the early fifteenth century, tax-collector, member of the city council and eventually bailiff, who was dead by 1457. Since then, further documentary research has all but confirmed that the skeleton was indeed Sutton's, showing that he was at least 54 when he died; that he requested burial in the cathedral before the image of St James and also evinced a powerful devotion to that cult by endowments in his parish church. Moreover, the skeleton's boots, which were once thought to belong to the sixteenth century, are now seen as consistent with a fifteenth-century date.[9] These are the kinds of problems and opportunities which Barrie Trinder had in mind when he wrote of historical and archaeological evidence coming 'fruitfully into conflict'.[10]

---

[9]   K. Lack, 'A Dyer on the Road to St James: An Identity for the Worcester Pilgrim', *Midland History*, xxx (2005), 112–28.

[10]   B. Trinder in A. Rogers and T. Rowley (eds), *Landscapes and Documents* (SCLH, 1974), p. 79.

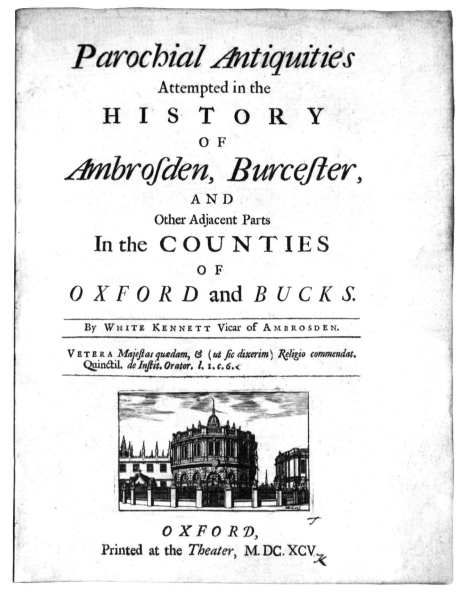

Parochial Antiquities
Attempted in the
H I S T O R Y
O F
Ambroſden, Burceſter,
A N D
Other Adjacent Parts
In the C O U N T I E S
O F
O X F O R D and *B U C K S.*

By WHITE KENNETT Vicar of AMBROSDEN.

VETERA *Majeſtas quædam,* & (*ut ſic dixerim*) *Religio commendat.*
Quinctil. *de Inſtit. Orator. l. 1. c. 6.*

O X F O R D,
Printed at the *Theater,* M. DC. XCV.

PLATE I. Clerical history

White Kennett's *Parochial Antiquities of Ambrosden, Burcester and other adjacent parts* appeared in 1695, and is generally regarded as one of the first published parish histories in England (see p. 126). It contains 703 pages plus an index and an impressive glossary of terms. The author was vicar of Ambrosden and later became bishop of Peterborough. It is worth remembering that Anglican clergy have not only been avid students of local history, particularly in the eighteenth and nineteenth centuries, but that they also wrote many primary documents which local historians now regularly study (for example parish registers, visitation returns, glebe terriers, tithe-books and personal journals).

AN

ACCOUNT OF

The Oakleys
[SUFFOLK.]

WITH

A

COMPILER'S VAGARIES ABOUT SOME INHABITANTS THERE

WHOSE NAMES

HAVE BEEN FOUND

IN VARIOUS RECORDS

Dating From Early

TIMES.

———◆———

Privately Printed Between The Years 1936 and 1942

being now

Offered to the STUDENT of such matters,
for Correction and Completion, if ever the task
be WORTH WHILE.

2

PLATE 2. The antiquarian approach

This book on the adjacent parishes of Great and Little Oakley in Suffolk first appeared serially in the years 1936–42, and was then published anonymously. Like so many examples of local history in the pre-Hoskins era, it now appears unredeemably antiquarian, sentimental and uncritical in its approach, as is clearly reflected on the title-page. Sad to say, it still has its counterparts today, written by well-meaning authors who dedicate many hours and considerable expense to their projects. Giving no shape or direction to their writing, they pile up miscellaneous pieces of information, throw in over-long quotations, and fail to give references.

PLATE 3. Upper-crust history

Early antiquaries focussed their histories on the lives of landowning gentlemen and aristocrats, and among their primary sources were funerary monuments in churches bristling with effigies, heraldry and fulsome inscriptions. From the mid-twentieth century, however, their successors deliberately switched attention to the 'common people' (farmers, labourers, craftsmen, traders and paupers, with their wives and families) and a new range of sources came into vogue such as wills, inventories, poor-law records, tax returns, rate-books and census enumerations. Much of this 'new' local history was concerned with occupational, social and religious groups rather than with individuals. Since the 1970s, renewed interest in landowning families, great estates, local administration and the dispensing of justice has given the study of local communities a more balanced and coherent framework. (Tomb of Sir Ralph Fitzherbert and his wife, St Mary's Church, Norbury, Derbyshire. Photograph: Carnegie.)

PLATE 4. Perishing documents

Written documents of any material, particularly those made of paper, parchment and vellum, have always been subject to damage, as this sad collection from the Wiltshire and Swindon History Centre at Chippenham, powerfully illustrates. They have frequently suffered from damp, fading, the attacks of vermin and insects, erasure, re-use, careless storage, theft and fire. Every piece of historical research reveals that evidence has been lost, and today one still hears of new losses and careless acts of destruction. Even documents made of stone, such as gravestones in churchyards, often perish as a result of natural erosion or human vandalism. Therefore any methods for accurately recording or duplicating the texts carried by such documents are to be welcomed. (Wiltshire and Swindon History Centre, Chippenham.)

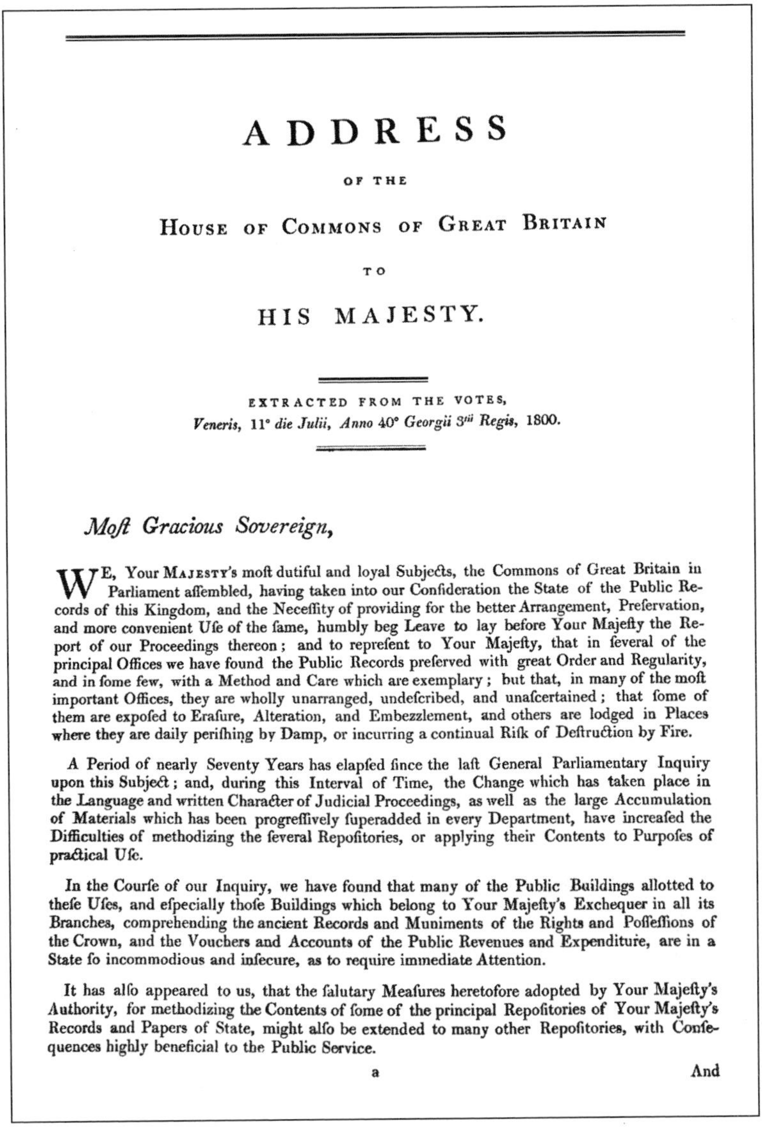

ADDRESS

OF THE

House of Commons of Great Britain

TO

HIS MAJESTY.

EXTRACTED FROM THE VOTES,
Veneris, 11° *die Julii, Anno* 40° *Georgii* 3*tii* *Regis,* 1800.

Moſt Gracious Sovereign,

WE, Your MAJESTY's moſt dutiful and loyal Subjects, the Commons of Great Britain in Parliament aſſembled, having taken into our Conſideration the State of the Public Records of this Kingdom, and the Neceſſity of providing for the better Arrangement, Preſervation, and more convenient Uſe of the ſame, humbly beg Leave to lay before Your Majeſty the Report of our Proceedings thereon; and to repreſent to Your Majeſty, that in ſeveral of the principal Offices we have found the Public Records preſerved with great Order and Regularity, and in ſome few, with a Method and Care which are exemplary; but that, in many of the moſt important Offices, they are wholly unarranged, undeſcribed, and unaſcertained; that ſome of them are expoſed to Eraſure, Alteration, and Embezzlement, and others are lodged in Places where they are daily periſhing by Damp, or incurring a continual Riſk of Deſtruction by Fire.

A Period of nearly Seventy Years has elapſed ſince the laſt General Parliamentary Inquiry upon this Subject; and, during this Interval of Time, the Change which has taken place in the Language and written Character of Judicial Proceedings, as well as the large Accumulation of Materials which has been progreſſively ſuperadded in every Department, have increaſed the Difficulties of methodizing the ſeveral Repoſitories, or applying their Contents to Purpoſes of practical Uſe.

In the Courſe of our Inquiry, we have found that many of the Public Buildings allotted to theſe Uſes, and eſpecially thoſe Buildings which belong to Your Majeſty's Exchequer in all its Branches, comprehending the ancient Records and Muniments of the Rights and Poſſeſſions of the Crown, and the Vouchers and Accounts of the Public Revenues and Expenditure, are in a State ſo incommodious and inſecure, as to require immediate Attention.

It has alſo appeared to us, that the ſalutary Meaſures heretofore adopted by Your Majeſty's Authority, for methodizing the Contents of ſome of the principal Repoſitories of Your Majeſty's Records and Papers of State, might alſo be extended to many other Repoſitories, with Conſequences highly beneficial to the Public Service.

a　　　　And

PLATE 5. Milestones in record publication

In 1783 a full transcription of Domesday Book was published in two handsome volumes (using special type); two more containing related documents and indexes were to follow decades later. In July 1800, following an address by the House of Commons to George III, Record Commissioners were appointed to supervise the publication of other major documents. This extract comes from their first volume of 1802 which was entitled *Taxatio Ecclesiastica Angliae et Walliae* or 'Taxation of Pope Nicholas'. For the year 1291 it listed all English and Welsh parishes under their respective dioceses, archdeaconries and deaneries, with their valuations and, if applicable, the portions owned in them by religious houses. The address to the king reproduced here expresses anxiety about documents being stored chaotically and exposed to various kinds of damage. Since then many other sources have been edited, published and calendared at national, county and local levels. Even so, a huge amount of such work remains to be done.

PLATE 6. The Strong Room

This photograph of Strong Room 2 in the Lancashire Record Office at Preston reminds us of the prime responsibility of archivists, to keep records safe and secure. It shows how original documents of different shapes and sizes are shelved, boxed or wrapped and kept in carefully controlled conditions which involve steel doors, mobile shelving, damp-proofing, temperature controls and the use of argon gas as a fire-retardant. In recent years entirely new record offices with impressive modern facilities have been built in Essex, Hampshire, Norfolk and elsewhere. Similarly the two great central institutions in London, The National Archives and British Library, have been moved to more spacious premises at Kew and St Pancras respectively. (Jacquie Crosby and Lancashire Record Office.)

PLATE 7. The Search Room

This is the space, or series of spaces, in a record office where the public come to consult historical archives and published sources. It symbolises the 'democratisation' of history because searchers can include all ages from schoolchildren to pensioners, and all types from beginners searching their family histories to scholars of international repute. As well as basic tables and chairs, facilities normally include catalogues in several different forms, access to the internet, microfiche and film readers, map presses and a working library. For the average searcher, much depends on the helpfulness and expertise of the staff 'behind the desk'. It has been argued that in the next 50 years, record offices and their search rooms will change markedly as personal visits become fewer and ever more documents become available online or are 'born' electronically. (Photograph supplied by the Wiltshire and Swindon History Centre, Chippenham.)

	Surname	Other names	Directory Heading — The Post Office Directory of Hertfordshire, 1870	Census Heading 1871 Census	CEB Ref	Address	Census/Age,Origin
	Chamberlain	James	*PH, Fox & Duck* /Furniture Dealer		2,34	Great Lane	62, London
WID	Clambert	Elizabeth (Mrs.)	Shopkeeper	Marine Store Deale	2,26	River Green	53/W, Therfield
	Clayton	Joseph	General Dealer	Carrier	2,13	High St	45, Buntingford
SON	Clayton	Walter	Shopkeeper	Grocer	4,1	Wyddial/High St, B	21, Buntingford
	Cocks	Benjamin	Surgeon/Medical Officer, Union North-eastern & South-eastern D		2,11	High St	38, Middx: Kensington
	Copeland	William	Shoe Maker	Bootmaker	1,6	Buntingford/Aspen	65, Herts: [Furneux] Pel
	Coxall	Levi	*PH, Bell*	Farmer of 20 acres	2,37	Baldock Lane	53, Herts: Anstey
	Croft	George Edmund	Master, Union House		2,22	Union Workhouse	37, Middx: Hayes Married
	Croft	Mary Ann Crock	Matron, Union House		2,22	Union Workhouse	34, Devon: Newton Abb
	Dellow	William	Insurance Agent, Railway Passengers'/E	Miller, Baker & Corn Me	2,10	High St	34, Herts: Gt Hormead
Fam?	Dellow	Henry	Miller	Father, John Dellow, fori	2,39	The New Mill	29, Buntingford
	Dodd	Jane (Mrs.)	Haberdasher	Fancy Shopkeeper / Leather Cutter's Wife	2,15	High St	43, Wilts: Wroughton / See 1861/1881 !
	Farrington	Thomas	Boot & Shoe Maker [Master]		2,17	High St	46, Layston
	Flint	John	Tailor/Draper	Tailor [Master]	4,1	Wyddial/High St, B	37, Beds: Shillington
	Fordham	Alfred	Beer Retailer/Veterinary Surgeon	Publican & Farrier	2,9	High St, *Star Beer*	30, Sandon
	Froode	William	Inland Revenue Officer			*George & Dragon*	
	Gayler	John Rogers	Watch & Clock Maker		2,15	High St	32, Herts: Stevenage
	Gibbons	William	Insurance Agent, County Fire & Life/Buil	Builder emp 60 me	2,14	High St/Layston	56, Suffolk: Bramford
	Gisby	George	Clerk to Magistrates/Clerk to Association for Prosecution of Felons				
Fam?	Gray	Edward	Bricklayer				
	Green	William	*PH, Crown*				
	Grout	George & Willia	Saddlers & Harness Makers				x2
WID	Hamilton	Maria (Mrs.)	Ironmonger/Brazier/Smith	Ironmonger emp 5 men	2,14	High St/Layston	68/W, Essex: Chelr SON
	Hankin	William	*PH, White Hart* /Butcher (Pork)	Publican	1,3	High St, Buntingford/Asp	53, Royston
	Horsnell	George	Blacksmith				
	Houchin	John	Plumber & Glazier & Painter	[Master]	2,15	High St	58, Buntingford
	Howard	Richard	Chimney Sweeper [Master]		1,5	High St, Buntingford/Asp	34, Hitchin
Fam?	Hoye	Esther (Miss)	Confectioner		1,2	High St, Buntingford/Asp	50, Aspenden
	Hunt	William	*PH, Adam & Eve*	Carpenter	3,2	Throcking/Buntingf	58, Throcking
	Hunt	Joseph	Clerk to the Guardians				
	Jones	Charles	Station Master		1,12	Buntingford/Aspen	38, Norfolk: Norwich

A computerised analysis (using Excel) of tradesmen and professionals in the small town of Buntingford (Herts) in the later nineteenth century. In his doctoral thesis, Peter Bysouth has here assembled data from two trade directories of 1870 and 1882 and from the censuses of 1871 and 1881. (See p. 148.)

Surname	Other names	Directory Heading	Census Heading	CEB Ref	Address	Census/Age,Origin
		Kelly's Directory of Hertfordshire, 1882	1881 Census			
Chamberlain	James	*PH, Fox & Duck*	& Upholsterer	2,19	GreatLane	74, Herts: Sawbridgeworth
Clayton	Joseph	Draper/Stationer/Fruiterer/Furniture Dea	General Dealer & Fancy	2,16	High St	56, Buntingford
Clayton	Walter	Coach Painter	Joseph's Son	2,16	High St	31, Buntingford
Clowes	John	Baker				
Cocks	Benjamin	Surgeon & Medical Officer, Union North-eastern & South-eastern		2,16	The Court/High St	48, Middx: Kensington
Coxall	Levi	*PH, Crown*	Publican & Laboure	2,1	Market Hill	63, Herts: Anstey Wid?
Dellow	William	Insurance Agent, Railway Passengers' /	Miller & Baker emp	2,2	Market Hill	45, Herts, Gt Hormead
Dodd	Jane (Mrs.)	Berlin Wool Repository	& Fancy Shop Kee|	2,14	High St	53/W, Wilts: Elcom[b]e
Dunn	Edmund George	Police Inspector			Police Station	
Farr	John	Beer Retailer	& Dealer	2,6	*Globe Beerhouse* ,	28, Hitchin
Farrington	Thomas & Son	Boot & Shoe Makers	Thomas	2,12	High St	55, Buntingford
	Henry	Bootmaker [Journeyman]		2,12	High St	26, Buntingford
	Joseph Ironmon	See Ironmonger below				
Feasey & Ironmonger		Insurance Agents, Norwich Union Fire/Grocers (Family) & Provision Merchants/Wine & Spirit Merchants				
	Fredk Feasey		Grocer	1,2	Aspenden /Bunting	36, Bucks: Olney
Flint	John	Tailor/Woollen Draper	Tailor	2,3	High St	47, Beds: Shillington
						Fam?
Gaylor	John Rogers	Watch & Clock Maker		2,14	High St	42, Herts: Stevenage
Gibbons	William & Co.	Insurance Agents, County Fire & Provident Life/Builders&Contractors/Surveyors/Lime Burners/Brick, Tile & Drain Pipe Makers				
Gotobed	Charles Cropley	Painter &c.	Plumber emp 1 ma	2,3	*Bell Public House* ,	35, Cambs: Ely
	John	Bell Hanger		2,15	High St	48, Buntingford
Hamilton	John & Charles	Ironmongers	See Maria below			
	Charles			2,14	High St	40, Buntingford
Hamilton	Olivia (Mrs.)	School Mistress, Adams' Memorial School for Girls & Infants				
Hankin	William	*PH, White Hart*	Pork Butcher	2,19	Great Lane	63, Royston
Hancock	William Joseph	Station Master		1,4	Aspenden/Buntingf	37, London: Whitechapel
Howard	James	Miller	& Corn Dealer emp	2,41	Mill House	35, Royston
Howard	Richard	Chimney Sweeper		2,36	Chapel End	45, Hitchin
Hoye	Esther (Miss)	Confectioner		1,2	Aspenden/Buntingf	60, Aspenden
Hunt	William	*PH, Adam & Eve*	Farmer	3,3	Throcking/Buntingf	67, Buntingford
Hunt	Joseph	Clerk to the Guardians & RSA			Ware/Excluded	
Ironmonger	J. & Co./Jose	Grocers & Provision Dealers/Ale & Porte	Grocer emp 2 men	2,4	High St	48, Beds: Luton
King	Robert	Saddler		2,12	High St	68, Cambs: Melbourn

PLATE 8. The National Archives (TNA)

Formerly the Public Record Office (PRO), this important institution moved in 1977 from its Victorian quarters in Chancery Lane to extensive new riverside premises at Kew in west London. For many users the site is inconvenient, being well away from mainline rail termini, but the service, once you have arrived, has certainly changed for the better. Many of us can remember how forbidding the atmosphere used to be in Chancery Lane, but now the TNA welcomes searchers of all kinds, and the majority are family historians in what has truly become a public service. No local historian can neglect the riches which are kept here, or fail to use the various finding-aids increasingly available in printed and digitised forms. (The National Archives of Scotland (NAS) is the equivalent in Edinburgh.)

PLATE 9. The British Library (BL)

Equally important for local historians, this magnificent and many-faceted collection of both printed and manuscript works moved in 1997 from its traditional base in the British Museum in Bloomsbury to new premises in the Euston Road (close to several major rail termini: notice St Pancras station looming in the background). While the exterior and forecourt evoke mixed feelings, most visitors seem to enjoy the light, roomy and well-appointed interior spaces as places in which to work. Here also is the National Sound Archive. (The Libraries of Scotland and Wales are in Edinburgh and Aberystwyth.)

Mrs A.3.B [born 1892, Barrow in Furness]

ER   Did you ever have rabbit?
R   Oh yes, I've had a lot of rabbit. M'father used to go rabbiting.
ER   How did he catch them?
R   He had a ferret. Then mother used to clean them, skin them and stuff inside it, get a needle and cotton and sew it all up and put it in the cooker.
ER   How often would he go ferreting?
R   Just when he felt like it. Then she would go to the market and get a sheep's head or a pig's head and cut the chawl off.
ER   That's the cheek, is it?
R   The cheek, and she used to roast them. She used to cut all the snoffal out and soak it in salt and water, boil it and make brawn of it. She used to put it in a basin with a two pound weight on and put it on the stone cold floor and then it used to turn out. She used to cut it and make our sandwiches. For father, she used to say, "When you're coming home from school, call and get a pair of kippers at three-ha'pence a pair or a penny bloater". That was for dad's tea and we used to have an egg.
ER   The children had an egg?
R   Yes. One would have the top of m'dad's today and another would have it another time. We used to suck the top and that was teatime.
ER   Was the brawn a teatime dish as well?
R   It was just a sandwich, not a knife and fork, just a sandwich at teatime and then, perhaps tomorrow, we'd have a jam sandwich.

Mrs H.4.P [born 1903, Preston]

And it was all the same pattern. Getting drunk coming home from work and giving her what was left. This was a more intimate life that was told to us by my mother's friends, the ones that used to come in and help her. One of them said many a night she's sat in their lavatory all night. I've known the second wife do the same—I don't say sat on the toilet but had to go out to a neighbour's house. He used to get the blues or something when he was drunk and he with was always threatening her with a knife or the axe. This is God's truth, every time she was pregnant she daren't tell him because he would start all over again, and naturally it was his child. She never got out and she wasn't even a drinker. She didn't know what it was to go and sit in a pub but he accused her all the time and it led from one thing to another. It hurts me to repeat it but nevertheless it's true, to think that your mum that's gone through all that. When the confinement happened he stood over her with a burning lamp threatening her, not doing it, terrifying her, revelling in terrifying her. He is dead, may God rest his soul!

PLATE 10. Oral evidence

Personal reminiscence and memory are important forms of evidence which have always been part of the study of history. They were used, for example, by classical writers and medieval chroniclers when writing about their own times or the recent past. In so doing, they drew on their own direct experience or on observations passed through to them by older generations. Yet, since the 1960s, academics such as Elizabeth Roberts of Lancaster University and local historians such as George Ewart Evans have taken oral history to a new level in Britain, in order to penetrate the lives of ordinary working people born in the nineteenth and twentieth centuries who have left few, if any, written records.

These two extracts come from careful transcriptions of oral interviews conducted by Dr Roberts. In the first the interviewer skilfully questioned a working-class woman from Barrow-in-Furness about the diet of her family when she was a child in the early years of the twentieth century. In the second a woman from Preston, born a decade later, needed no prompting as she reminisced with fluent emotion about her father's drunken brutality towards her mother. (Reproduced by kind permission of Elizabeth Roberts.)

PLATE 11. Rural history

Nothing could appear more English than the village of Taddington (Derbyshire) with its lanes, houses and church nestling in a natural hollow and surrounded by its own rolling fields. Here, surely, is a community conscious of itself against a slightly threatening outside world. It is hardly surprising that most books on local history, whether by amateurs or professionals, have been written about single rural parishes and villages. In 1964 this approach was famously encapsulated in Finberg's dictum that local history is about the 'Origin, Growth, Decline and Fall of the local community'.

Today, however, most historians emphasise the massive changes which transformed village life in the nineteenth century, without seeing them necessarily as a 'fall'. Rural communities usually survived these changes and many have since grown in area and in population. Also, moving forward, we begin to see huge potential in studying how villages changed after World War II as a result of new revolutions in agriculture, population, living standards and transport, and of values often described as 'gentrification' and 'suburbanisation'. Lastly, it is now widely realised that rural communities can never be considered in isolation from surrounding parishes, towns and regions. (Photograph: Alan Crosby.)

PLATE 12. A slice of industrial Lancashire

Although against a backdrop of traditional moorland farming, this scene taken at Lower Darwen near Blackburn will not be alluring to the average tourist or guide-book writer. The sprawling housing of different dates, pylons, huge white 'sheds' for commercial and industrial purposes, the M56 motorway with its signs and lamp standards, all contribute to what some people would call a 'blighted' landscape. On the other hand, it represents several generations of human decision-making and labour in the nineteenth and twentieth centuries, and that surely deserves study in its own right. Unfortunately, a deep-seated prejudice against industrialisation and urban life, and in favour of 'pretty' and 'historic' places, has for generations been characteristic of many local historians. This is partly why various groups have left the fold since the 1950s to found their own specialities such as 'regional history', 'industrial archaeology', 'community history', 'oral history' and modern 'urban history'. (Photograph: Alan Crosby.)

PLATE 13. Vernacular buildings

The study of domestic buildings was begun by earlier local historians, but since the 1950s has become a speciality with its own journal, national society and local groups. This small brick cottage (Gingerbread Cottage in New Buckenham, S. Norfolk), sits within a planned Norman market-town and graphically demonstrates how misleading the exteriors of buildings can be. As is common elsewhere, a nineteenth-century brick skin conceals a much earlier history (although an observant person might have wondered about the eccentric placing of the windows and door). Inside is in fact the perfectly-preserved frame of an early sixteenth-century house, consisting of a hall and service bay. The chimney stack, now sporting a modern TV aerial, was inserted in the seventeenth century into an earlier smoke bay, a primitive form of timber-framed chimney. The house also contained a well-preserved (and very rare) plank-and-muntin screen associated with the cross-passage, the position of which is marked by the door. The hall, with its smoke bay, was to the right. The exciting history of this house was revealed during a long-term study of houses in the town led by members of the Norfolk Historic Buildings Group. (Photograph supplied by Adam Longcroft, with the houseowner's permission.)

PLATE 14. The strange status of maps

Maps, whether manuscript or printed, present the historian with a special kind of hybrid evidence. On the one hand, by patterns of lines, shapes and symbols, and often by colours, they represent aspects of our physical environment, rural and urban. On the other hand, they contain verbal statements in the form of personal names, field and street names, measurements, keys and schedules. Cartography is therefore an extremely important way of relating the physical to the verbal, the topographical to the human, and therefore of actually putting 'people in their place'. It is clear that maps, as a form of evidence, are closely related to those paintings, drawings, engravings and photographs which also bear verbal messages. (Map of Clyffe Pypard (1742) drawn by John Overton of Devizes; photograph supplied by the Wiltshire and Swindon History Centre.)

7

Creative interpretation

Records, like the children of long ago, only speak when they are spoken to, and they will not talk to strangers.

(C. R. Cheney, *Medieval Texts and Studies*, Oxford, 1973, p. 8)

A T THIS POINT an especially venomous nettle has to be grasped. How do we as historians undertake our most demanding and creative task, that of shaping our own interpretations of the past? What is happening in our brains as we try to formulate our overall conclusions, and gird ourselves for the demanding business of writing? Of course it is true that an alarming number of people are content to guess and 'make up' their history. Examples can be regularly heard on television and radio, often given away by use of the speculative tenses 'would have' and 'could have'. Evidence does not bother such people, for they inhabit a perfumed and technicolour world of unfettered imagination. Others approach history as mere collectors, assembling and pasting together snippets of information without any attempt to analyse or synthesise them. Real historians, however, are intellectually and morally bound to penetrate the past in a much more thoughtful and painstaking way.

As was discussed in the last chapter, our first objective must be to argue with our documents and other evidence, until we have a satisfying picture of their combined significance. The result is a mass of factual and judgmental material, which is the essential basis for broader interpretation. When one is trying to tease out the significance of an historical event, one soon learns that some questions are easier to answer than others. For instance, it is relatively easy to appreciate *what* happened and *when*, but much harder to say *how* it happened, and almost impossible to say *why* it happened.[1]

---

[1] For these important distinctions I am deeply grateful to Alan Crosby (private correspondence).

It may seem dangerous to assert that we are also, in pondering our evidence, using our imaginations. Of course this does not mean that at a certain point we cut loose and romance wildly. In fact, imagination is used only as a way of breathing life into historical 'facts' and extending the scope of our critical faculties. It is, frankly, a form of speculation but *only* on the basis of known evidence. At the same time we confess our ignorance, by pointing out what sources do *not* say, what is unknown about the past and what, nevertheless, may have happened – though no evidence has been found to prove or disprove it, and only time and later historians may tell (or not).

But historical interpretation involves more than detailed attention to sources, vital though that is. Pieces of evidence are merely raw materials which the historian controls and uses for his or her own creative purposes, and they recede in importance as an over-arching reconstruction begins to crystallise in the mind. This is the 'interpretative', 'conceptual' and 'historiographically aware' history which so many tutors and examiners demand of their students, especially when they persist in writing of events and sources in a dull and descriptive way. The emphasis should now be on one's own vision of the past and how it relates to existing historical knowledge: not only describing what is known about a particular subject, but trying simultaneously to explain its wider significance. As Kate Tiller has written, 'Local history is always a balancing act in relating the particular and the general, judging the significance of the specific detail as part of an overall picture.'[2] The task is undeniably difficult and time-consuming, for one's interpretation has to be in the form of a logical and systematic debate, full of ideas, questions, uncertainties and judgements. Moreover, one's views may take some time to settle down, and even while writing one may still be refining the argument. Nor is it uncommon after publication to wish one had said something rather different!

It cannot be said too often that good history, whether spoken or written, has shape, purpose and direction. Because it has been logically designed, it is not choked with masses of ill-digested fact and quotation. Many bits of evidence and opinion will have been considered, but only as the raw material for broader statements or judgements. Some factual material will of course appear in our interpretation, but only to substantiate historical points and to sustain particular arguments. In other words, proper historians, although they are always thinking about evidence and sometimes quoting directly from it, are always trying to 'see the wood for the trees'. Their basic intention is to make connections, to clarify, generalise and draw conclusions – which does not mean over-simplifying, for

---

[2]   K. Tiller, 'Local history brought up to date', *TLH* (2006), 149.

nothing must be deceitfully omitted which is inconvenient or contradictory to one's case.

Vital to the shaping of our interpretations is the realisation that historical work is provisional and cumulative, never final and definitive. While doing research we obviously hope that our discoveries will to some extent stand the test of time, and turn out to be of interest and value to others (otherwise we would not want to publish). The converse is that we cannot ignore what other historians say and write. They can teach us about new sources and techniques, and offer studies to compare with our own. More importantly, they bring us into contact with a range of priorities, standards, opinions and arguments, and remind us of those general concepts, models and theories which lie behind all serious research. Consider, for example, the great interest today in family and community history. This is an emphasis which arises from both popular interest and academic research, and its influence has filtered through to almost every other form of history. Whatever our chosen subjects, we are now much more conscious of the structure of families, the importance of kinship, the extent to which people moved house and job, the extent to which others stayed put, variable expectations of life, the amounts of child mortality and illegitimacy, the effect of birth control, the prevalence of re-marriage, the roles of godparents and friends, and many other issues. In other words, ideas have the habit of spreading from one field of endeavour to another and, in so doing, they stimulate new thinking, new research and frequent re-assessment.

It is therefore a crude simplification to regard history as the creation of solitary researchers, with their heads down in private studies, faintly humming libraries and rather noisier record offices. Of course in one sense historical research *is* a lonely business (far more so than, for example, the pursuit of archaeology which by its very nature is more gregarious and noisy), but a good piece of history is the brainchild of someone who has deliberately sought contact with other minds – by means of conversation, correspondence and, above all, reading. Historians who ignore the work of other toilers in the same or related fields, are bound to be crippling their own appreciation of the past. No matter what the subject, we should always try to measure our discoveries against current historical opinion, to see how far they might confirm, challenge or amplify that opinion. That is why, at the start of our writing, we usually refer to other people's work, trying to move logically from the (fairly well) known to the (completely) unknown. It is also why, as we later develop our own detailed arguments, we still repeatedly refer in both text and footnotes to what others have put into print.

Of course the process of interpretation will have begun long before writing is seriously contemplated. While evidence is being found and analysed, one will already be thinking about possible uses and lines of argument. However, to get one's historical opinions into anything resembling a final shape, it still helps to communicate with others. One way of clarifying the mind, for instance, is to prepare a short talk or lecture. A much more effective way, without any doubt, is to commit oneself to writing.

To end this rather theoretical discussion, and to turn our minds towards the practical demands of writing, let me quote a specific example of interpretation from Pamela Sharpe's book on the Devonshire town of Colyton in the aftermath of the Monmouth Rebellion and battle of Sedgemoor in 1685.[3] Footnotes are not reproduced but indicated by asterisks.

> It is easy to romanticise this period but a general pardon was not issued until March 1686. Before this many fugitives had been camping out in the woods and some were forced in by the winter. The soldiers' searches through the houses of Colyton sound benign or even comical in the accounts of their examinations of the households of the Clapps or the Drowers, but there is every evidence that they shared the brutality of the Judge Jeffries trials, raping and pillaging as they searched. For three-quarters of the old style year of 1685 Colyton was, in effect, under a military occupation. The Calendar of State Papers records that in December 1685 the King requested a full enquiry into the holding force in the West and specifically ordered an enquiry into the looting of lace from the house of an honest citizen in Colyton, 'intending that the offenders should be punished according to the utmost severity of the law and that full reparation should be made'. Thirty-three out of the eighty-six Colyton rebels had been captured and their whereabouts and fate would have been largely unknown to their families.* There is also evidence that in towns as politicised of those of south-east Devon, rebels had many local enemies only too ready to turn them in. On return to Axminster, eight fugitives were caught and captured by fellow townsmen who were paid at the rate of £1 per rebel and 5d. for the cord to bind them.* The Lyme magistrates records show other evidence of 'treachery'. John Bailes of Axminster gave the names of twelve men from his own town and four from Colyton whom he had seen in Monmouth's camp and he provided more evidence to incriminate the minister Towgood, construing him as a political leader 'and saith that one Toogood a minister did often use the house of one Bryan a clothier in Axminster before Monmouth's landing'.*

---

[3]   P. Sharpe, *Population and Society in an East Devon Parish* (Exeter UP, 2002), p. 58.

We may question some of the writer's conclusions and, faced with the same evidence, each one of us would have made a different choice of words. Nevertheless, in one paragraph Sharpe has deployed the work of other historians, quoted primary and secondary evidence, changed focus from the local and personal to the regional and national (and back again), and drawn her own conclusions. She has remained clearly in control of her own knowledge, and imposed her own thinking on the subject – creating her own objective yet personal interpretation. This is history.

8

Starting to write

Historical writing is essential to historical understanding, and those who shrink from undertaking it are something less than historians.

(J. Tosh, *The Pursuit of History*, Longman, 2002, p. 94)

D O N O T postpone writing for too long because it can so easily be for ever. Some people procrastinate by saying that they have not finished their research, but this is usually an excuse rather than an explanation. It almost goes without saying that if one is facing a deadline, as with a dissertation or a publisher's timetable, it is even more important to begin writing in good time. Of course our evidence never seems enough in quantity or quality, and no research is definitive for all time. Indeed, we sometimes change our minds and come to different conclusions on specific points of interpretation. There is no disgrace in that, for the search for historical truth demands honesty and open-mindedness, and it never ends. Similarly the hunt for background reading to illuminate what we are finding locally, and for studies which are comparable to our own, is also never-ending. Yet beyond a certain stage our approach is not likely to alter significantly, and we should take the plunge. The longer writing is delayed, the more difficult it becomes to find motivation and to organise a formidable mass of material. As R. H. Worth wisely said, 'One always writes too soon; but if one puts it off, one may not write at all'.[1] Or, as an adult student once put it to me with quiet fatalism, 'It's a race with mortality'. In practice we do not necessarily have to write the whole study consecutively from A to Z: sections of text, dealing with distinct aspects of the total subject, can be written separately and later incorporated (with adjustments) into the larger work.

---

[1]   H. P. R. Finberg quoting R. H. Worth in J. Thirsk (ed.), *Agrarian History of England and Wales*, iv (CUP, 1967), vii.

Preliminary planning and the first draft

Before attempting to write on any subject, we should re-assemble all relevant information – whether in the form of printouts, facsimiles, transcripts, slips, cards, analyses, notes from secondary reading, or whatever. I find it immensely helpful to spread these things out physically, on a large table or on the floor. For increasing numbers of people, this stage involves the sorting of electronic documents and files, and the printing-out of hard copies (which for most of us are easier to study than successive texts on a screen). The mere act of finding and re-reading all these bits of evidence helps to clarify their relative significance and their interplay, and may lead to the rejection of marginal or irrelevant items. Furthermore, while the raw materials are spread out, we can experiment (for as long as it takes) with their physical arrangement, in the hope of finding a satisfying sequence which will form the basis of a piece of writing.

With all the evidence brought back to mind, and already to some extent ordered, we are in a position to draft an 'outline plan' or skeleton of ideas which can be later expanded into continuous prose. The purpose of this plan in note-form is not merely to condense bits of evidence which seem important, but to establish the main twists and turns of an historical argument, the logical framework around which we hope to build a piece of original history. The actual length of these vital notes is a matter of personal choice and experience. Some practised writers do no more than jot down the principal ideas, but most of us will probably prefer a more detailed approach – at least sketching the nub of each successive paragraph (see Appendix 7, pp. 150–1). It is important to realise that these notes are not a straitjacket but a stimulus to get our thoughts moving: we may need several versions before we are satisfied, and even then the final version may not be slavishly followed but adapted as we write.

All forms of written history, from books to short articles, contain the following general elements, in roughly this order:

- A clear statement of the basic subject, or problem, to be investigated.
- A discussion of the historiographical context, because new work needs to be related to the writings of other historians, both living and dead. (In this way, we acknowledge the cumulative and reactive nature of research.)
- The topographical context, because we usually need to depict the landscape or townscape within which our human drama took place.
- An explanation of the evidence and methodology to be used.
- Forming the greater part of the piece, a detailed 'development' of the

subject, breaking it down to its constituent parts, analysing a volume of varied evidence and presenting an interpretation.

- Lastly, a summary of the results and broad conclusions.[2]

Within such a structure, our 'outline plan' needs further division into manageable, reasonably self-contained lengths. As everyone knows, a book is normally divided into chapters; it may also have major 'parts' grouping chapters. These divisions too carry titles. Shorter works such as articles generally have sub-headings, or physical breaks which may or may not be titled or numbered. Two principal ways of naming chapters or sections are observable in historical literature. The first, frequently seen in older parish and county histories, is by *period* or *royal dynasty* such as 'Before the Norman Conquest' or 'Tudor Times'. The second method, now adopted by the majority of working historians, is to put the main emphasis on *theme*, for example 'Earning a Living' and 'Religious controversy', sometimes including a chronological reference such as 'Commercialism in the Georgian Town'.[3] Whatever divisions are chosen, they should grow organically out of the subject and material, and not be imposed arbitrarily upon them. Finally, having divided our subject, we will find junctions and overlaps which necessitate minor repeats, cross-references and carefully constructed seams.

Having spent time on constructing an outline plan, one is in a good position to plunge into a first draft. While the ideas flow, write quickly and be thankful. If you are writing long-hand, be sure to leave plenty of space between lines, because sooner or later you will want to make alterations (crossings-out, insertions, arrows moving text around, etc.). The great advantage of the modern computer is that one can alter text very easily, and all the unwanted verbiage immediately disappears. At this drafting stage, however, it is vitally important that you do not torment yourself with niceties of style and grammar. Nor should you spend a long time trying to compose a perfect first paragraph. Experienced writers will often say that in first drafts they bang out anything which comes into their heads, in order to get the prose moving. Above all, do not fall for the temptation of stopping every few minutes and reading over what you have just written.[4] This may occasionally

---

[2]   An effective way of getting the measure of any piece of history is to read the conclusions first.

[3]   In his *Local History Research and Writing* (Morley, 1974) David Iredale recommended the following headings: Lie of the land, Settlement, Population, Work, Transport, Property, Government, Social Welfare, Education, Law and order, Society, Religion and Recreation. However, it would be wrong to impose these frameworks on all local studies.

[4]   One is often tempted to scroll back to re-read one's text, and to print-out with extravagant frequency.

be useful to confirm a train of thought, but can easily become a sort of nervous paralysis which seriously delays progress. Constant spell-checking is also wasteful of time, and in any case is best done when a draft is completed. At all costs keep the text moving and – in spite of the temptation – do not get bogged down honing fine detail or perfecting footnotes. While writing quickly, especially on a computer, you may produce very inflated, repetitive prose, or you may miss out parts of the argument and slide over complications. These defects do not matter because they can be repaired later.

After any sort of break in writing, as a way of getting one's thoughts moving again, it certainly pays to re-read (and perhaps revise) what was written in the previous session. William Hoskins advised leaving off each day's work 'without completely exhausting the subject in hand'; the next day the threads can be picked up with far less trouble than if beginning a new subject.[5] However, it has to be remembered that although professional authors can sit down to the task fairly regularly, if not daily, many lay historians are obliged to write intermittently in spare moments. In that case, it is important not to leave off for too long. It is better to write a little once a week, than to rely on more widely spaced bursts of activity. On each occasion one usually needs a minimum of several hours to make real progress. The odd half-hour is simply not long enough to get the creative juices working.[6]

In spite of this emphasis on the value of regular writing, one major exception must be conceded. If it proves difficult to write up a particular topic, you should temporarily abandon the attempt – certainly for several days – and then return with a fresh mind. By this strategy a solution is often found which at first seemed so elusive.

If you are writing long-hand, it is advisable to use only one side of the paper, in case you want to do any cutting and pasting at a later stage. Also, remember to number your pages, or you will be in a muddle by the day's end. The same point applies when you print out electronically, for these pages too should be numbered. While notes and transcripts are still available, it makes sense to put in as many references as possible. If the details are not to hand, however, leave a gap which can be filled later, and do not break that precious flow of thought and effort by embarking on a disruptive search.

Try to make sure, even at this early stage, that each paragraph is reasonably self-contained and built around the making and development of one major point. In

---

5   W. G. Hoskins, *Local History in England* (3rd edn, Longman, 1984), p. 227.

6   I have long admired authors who habitually rise early and begin the day by writing for a few hours, but am not one of them!

Ernest Gower's words, 'the paragraph is essentially a unit of thought, not of length' and 'must be homogeneous in subject matter'.[7] Skilled writers generally convey their gist in a key sentence at, or near, the beginning of each paragraph – thereby stating the point early and clearly (Appendix 9, pp. 155–6). It is also important that each paragraph connects logically with its neighbours, and thus appears part of an organised and progressive discussion. In practice this often means using words and phrases which at the beginning of paragraphs link backwards ('Another strong trend in this period …') and which at the end point forwards ('An even worse tragedy was about to happen'). Sure signs of sloppy writing are overlong rambling paragraphs which have no obvious shape or core of ideas. If a printed page has no paragraph-break in it, you can be sure that it will be difficult to read. Equally suspect are very short paragraphs consisting of single sentences, because they avoid discussion and amount to a form of purely descriptive listing.[8]

The shape of this book so far has probably given the impression of a linear system in which one clear-cut stage succeeds another. In real life, however, research and writing regularly overlap. Ideas are sometimes written up while evidence is being studied, and are later – with appropriate topping and tailing – slotted into the emerging text. On the other hand, historians in the midst of writing are often driven back to their documents because new questions arise or because earlier note-taking was in some way unsatisfactory. Moreover, documents have an irritating habit of turning up late in the day, and this too can lead to heart-searching revision.[9] In practice, therefore, you may in the same day be consulting original sources, reading other historians, and writing your first draft.

Some guidelines for writing

When one is writing history, several well-recognised 'modes' should be kept in play. *Description* portrays an event or scene at a particular time; *narrative* presents a chain of events and, by emphasising time and change, helps to give a text movement; and *analysis* is the attempt to show why events happened and

---

[7]   Ernest Gowers, *The Complete Plain Words* (HMSO, 1986), p. 170.

[8]   Nowadays, sadly, the single-sentence paragraph is a marked feature of the provincial press. For the shaping of paragraphs, see Appendix 9, pp. 155–6.

[9]   Margaret Spufford has described 'the historian's ultimate nightmare'. After her book on seventeenth-century Eccleshall was finished, a highly relevant stray document came to light. It necessitated the writing of a special postscript: M. Spufford, *Poverty Portrayed* (Keele University, 1995), pp. 69–70. Sometimes delays in publishing mean that material is outdated before it appears. This often happens with conference proceedings and with some book reviews.

how they were connected.[10] Every student of history has to learn not to write long passages of description or narrative, and then as an afterthought insert small pieces of analysis. All three dimensions must be kept in regular, though not necessarily equal, play as one attempts to survey and explain the past. Other kinds of balance must be preserved as well: the reader should be moved frequently, forwards and backwards, between detail and broad generalisation, between facts and judgements, and between the locality and the wider world (Appendix 16, pp. 174–83).

Another important device is *comparison*. Thus, in describing how a town was governed in the seventeenth century, we may profitably compare it with other towns at the same period, or compare it with the same town in earlier and later centuries. This movement through time and space helps to measure the significance of what is being studied, and gives life and bounce to an historical text. The need to compare, and to place work in a wider framework, explains the use of 'general' sources like hearth-tax returns, returns of poor-law expenditure, and census abstracts. Their great virtue, apart from the fact that they are often in published form, is that they survey whole counties and regions, at one time and in a reasonably consistent manner. Therefore they enable us to judge local communities relative to each other (Appendix 6, pp. 146–9). Furthermore, we usually discover that other historians have drawn conclusions from these sources, and that gives further scope for meaningful comparison.

The ultimate aim is to write an unbroken chain of systematic argument, which not only describes what happened in the past but almost simultaneously tries to explain why it happened. This can be done only when the evidence has been wholly assimilated and when the logic of an historical interpretation has been thoroughly worked out. What we write is also truly personal and unique, and can never be repeated by another writer, or even by ourselves at a later date. This duality, blending the objective and personal, makes the historian's task a particularly fascinating and demanding one. Ironically, while many of us are reluctant to start writing, we then spend insufficient time on the job and publish too soon!

Nobody can give a detailed formula for writing history, because in the last analysis good style reflects the individual personality and can take so many different forms. Nevertheless, a few general principles can be hazarded.

---

[10]   G. R. Elton, *The Practice of History* (London, 1984), p 118; A. Marwick, *The Nature of History* (3rd edn, Basingstoke, 1989), ch. 6.

Shaping the past

Writing in 1691, John Aubrey proudly described his research method as follows: 'I now set things down tumultuarily, as if tumbled out of a sack, as they came to my hand.'[11] Since then, legions of historians have copied Aubrey's example and written 'tumultuarily'. This is the kind of history which Joseph Hunter, the nineteenth-century Yorkshire historian, brilliantly described as 'a succession of facts detached, like a rope of sand'.[12] Proper history, by contrast, has to be leavened by ideas, judgement and discussion. We must give shape to the past, and not present mere catalogues of miscellaneous facts, trivial anecdotes and lumps from original sources. Nor must we drop slabs of national history into the story of local life, inadequately related to it. As John Marshall has warned, 'The local historian is only drowned in information if he or she has no ideas to act as life-saving equipment'.[13]

The shorter the study, the more selective it should be (see pp. 44–5). It does not follow that we should write only about the unusual or the dramatic, such as royal visits, fatal accidents and those wretched murders which feature so prominently in many local publications.[14] Murders may actually be of some importance, but only when they are embedded in a wider study of crime, law or morality. In a balanced account, we must also emphasise the typical and the ordinary. Indeed the regularities and slow-moving trends of life (the *longue durée* to cite a fashionable phrase) are usually more important than isolated events.

Unfortunately many local historians do not exercise sufficient control over their evidence. They dutifully but unimaginatively summarise each document in turn, and thus allow the sources to dictate their thinking. To write well, we must remain firmly in charge and draw out the evidence which suits our own critical purpose. At times this may, indeed, involve bringing certain documents under very close scrutiny, especially when they present problems of meaning and interpretation. Usually, however, the evidence is kept at greater distance as we survey clusters of miscellaneous sources, and use only those parts which seem telling and relevant to the case being presented.

---

[11]   J. Aubrey, *A Perambulation of the County of Surrey*, I (London, 1718), foreword 'To the Reader'.

[12]   Quoted in Thomas Helsby (ed.), *George Ormerod's History of the County Palatine and City of Chester*, vol.1, 2nd edn (London, 1882), p. xi.

[13]   Marshall, *Tyranny of the Discrete*, p. 29.

[14]   Another temptation is to dwell on famous sons and daughters who spent most of their lives elsewhere, even those who merely had locative surnames. Many older parish histories and early VCH volumes abound with such 'worthiness' and hagiography.

Asking questions

As with the analysis of documents, the best way of giving shape to writing is to ask penetrating questions. How many people lived there? Was the population rising or falling? How did people earn their living? Were there marked differences of wealth? Primary enquiries of this kind lead to others of a more detailed nature. Here, for example, are ways in which Alan Rogers suggested that a local historian might probe the subject of religion:

> … how important was religion among the community? How widespread was its acceptance? What proportion of the population was among the active or its more formal adherents? … What religious organisations did they enjoy? When and how did they originate? And what were their relations, the one to the other? What sort of persons predominated within each organisation? And … what sort of activity did they engage in? Were they inward-looking or 'full of good works'? What attempts did they make to deal with the problems of contemporary society, to reach those outside? [15]

In a piece of published history, such questions need not be stated overtly. Normally, in fact, they are not.[16] The real value of our questions is that they guide our thoughts as we ponder the evidence and write. As a consequence, the history that we write will contain strong threads of logic and order, of analysis and discussion.

Confessing doubt

Given the patchy and uneven nature of historical evidence, our knowledge of the past inevitably displays gaps and doubts. We should candidly acknowledge the flaws in our sources and interpretations, and refrain from wishing for documents which do not exist. Good history is liberally sprinkled with actual or implied question-marks, because the historian can never expect to uncover the whole truth. In other words, questions are always more numerous than answers. The related issue of what kind of language should be used to express complicated judgements and degrees of possibility and probability is discussed in Appendix 10, p. 157.

---

[15] A. Rogers, *Approaches to Local History* (2nd edn, Longman, 1977), pp. 127–8.
[16] *Rhetorical* questions can be effective in historical writing, but need to be used more sparingly than genuine ones.

Controlling detail

Historians should not bombard their readers with endless details, but select those which best illustrate their arguments. In other words, we must always make detail count by explaining its relevance. By doing so we escape, as Lionel Munby sagely expressed it, from the prison of our own knowledge.[17] Selection also implies rejection; in writing we cannot expect to use all the evidence we have found, however painfully it was gathered or joyfully found. Although an historical interpretation should be based on all relevant evidence, many facts and references will turn out to be inessential. On the other hand, we must certainly not suppress any evidence which is inconvenient or contradictory to our case – that would be intellectually dishonest. Chris Lewis's assessment of William Hoskins summarises the importance of controlling detail:

> His strengths as a local historian, which should be a model for all, are precisely the ability to sum up the general development of a particular place without getting bogged down in the mire of detail, and then go on to show how the lessons of one place could be applied to others and to English history generally.[18]

Mastering chronology

As has been said, a strong chronological thread must run through any piece of historical writing, simply because history records the passage of time and is concerned with those two precious dimensions of *continuity* and *change*. Passages of pure narrative frequently introduce events in strict chronological order. Nevertheless, in designing an historical argument, it is a mistake to make time a straitjacket. It is sometimes more effective, both for historical and literary reasons, to move around chronologically. Many a biography, for example, begins with the death or funeral.[19] Similarly, investigations of riots and rebellions usually begin by describing the dramatic events, and then move backwards to investigate their antecedents and causes.

---

[17]   L. Munby, review in *TLH*, 13, 4 (1978), 240.

[18]   Lewis, *Particular Places*, p. 45.

[19]   Frank Barlow's book *Thomas Beckett* (London, 2002) begins with this arresting sentence: 'On the fifth day of Christmas 1170, the morrow of the festival of the Holy Innocents, that is to say, Tuesday, 29 December, Thomas, archbishop of Canterbury, primate of the whole of England and legate of the Holy See, was murdered in his cathedral church by four noble knights from the household of his lord and former patron and friend, King Henry II.'

The mention of a date is often of critical importance in understanding the full significance of a statement or judgement. Therefore in most circumstances it is good policy to mention dates at, or close to, the beginning of sentences, rather than at the end where they may lose impact, or take the reader by surprise. Do not, however, begin a sentence with a raw date; at the very least precede it with a word like 'In', 'On' or 'During'.[20] Also take care to bring together all phrases and clauses implying time.[21] Note that when dates are cited in an historical account, the normal and clearest form to use is 25 March 1307, rather than March 25 1307 or March 25th 1307.

A related problem lies in our choice of tenses for verbs. We live in an age when it is becoming more common to describe the past by using the present tense. This can be an effective literary device, if used sparingly, but should not become the norm. Generally one writes about the past in a past tense, but about surviving evidence in the present. Some writers overuse 'would have', 'could have' and 'must have', dangerous tenses which usually betray guesswork.

Polishing quotations

Quotations, either from original sources or from the work of other historians, can be a highly effective device in writing because they introduce different, fresh voices. They must be long enough to make a telling point, but not so long as to bore the reader and unbalance the text. Many writers use excessively long quotations (Appendix 13, pp. 162–4). Presumably they do this in the hope of giving authenticity to their work, but in fact they merely expose their own inadequacies. In Finberg's words, 'there is no better way of unnerving the average reader at the outset than to hurl a chunk of Domesday Book at him, without any explanation of its terminology or so much as a hint that scholars are not altogether certain what some of the entries mean.'[22] Yet (it is worth saying again) the crude stitching together of extracts from primary and secondary sources is the most common mistake made in the writing of history. Quotations can greatly improve the texture of historical writing, but they should be used judiciously and, like jewels in a crown, be securely embedded in a text which debates and explains them. They should also be fully and accurately referenced (see Appendix 17, pp. 184–90), for it is unethical, and indeed insulting, to use the words and ideas of somebody

---

[20]   One should not use numbers, of any kind, at the beginning of sentences.
[21]   Instead of 'A few months after her excommunication, Abigail died in 1639 ...', one would do better with 'In 1639, a few months after her excommunication, Abigail died ...'
[22]   Finberg in Finberg and Skipp, *Local History, Objective and Pursuit* (1967), p. 85.

else – whether living or dead – without giving due acknowledgement. Finally, quotations should not be 'corrected' but reproduced exactly as we find them in the source.[23]

Writing humanely

Above all, we should try to produce history which is humane in both content and style. The central concern is with people – thinking, sentient human beings in all their diversity – and not with places, objects or even sources. Unfortunately, many original documents are primarily concerned with legal and administrative matters, and reveal little about human opinions, beliefs and emotions. Nevertheless, by working in a detached yet sympathetic way, we must get as close as we can to reconstructing what it felt like to be alive at that time. Even though our writing will inevitably mention sources, methods of analysis, statistics and the physical world, these ought never to be regarded as ends in themselves but as merely contributing to the complex story of mankind. In a sense, however difficult the task, we are aiming at personal and social biography.

Yet the opposite is frequently the case. As John Marshall once remarked, 'Plenty of people have written about the Poor Law, but very few, convincingly, about the poor.'[24] Similarly economic, architectural and landscape historians have tended to write in a totally de-humanised way. Timber-framed buildings, for example, or the earthworks of shrunken villages, have no historical value in themselves, unless they are explained as the results of human thoughts and actions. The prices negotiated between sellers and buyers are not simply statistics: they show the value which people put on certain commodities, a value which the historian's language should reflect. In the study of local history, we are usually thinking about ordinary, relatively obscure and unsung people and trying, with compassion yet without sentimental gush, to reconstruct something of their lives. The local historian has no greater reward than to be able to show that the lives of 'ordinary' people had meaning and dignity; that they were individuals and certainly did not regard themselves as equals, socially or morally; that they, like the great and famous, had hopes and fears, joys and pains, achievements and failures. In a recent television programme Melvyn Bragg was surely right when he spoke of 'the extraordinariness of ordinary people'.

---

[23]   It is, however, permissible to omit unnecessary and clogging words by using the appropriate convention (thus: …).

[24]   I regret that I have never been able to find where this memorable remark was made or published.

Because of the nature of historical evidence we often concentrate on human groups, for example those who pursued the same occupation, had a common faith, or regarded themselves as belonging to the same social stratum, but we must also seize those rarer opportunities of writing about individual men, women and children.[25] This does not mean throwing in every personal titbit we happen to know: simply that where we are able to say something of personal importance, we should do so with appropriate empathy. 'I am an historian,' said Henri Pirenne, 'Therefore, I love life.'[26]

Avoiding moral superiority

Some historians, with the benefit of hindsight, write from a predominantly modern perspective which presupposes that everything which happened in the past was quite inevitable. They adopt a superior tone over earlier generations, pitying them for their superstitions and prejudices, and unfairly blaming them for not seeing the full consequences of their actions. Worse still, they judge historical individuals and communities by the moral and intellectual values and perceptions of today, or of their own generation, and make little attempt to understand how it felt to be alive at a particular period, as events unfolded uncertainly and new problems arose without warning. What, for example, was it like to be an overseer of the poor in a period of growing unemployment and economic recession, caught between the increasing demands of desperate paupers and the complaints of angry rate-payers? Parallels with the present can be very instructive, but our writing should have no place for condescension and moral superiority.

Revealing background and personality

Aiming to study the past objectively, we as historians will certainly strive to keep our own beliefs and prejudices under control. On the other hand, our personalities and contemporary involvements will inevitably influence what we write, and we should not be afraid of revealing them. It is better to write one-sided and partial history, and to be frank about it, than to have a secret agenda or to try any form of deceitful indoctrination, political, religious or otherwise. When Edward Thompson wrote that 'Enclosure ... was a plain enough case of class robbery,

---

[25] The opportunity of writing about individuals at some depth does sometimes present itself to the local historian. See D. Dymond (ed.), *Parson and People in a Suffolk Village: Richard Cobbold's Wortham, 1824–77* (Wortham Research Group, 2007).

[26] M. Bloch, *The Historian's Craft* (Manchester UP, 1954), p. 43.

played according to the fair rules of property and law laid down by a parliament of property-owners and lawyers', he may not have achieved the highest standard of historical impartiality, but at least he was giving a useful and thought-provoking way of looking at a familiar problem.[27] However objective we try to be, our writing remains to an important degree an expression of our own individuality.

Because it was then thought entirely wrong to use words like 'I' and 'mine', some older academic historians relied heavily on the regal 'one' or on phrases like 'this present writer'. Another option was to employ the passive tense and impersonal constructions like 'It can be argued that ...' Now, however, the first person singular is seen more frequently and can be an effective way of emphasising history as a personal quest. This device should not be used too liberally, however, for it can easily give the impression of self-centredness or arrogance.

---

[27]   E. P. Thompson, *The Making of the English Working Class* (Pelican, 1968), p. 13.

9

Producing a final draft

No language has better ingredients than English; no language has
ever been more monstrously ill-treated and deformed by vandals and
incompetents.

(Kenneth Hudson, *Dictionary of Diseased English*, London, 1977, p. xiii)

Writing must not be regarded as a mere chore, a second-rate activity to be
done in the odds and ends of one's time …

(R. M. Robbins, *Antiquaries Jour.*, lxviii, 1988, 5)

I N second and later drafts, a writer is normally concerned with the refinement
of prose so that it is lucid, coherent and elegant. Again, nobody can give a
precise formula for success, but we can find plenty of examples showing what to
aim for, and what to avoid.

Revising and re-drafting

Those of us who use desk-top computers and laptops are continually revising
and tinkering as we write: this is a massive advantage of the new technology.
Nevertheless, when the first draft is supposedly complete, we must be prepared
to re-read it with the greatest attention to detail, and to revise as much as is
necessary. After all, it is usually possible to write the same thought in several
fundamentally different ways (try it!). The number of revisions will vary from
individual to individual, but most of us need several. It is also worth saving the
various versions, distinguishing and dating them adequately, in case at a later
stage material needs to be reinstated or arguments reconsidered. Very rare is the
writer who can produce a publishable draft at the first attempt, and anyone who
claims that gift should be regarded with polite suspicion. Revision may mean

changing the order of words, inserting new material, deleting overblown prose, or totally restructuring whole sections. When a passage has been re-thought and recast, it is important to check the surrounding prose in case other adjustments prove necessary. One major reason for the ugliness and confusion of much modern writing is an unwillingness to undertake careful revision. 'Prose is like hair; it shines with combing.'[1]

Expanding and condensing

One is frequently dissatisfied with a passage, without knowing exactly what is wrong. This 'inner voice' of criticism should be heeded because it is invariably right. On maturer reflection, one realises that the logic of an argument has not been worked out thoroughly enough. Something may be missing or an idea, though mentioned, may not have been given sufficient weight. A comment which began as a subordinate clause often has to be given the status of a separate sentence. On the other hand, it is an even more common experience to have to prune and tighten.

In a first draft nearly all writers use unnecessary words, phrases, sentences and even paragraphs. For example, we often commit the sin of tautology by using two or more words which are identical or very close in meaning, such as 'the inexperienced beginner'. It is also easy to leave behind more of our 'mental scaffolding' than can be justified: 'Now let us turn, as in the last chapter, to the subject of ...' Or we may find that we have included facts, ideas and references which impede the flow of an argument and are better placed in footnotes or appendices, if not rejected altogether. The more compact our writing, the more forceful and effective it becomes. We cannot afford to waste space as older antiquaries did with their more egotistical and ruminative styles (p. 174, no. 1). Pascal wisely said that if he had had more time, he would have written less![2]

Choosing words

In the hope, as they think, of giving their prose greater weight and academic gravitas, many writers complicate their message quite unnecessarily. They actually

---

[1] I cannot find the origin of this neat simile; it may be attributable to Gustave Flaubert. The need for careful last-minute revision is illustrated in the preface of an important book published in 2007: 'In the later stages, we have incurred a debate [*sic*] to ..., our copy editor, who brought polish and conistency [*sic*] to a manuscript assembled over many years and attempted to save us from our worst errors.'

[2] *Oxford Dictionary of Quotations* (4th edn, 1996), p. 507.

prefer the complex to the simple, the oblique to the direct, the pompous to the plain. They choose the rare word where a common one would serve better, and they observe Finberg's tongue-in-cheek rule 'never to use one word where you can possibly use four'.[3] To fall for these temptations shows a careless disregard for the reader. Heaven knows that historical truth is complicated enough without being further obscured by our choice of words.

Every writer of history has a duty to choose words which are as precise and concrete as possible. We should not use dangerously vague terms like 'the people' or 'progress' when it is usually possible to say which people we have in mind, and what kind of progress. We must also be wary of historical labels such as 'The Middle Ages' and 'capitalism' which can mean different things to different minds. Linguistically and stylistically the greatest difficulty arises when we have to express judgements and opinions – with which history abounds. That is why the literature is full of adverbs like 'perhaps' and 'probably', of adjectives like 'uncertain' and 'ambiguous', and of phrases such as 'The evidence suggests …' or 'On balance, it seems likely that …' (see Appendix 11, p. 158). The increasing use of numbers has certainly given more precision to historical writing, but our main tools remain words, and they have to be used as responsibly and accurately as possible. Indeed, as journals of demographic and economic history amply demonstrate, we are now struggling with a new challenge today: that of developing a civilised literary style that will express the increasing numeracy of our interpretations. Sentences heavy with statistics often prove indigestible to the reader: that it why a convincing balance has to be found between numerical tables and the prose which surrounds and interprets them.

Sentences vary in length and rightly so. It has been suggested, however, that their *average* length should be no more than fifteen to twenty words.[4] Whether or not this rule is seriously adopted, the underlying point is a good one. In the heat of composition, we often draft sentences which are far too long, and loaded with subordinate clauses, weak participles and other clutter. When such agglomerations are re-thought and broken down into shorter sentences, the message can usually be put across more economically and persuasively.[5] Remember too that computers can count words, and warn us of stylistic and grammatical infelicities.

---

[3] Finberg, in Finberg and Skipp, *Local History: Objective and Pursuit*, p. 85.

[4] Martin Cutts, *The Plain English Guide* (Oxford, 1995), p. 11.

[5] Students writing dissertations often worry about being limited to, say, 20,000 words. In my experience, a fifth of the verbiage of early drafts can usually be pruned away, and sometimes more.

The importance of style

Although not writing literature in the strict sense, most historians care about their readers and strive to write prose which is smooth, shapely and economical. To convey ideas unambiguously they choose the minimum number of effective words, and think constantly about their arrangement – if necessary changing the word-order many times. For example, it is generally good practice to place the subject at or near the beginning of a sentence, and to keep subject and verb as close as possible. Another important consideration is to give prominence to the words which matter most. Frequently an important word is lost in heavy choking verbiage, or appears early in a sentence and is weakened by later qualifying clauses. Though not an invariable rule, it can help to reorganise sentences so that salient words come toward the end, as a sort of climax.[6] Similarly, in giving a string of examples it can pay to keep the most effective until last ('but above all …'). In this quest for better shape and flow, it can be very helpful to read one's work aloud, or slowly in the head as if publicly declaiming.[7]

Therefore, as conscientious writers we must constantly seek opportunities for cutting, tightening and strengthening our prose. For example, when referring quite properly to the work of other historians, we should not clutter a text with titles of articles and books: such details belong in references and bibliographies. The text, with an appropriate reference number, may simply say, 'A. B. Smith argues that …'[8] Similarly, all writing is carefully combed for sentences beginning with impersonal and unnecessary constructions like 'It can be argued that …' or 'It should go without saying that …', and for colloquial expressions which make the language flabby and less direct. Perhaps the worst traps of all are colloquialisms such as 'there is', 'there were', etc., which many people transfer unconsciously from speech to writing.[9] We must be prepared to mould and re-mould our writing until it flows with ease and dignity, and until key words and phrases have the prominence and impact which they deserve. In this sense, style is not an optional extra or a cosmetic: it is part of the basic craft of communicating with the widest possible readership.

-----

[6]   In this and the next sentence, for example, I have endeavoured to highlight 'climax' and 'last'. This does not invalidate the point made earlier about the value of putting dates at the *beginning* of sentences; see above, p. 95.

[7]   One should avoid the jerky effect of too many short words in succession ('He put it out that at the time he could not come'), and the repetition of sounds when words begin with the same letter ('… barely been begun before …').

[8]   This assumes that we are not forced to use the Harvard system; see above, p. 110–11.

[9]   Sometimes one encounters sentences which double the offence: 'There is reason to believe that there was …'

Avoiding jargon

In his inaugural lecture at Leicester in 1966 William Hoskins drily observed, 'I once wrote a book with the simple title of *The Making of the English Landscape*, but I ought to have called it *The Morphogenesis of the Cultural Environment* to make the fullest impact.'[10] He would have chortled to hear that a course on Garden History in an English university was once entitled 'Ornamental and functional space: the aesthetics and conceptuality of horticultural activity in past social contexts'. In the *Oxford English Dictionary* one definition of the word 'jargon' is 'the cant of a class, sect, trade or profession'. It is, in other words, a terminology adopted by a specialised group to enable its members to communicate with each other. Deliberately or not, it has the simultaneous effect of deterring and excluding outsiders. Jargon is a curse in all academic disciplines, but is particularly reprehensible in the record of human life and society. Not only does it make wider communication difficult, but it frequently prevents us from thinking clearly in the first place. Examples of ugly jargon are regularly adopted or coined, usually by professionals who should know better. Indeed, historians in the van of the computing revolution are fast developing their own brand of verbal fog and gobbledegook. In recent decades we have been asked to swallow:

- non-migratory mobility
- residential propinquity
- multi-source nominal record linkage
- commensality
- commodification
- prosopography
- liminality
- reification
- female net native out-migration

and many others.[11] It is no accident that those in the habit of using jargon are poor writers anyhow. The seductive power of bland but fashionable words such

[10] W. G. Hoskins, *English Local History: the Past and the Future* (Leicester UP, 1966), p. 21.
[11] 'Commensality' means 'eating together'. 'Commodification' appears to mean 'the increasing consumption of material goods'. 'Prosopography' is especially popular with ancient and medieval historians: it means the study of individual lives by putting together miscellaneous pieces of evidence, in other words, 'Biographical Notes' or 'Notes on People'. 'Liminality' refers to the effects, physical and mental, of boundaries around spaces. Amazingly,

as 'function', 'situation' and 'activity' can have similar deterrent and nonsensical effects. Thus, one recent writer solemnly concluded that 'the main reason why so many parish registers were unreliable was probably a function of the system of registration'.

Nevertheless, a distinction should be made between jargon and technical language. Jargon is *unnecessarily* obscure language, generally characterised by a dense accumulation of nouns, written by members of specialised groups who have no interest in communicating with outsiders. By contrast, technical language derives from inescapably specialised areas of life (for example, industrial processes such as 'tawing', legal instruments such as 'recognizances' and theological concepts such as 'transubstantiation'). They are therefore perfectly acceptable in the writing of history providing they are explained when first used – either in the text, in a footnote or in a special glossary. Another kind of technical language is adopted or coined by historians themselves to cover concepts which they wish to investigate. Thus they legitimately refer to the 'cost of living index', to 'mean household size' and 'age at first marriage'.

The abuse of nouns

A useful characteristic of the English language is that two nouns can be put side by side. Phrases like 'income tax' and 'church tower' are a precise form of expression in which the first noun acts as an adjective. Unfortunately, this device is increasingly abused by a wide variety of writers, not least by journalists, bureaucrats and academics. Instead of using appropriate adjectives, participles and prepositions (particularly those vital little words, 'of' and 'for'), these new barbarians string nouns together with careless abandon – three, four, five or more in a row. They are not even capable of inserting the occasional hyphen or apostrophe to help the tormented reader, but glory in the fact that such strings can be converted into fashionable acronyms. Published history now teems with coarse and ponderous rows of nouns (perhaps they should be called 'noun-strings' or 'noun-clumps') which make the language thick and obscure. One can invariably think of clearer, more logical and often shorter ways of expressing the point. For example:

- birthplace location analysis (meaning 'analysis of birthplaces')
- house plan classification types ('types of house-plan')

---

that much overused jargon-word 'data' is still assumed by many writers to be singular: 'Much data has been collected …' English Heritage, heedless of the *double entendre*, now talks of 'visitor interpretation schemes'!

- volume analysis completion rate ('rate at which volumes were completed')
- labour force participation rates ('proportion of people at work')
- case fatality rate ('proportion of those infected who died')
- wall painting condition audit ('survey of the condition of wall-paintings')
- census data capture sheet ('form for analysing censuses')
- stakeholder consultation forum ('for all interested parties')

The fact that some nouns in this kind of writing are superfluous or actually mistaken, underlines its basic sloppiness. But the most obvious objection is that it distorts logic: the meaning of such strings does not dawn on the reader (if at all) until the *last* noun has been reached. In languages with a more precise structure, such clumsiness is impossible because the word-order is more logical, but in English we are witnessing the illiterate abuse of greater freedom. Perhaps, as part of our education, a warning system should be fitted inside our brains: a bell should clang, or a red light wink, every time we write three or more nouns in a row![12]

Promoting verbs

An undue stress on nouns leads to the devaluing of verbs, and therefore to an unpleasant lumpiness in writing. After a few moments of self-criticism, a noun-laden phrase like 'in a period of acute population pressure and increasing conversion to arable' will spring to life as, 'in a period when the population grew fast and ever more land was ploughed'. As Martin Cutts has advised, you should 'use the clearest, crispest, liveliest verb to express your thoughts'.[13] Yet nowadays many historians choose verbs which are passive, weak and sometimes over-complicated, such as 'is indicated', 'will be discussed', 'occurred' and 'are being found'. Furthermore they often place them at the ends of sentences, like a feeble death-rattle.[14]

The devaluation of verbs advertises itself in two other regrettable habits. The first is the persistent and zombie-like use of abstract nouns such as 'factor', 'structure',

---

[12]   Of course noun-strings are characteristic of the German language, and the habit appears to have seeped into Britain through the USA. One of the worst examples I have ever read, though not in the field of history, is: 'Canary Wharf Borough Council Library Users Facilities Survey Project'. Nine nouns in a row!

[13]   Cutts, *Plain English Guide*, p. 56.

[14]   In academic journals, this is a common feature in abstracts introducing articles (see pp. 59–60).

'activity', 'index' and 'situation'. It is significant that these words are usually embedded in ponderous noun-strings. The second habit concerns that important part of speech, the adverb, which can be overused in an effort to compensate, consciously or consciously, for the weakness of verbs. A good example is 'becomes effectively'. Furthermore, adverbs can be used too automatically. Why do we always have to 'readily admit', 'fully confess' and 'richly deserve'? In a final revision therefore we should only pass adverbs which are apt and strong.

Care should also be taken with present and past participles. These can seriously unbalance one's writing, when it would be better to use either shorter sentences or better-constructed subordinate clauses. Many people, for example, write in this way: 'The battle lasted all day, *making* it impossible for anyone to help the wounded or comfort the dying and *meaning* that the omission lay heavily on their consciences for the rest of their lives.' This stylistic habit is fairly general but particularly afflicts the more senior among us. Of course, the worst possible misuse is the 'hanging participle' which creates total nonsense: 'Having lost his capital, the estate was sold'.

The final revision

After writing a passage, and getting as close as possible to a final draft, put the text away for a fortnight or more. On re-reading it, you will invariably spot imperfections which you had previously overlooked, such as:

- mistakes in spelling,[15]
- inconsistencies in using numbers,[16]
- mistakes in punctuation,[17]
- choice of wrong tenses, and mixing of tenses,[18]

---

[15] Perennials are 'privelege', 'seperate', 'independant', 'benefitted'. Remember that most spell-checks on computers would pass 'laud of the manner'!

[16] Manuals vary in their advice about spelling out low numbers, unless in a sequence of statistics; some recommend spelling up to ninety-nine, others to nineteen or nine. Obviously it is important to be consistent.

[17] Many writers do not use enough punctuation, particularly commas, hyphens and apostrophes, and think it trendy to do so. In references and bibliographies the tendency is to omit commas and stops. Normally one writes 'In the seventeenth century' but 'in a seventeenth-century book'. A common error results from confusing 'its' (meaning 'of it') and 'it's' (meaning 'it is'). See M. Ritter (ed.), *Oxford Style Manual* (2003), ch. 5, 'Punctuation', pp. 112–53.

[18] Mixing present and past in the same sentence is common: 'In 1694 John had only a few acres, but by 1697 he is expanding his estate.' See p. 95 above.

- words that beg to be deleted,[19]
- stilted expressions such as 'with regard to' and 'in respect of',
- the old-fashioned use of capital letters with common nouns such as Parish, Borough, Church, Overseer and Lord (of manor),[20]
- mistakes in the order of words,[21]
- the awkward juxtaposition of two or more prepositions,[22]
- the confusion of 'less' and 'fewer',[23]
- careless use of adverbs such as 'happily', 'frankly' and 'hopefully',[24]
- using 'however' and 'nevertheless' instead of 'but',[25]
- the loose spraying of 'it', a dangerous little word often used in different senses in the same sentence,
- using the word 'only' too early in sentences,[26]
- overuse of 'the' which frequently retards the flow of writing when 'a', or no article at all, would be preferable.[27]

All of us tend to overdo certain words, phrases and constructions (a godsend to analysts of literary style), but may not be conscious of them until we later re-read the text, or until someone else points them out. Fortunately computers provide another way of spotting repetitions through its 'Find' key, and it does not take long to think of alternative expressions and remould a flawed sentence.[28] This is also the time to consider using an array of important words which help

---

[19] 'In spite of the fact that ...' can be replaced by the single word 'Although ...'

[20] This habit was very noticeable in Victorian times, and persists in higher age-groups and among Americans. See A. F. Pollard, 'The use and abuse of capital letters', *Bulletin Inst. Historical Research*, v (1927–8), 1–12. Remember, however, that capital letters are retained for special usages such as World War I and the New Poor Law.

[21] '... suspected signs of arson.'

[22] '... referred to in ...'

[23] The correct usage is 'less cheese' and 'fewer cheeses'.

[24] In a sentence like 'He was frankly an evil influence', the writer is being frank, not the evil person. Such misleading colloquialisms are best avoided in writing.

[25] 'It was raining, however I walked home.' 'However' and 'nevertheless' are adverbs, not conjunctions.

[26] 'He only wrote in the early morning.' This is a persistent failing of mine, pointed out by a colleague reading a draft of this book.

[27] Why, for example, do demographers refer so often to 'the' or 'a' plague when neither article is needed?

[28] Among my weaknesses is a tendency to overuse the adverbs 'clearly', 'often' and 'increasingly'. A friend of mine confesses that he overuses adjectives such as 'magnificent', 'superb' and 'outstanding'.

to sharpen one's writing. For instance, 'furthermore' strengthens an argument, 'similarly' helps to knit points together, and 'however' introduces contrast. One needs to bring phrases together which imply time or place,[29] and make sure that constructions have not been mixed in the same sentence.[30] At this stage too, one should check all references for almost inevitable errors and inconsistencies (see below, Appendix 17, pp. 184–90).

One final point needs stressing. Time must be found for comparing the start and finish of a piece of writing, whether or not we have used the formal headings of Introduction and Conclusion. Of course these two vital sections should be written as strongly and memorably as possible, but they should also have a circular, balanced relationship. In the first our purpose is to introduce the subject and to outline historical questions worthy of investigation, while in the second we summarise how far those questions have been addressed and, we hope, answered (Appendix 16, pp. 181–3).

Seeking criticism

When a text is finished, and before it is published, it should be read by at least two other people – but do not be surprised if their reactions differ. Ideally one reader should be a specialist who has experience relevant to the subject, and another a layman who will point out when the writing is less than clear. Such criticisms, which always need acknowledgement in a foreword, are capable of identifying not only poor writing but also major failings of structure and logic. It is therefore sad that many historians, having sought help in the earlier stages of their research, publish their findings without seeking further comment.

References

Footnotes and endnotes, the normal kinds of reference, are a vital part of the mechanism of history. They are not, as some people think, a form of masochistic generosity whereby we give away our best sources and hand a cudgel to our enemies. Nor are they a self-indulgent luxury, as some second-rate publishers assume. On the contrary, to give references is simply to declare one's good faith and to show that one has not invented the past. Because history is based on the interpretation of evidence, one must indicate the nature of that evidence and

---

[29] 'In 1810 John Smith left £200 when he died.'
[30] 'Edward Brown left his tenement to his son Thomas, while his daughter Jane was to have £5.'

give readers the chance of consulting it for themselves. Not to do so is to invite suspicion and criticism; that is partly why so much published local history is pooh-poohed by professionals.[31]

Of course readers will treat references in different ways. Some will ignore them altogether because they only want 'a good read'. Others may show interest in only an occasional reference, as something worth following up. Those heavily involved in research into that or related subjects will, however, scan the full range of sources behind a particular piece of writing, and may want to consult some of the manuscript and secondary works for themselves. Because no piece of history can ever be the final word, references are therefore an invitation to keep the debate open and to take the matter further. In this sense the work of historians is for ever cumulative and open to revision.

In giving references a balance has to be found. All quotations and all major facts and opinions, especially if they are major turning-points in the argument, must be supported by references. On the other hand, one's writing should not be over-burdened with great quantities of notes and extra comment, because that has a deterrent and intimidating effect on readers. For example, Eric Kerridge's seminal book on the *Agricultural Revolution* (1967) was famously marred by the number and length of its footnotes, which often occupied more space on the page than the text itself. Although published some forty years later, Keith Snell's stimulating and original *Parish and Belonging* (2006) exhibits the same tendency.[32] In such cases, it may be better to consider the creation of special appendices, or at least to reconsider the balance between text and references.

Four other points need to be remembered. First, several sources can be grouped into a single note – providing they follow the same sequence as in the text, and do not take up too much space. Secondly, a manuscript or printed source should not be referenced unless it has been specifically consulted. If you have merely seen its mention elsewhere, the honest policy is to give one source as 'quoted' in the other. Thirdly, while it is perfectly proper to supplement references with comment, and indeed to have notes consisting only of comment, you should not use this as an excuse for adding large chunks of extra text. Lastly, references in books, articles and students' essays show an increasing reliance on the new electronic media of websites and CDs. They too should be referenced consistently and in the approved fashion, always giving the date when they were last accessed (see p. 187).

---

[31] Ritter, *Oxford Style Manual*, Ch. 15, 'References and notes', pp. 504–33.

[32] E. Kerridge, *The Agricultural Revolution* (London, 1967); K. Snell, *Parish and Belonging* (Cambridge, 2006).

The traditional form of reference is the footnote which appears in smaller type at the bottom of the page. Its great advantage is that it is easily consulted when wanted, and just as easily ignored. For about twenty years from the mid-1960s, however, endnotes (grouped at the end of each chapter or whole book) became the accepted norm, probably because they suited the technology of the time. This method leaves the main text unbroken but causes the reader to flap pages in searching for a particular note. Finally, since about 1980 the endnote has been abandoned by most publishers, and footnotes have been brought back into fashion with the rapid spread of word-processing. By this method you can easily add or delete notes at any stage of writing or revision, and they are automatically re-numbered.

In the text references should be indicated or 'cued' by a small superscript number – thus.[33] Where possible it should be placed after the full-stop at the end of a sentence, but sometimes has to come earlier, after a particular word or phrase. As a general rule, the number should appear *after* punctuation. In the case of footnotes, the sequence of numbers can be by the page, the article, the chapter (as in this book) or the whole book. Where a whole book is given a single sequence, those numbers quite commonly run into the thousands.[34] Of course, by definition footnotes should appear on the relevant page, although occasionally a longer-than-average note may run over to the next page. By contrast, endnotes are printed after each chapter or article, or are grouped all together at the end of a book. In the latter case, to help readers find the desired information as quickly as possible, endnotes should be clearly divided by chapter (each time giving the number and title), and every column should be headed by a further reference to relevant pages in the text.

The so-called 'author-date' or 'Harvard' system is a form of referencing used in the academic world, especially in the physical and social sciences and in archaeology. Spectacularly unsuitable for historical writing, it creates ugly breaks in printed texts by the bracketed insertion of sources, for example (Harper-Bill, 2005: 33–51) and constantly threatens the reader's concentration. It is also fundamentally unsuited to the referencing of primary sources. One particularly regrets that the Open University and the journal *Family and Community History* are wedded to this ungainly convention, which drills students into a habit which

---

[33]   In older publications, one sometimes finds that reference numbers are bracketed, but this is now regarded as an unnecessary complication. In any case modern technology now does the cueing automatically.

[34]   H. R. T. Summerson's impressive book on *Medieval Carlisle* (2 vols, Kendal, 1993) has one chapter with no fewer than 2,386 endnotes.

they have to abandon when submitting articles to the great majority of historical journals (see p. 172, no. 36).

Because references contain fine and important details such as initials and numbers, they have to be accurate. Mistakes can so easily creep in, especially when notes are copied from one medium to another. To ensure accuracy and consistency, careful checking is therefore essential in the preparation of a final draft. To speed up this detailed scrutiny, computers give us the useful option of converting footnotes temporarily into endnotes, and of printing them out as such. Once checking has been done, the notes are easily restored to their original form.[35] Remember too that the majority of footnotes and endnotes are usually abbreviated: this is done on the assumption that the *full* details appear only at the first occurrence and in a final bibliography. (In Appendix 17, pp. 184–90, are rules recommended for references and bibliographies.)

Appendices

Where we judge that transcripts of documents, special tables and other background information would be of interest to the reader, but are too intrusive and unbalancing in the main text, we may choose to use appendices. These are perfectly acceptable, providing they are truly relevant to the subject and appropriate cross-references are given.[36] It is of course important to number appendices and to list them on the contents-page.

---

[35] I am indebted to Heather Falvey for this valuable observation.

[36] Items such as tables, diagrams, maps and plates are better integrated with the main text. They might, however, appear as appendices if they are mentioned repeatedly in the text.

10

Publishing

[NB. *This section is mainly concerned with the production of books, but it should never be forgotten that one of the best ways for a beginner or less experienced local historian to get into print is through a local journal or newsletter.*]

I N SPITE OF commercial takeovers, competition from the internet and the imminent threat of electronic books, the number of books published in Britain every year is still rising.[1] This includes many local histories, hardback and softback, written by both academics and non-professionals and produced by a range of publishers, national and local, academic and commercial. Thanks to improved technology, these books display standards of production and layout consistently better than was achieved, say, thirty years ago, although it has to be confessed that their contents vary enormously in standard. At the top end of the scale penetrating and original books, and even instant classics, appear on a regular basis and make genuine contributions to knowledge. At the lower end, however, many books are aimed at popular but highly localised markets in individual towns and villages. Journalistic rather than historical, they are in general poorly researched and appear without references or even short bibliographies, or they simply present a mass of historical photographs inadequately related to their social and economic background.[2]

Within the field of history, several different strategies are adopted to get work into print. Most professionals, as well as submitting articles to established journals, write books which were previously commissioned by academic or commercial

---

[1]   *The Writer's Handbook, 2007*, p. 1 records that the total number of new titles in 2006 was 161,000 (up by two-thirds over fifteen years).

[2]   Some books are shoe-horned by their publishers into series with formulaic titles such as 'The Book of …' or 'Memoirs of …'

publishers.[3] Non-professionals, however, quite frequently devote years to research before eventually investigating the possibility of writing a book. Then some of them experience great difficulty in securing the interest of publishers, or they find themselves caught up in 'vanity publishing', paying large sums of money to underwrite severely flawed books.

Self-publishing

Not surprisingly therefore, an increasing number of local historians, both as individuals and as research groups and societies, now decide to be their own publishers. They take complete control of the product from writing and editing through to design and layout, and undertake all the attendant responsibilities of advertising, marketing, storage and distribution. Their varied and increasingly attractive products range from full-blown books to newsletters, videos, CDs and DVDs, and form a major advertisement for local studies in bookshops, libraries, record offices, museums, information centres, conferences and fairs. In spite of the risk of copyright infringement, another option which is attracting ever more converts is publishing on the internet. This medium can be used on its own or side-by-side with a paper version.[4] To guide us through the technicalities of modern design, publishing and marketing, various manuals are helpful such as R. N. Trubshaw's *How to Write and Publish Local and Family History Successfully* (Heart of Albion, 2005).

If, as an individual or group, you decide to publish your own work, you have to face a host of difficult choices – practical, financial, technical and aesthetic. Decisions have to be made, for example, on matters such as paper-sizes, typefaces, layout, running heads, illustrations and types of cover.[5] One has to ponder on the number of copies wanted, the intended retail price (compared to the unit cost), and

---

[3]   The History Press now incorporates a string of previously independent publishers of local history such as Phillimore, Sutton and Tempus. Among the survivors with a wide coverage are Oxbow Books (now including the formerly separate Windgather imprint) and Carnegie. All regions have publishers who produce books on local history such as the Larks Press in Norfolk, Hobnob Press in Wiltshire and Brewin Books in the Midlands. In Wales, Llygad Gwalch is similarly active, as is Birlinn in Scotland. Some university centres of local and regional history also publish in this field (eg. at Hertfordshire and Lancaster). It should not be overlooked that books produced by purely academic publishers, such as Ashgate and Boydell and Brewer, are often based on local communities and regions.

[4]   For example, Thirsk, *Hadlow* (2007) has appeared in both forms.

[5]   See Ritter, *Oxford Style Manual*, Ch. 1, 'The parts of a book', pp. 1–28 for these essential technicalities.

how the product is to be distributed and marketed. To settle these issues, advice should certainly be sought from more experienced authors and computer-buffs, as well as from commercial firms.

The most fundamental issue is to decide whether to do a desk-top job with a PC or laptop, or to seek a commercial printer. In the first instance, you can be your own printer by using relatively cheap programs for desk-top publishing (DTP). Indeed, as the quality of programs and printing machines rises, home-publishing becomes easier, cheaper and therefore more tempting – especially for very limited runs. Alternatively, if you employ a firm of commercial printers, they will normally take responsibility for type-setting, layout, binding and other details. Nevertheless, it is worth remembering that you can save money by supplying your own complete copy on CD, DVD or memory-stick. Providing you use a specialised publishing program, and convert your work into a locked 'PDF format', your brainchild can be turned directly into plates (cameras are no longer involved). Modern printers can deal with any combination of text and illustrations, and for colour use a process involving four plates to the page. Anyone looking for a commercial printer should certainly shop around, because quotations can differ widely in this highly competitive field and it is always worth haggling over price. One should review the options by asking the costs of hardback and softback, of different weights of paper, and of different print-runs. Whether or not you are supplying plate-ready copy, always demand to see final proofs before binding begins, preferably folded into sections.

Local history is normally published in runs of 250 to 1500 copies which, although relatively low, still leaves the self-publisher with the problem of storing bulky packages. However, a new technology offered by some firms already makes it possible to order small batches of books as they are needed for selling or distribution (say, 30, 20, 10 or even single copies). This method, known as 'print on demand' (POD), may in the future become the normal method of publishing many kinds of local history. It certainly means that books can remain much longer in print, and need never be remaindered.[6]

---

[6] Other firms now offer 'assisted publishing'. They will take responsibility for everything from concept to distribution (even complete re-writes if necessary) and will then print on demand. This gives an alternative to 'vanity publishing', but will not attract most self-publishing authors who want to keep direct control of their projects.

Basic advice

- Correct all proofs with the greatest care, using standard symbols.[7] Ensure consistency in your use of punctuation, numbers, sums of money, percentages, capital letters and other details. Do a final check on your references, and make sure that they follow the normal conventions and again are consistent. (A remarkable number of writers make up their own eccentric referencing systems as they go along.) When in doubt consult the printed works of major authors and publishers.

- Do not use too complicated or lengthy a title, for that will make you unpopular with librarians and bibliographers. Although this sin was particularly common in previous generations, it still crops up today.[8] At present titles seem to follow three overlapping fashions. The first is to employ two or three abstract nouns which seem relevant to the contents, perhaps starting with the same letter (such as *Deference, Deviance and Defiance*). The second is to create a title which sounds general in scope, but misleadingly conceals the fact that the research is based on a single locality.[9] The third is is to construct a two-part title, usually separated by an actual or implied colon; the first part frequently outlines the general significance of the subject while the second is more localised and may bear dates (*Peasant Piety and Aristocratic Arrogance: Puddlecombe-up-the-Creek, 1500–1650*).[10] Certainly one should avoid sentimental titles which convey little to most readers, and probably deter them.[11]

- Make sure that your publication is dated on the title-page or on its reverse (imprint page). Many locally produced books do not bear dates,

[7] See *Writers' and Artists' Yearbook, 2006*, 'Correcting proofs', pp. 621–31, which is based on the advice of the British Standards Institute. Other useful sources are Ritter, *Oxford Style Manual*, p. 45, and 'Proof-reading marks' at the back of the *Concise Oxford Dictionary*.

[8] Antiquaries of the eighteenth and nineteenth centuries loved verbose titles: Charles Parkin, *A Reply to the Peevish, Weak and Malevolent Objections brought by Dr Stukeley in his* Origines Roystonianae, No. 2, ... *wherein the said answer is maintained; Royston proved to be an old Saxon town, its derivation and origin; and the history of Lady Roisia shown to be a meer fable and figment* (Norwich, 1748).

[9] For example, J. Lown, *Women and Industrialisation: Gender at Work in Nineteenth-Century England* (Polity, 1990) is based on a single factory in a small Essex town.

[10] See Edward Royle, *Need Local History be Parochial History?*, Univ. of Cambridge Inst. of Continuing Education, Occasional Paper 4 (2001), pp. 3–4.

[11] For example, 'My Own Place' or 'Where the Rainbow Ends'.

an omission which makes it necessary for others to use 'no date' (nd) in bibliographies and references.

- Your printer or publisher should be able to supply you with an International Standard Book Number (ISBN). Your brainchild can then be found by librarians, booksellers and readers, wherever they are.[12]

- Include a contents-page listing every section of the book, with page-numbers, and make sure that the details are accurate. Also, where necessary, add a List of Illustrations distinguishing categories such as Maps, Figures, Tables and Plates.

- Accurate maps and plans are helpful to readers of all kinds. Permission has to be sought and fees paid to reproduce modern Ordnance Survey maps, and so it is usually better to design one's own maps which concentrate on features mentioned in the text. Do not on any account publish scruffily drawn or hand-labelled maps, because drafts can be redrawn professionally or photographed and tidied up digitally. Maps of different periods and scales can now be overlaid and combined through the use of Geographic Information Systems (GIS). By integrating and analysing different kinds of spatial information such as contours, water-courses, differences of land-use and human settlements, these new digital techniques are capable of revealing historically significant patterns as they have changed over time.[13]

- Illustrations are welcome embellishments but must be strictly relevant to the text. Make sure that they are numbered (also listed at the beginning of the book), and that their significance is fully explained in carefully worded captions.[14] One often sees historical photographs with feeble captions like 'The High Street long ago', graphs without proper titles, and tables with inadequate explanation of what their numbers and axes represent. One even sees examples with no caption at all. In fact, illustrations with their captions should be self-explanatory and complete in themselves, so that they can be used independently (for instance, reproduced in other

[12]   ISBNs are obtainable in blocks of ten from UK Standard Book Numbering Agency, 3rd Floor, Midas House, 62 Goldsworth Rd, Woking, GU21 6LQ, which is why printers and publishers usually hold a stock. See *Writers' and Artists' Yearbook, 2006*, 'International Standard Book Numbering', pp. 292–3 which also gives advice about copyright libraries; also Ritter, *Oxford Style Manual*, p. 7.

[13]   See I. N. Gregory, *A Place in History: A Guide to Using GIS in Historical Research* (Oxbow, 2003); Portsmouth University's 'A Vision of Britain through Time', www.visionofbritain.org.uk

[14]   See Ritter, *Oxford Style Manual*, ch. 10, pp. 219–34.

publications, or converted into teaching aids). When you have two or more illustrations on a page, take care that each is clearly numbered and captioned: the text must be unambiguously adjacent to the relevant image. In trendy modern publications readers are frequently confused by complicated layouts involving images of different sizes, the unclear use of numbers and consolidated captions with silly formulae like 'clockwise from bottom right'.

Where illustrations, maps and figures are turned at right angles to the normal text, remember that the reader will feel more comfortable rotating the book *clockwise*. When you have only one such illustration to an opening, most designers would place it on the *verso* or left-hand page. An alternative is to place it on the thinner and less weighty side of the book, whether left or right.

- Your publication should have a good visual balance between black print and white background. In other words, it should have enough 'light and air' without being extravagantly wasteful of space. A single-column layout is usually acceptable, but with certain page sizes the use of two or even three columns is worth considering. The latter can look very attractive, especially when numbers of illustrations and captions (of varying sizes) are inserted. Many histories produced by private individuals and local printers look far too dense and crude, with over-large or gimmicky type, narrow margins and gutters, weak breaks between paragraphs and an insufficient number of headings and subdivisions. Sometimes lines are spaced too far apart, but more often pages look crammed with type. Particular attention must be paid to the spacing of plate-ready copy, because this directly influences the final appearance of the printed page. Any subsequent corrections add considerably to costs.
- Give thought to the type of paper to be used in your publication. You certainly want one thick enough to avoid show-through from one face to the other, but not so thick as to make the book heavy to handle. Many people choose glossy paper, which is better for the reproduction of colour plates. On the other hand, satin or matt surfaces are much kinder on the eyes – especially under artificial light. A method which saves money is to group illustrations together on paper of higher quality than in the rest of the book.
- In a substantial book, the discerning reader deserves an index (which indeed may be perused more than the text itself). You, as the writer, are best placed to provide this important aid, though occasionally it can be

entrusted to others.[15] Remember that an index should cover Persons, Places and Subjects, sometimes expressed as *Nominum, Locorum* and *Rerum*. In major publications these three appear either separately, or with the first two combined because they overlap (especially in medieval studies).[16] In shorter works all three elements are commonly merged. Whichever mode is adopted, it is worth remembering that Subjects are the most important ingredient historically, the most frequently omitted and the most difficult to compile. For example, one often has to devise key words which may not feature in the text itself, so that related subjects can be grouped under suitable headings (for example, 'Cattle' with indented sub-headings such as 'bulls', 'calves' and 'heifers'). Indexes used to be compiled laboriously by amassing thousands of paper slips or cards, and by careful subdivision and filing. Today a great deal of time is saved either by using a general program which contains indexing facilities, or by buying one of the specialised indexing packages now on the market.

- Much local history appears in the form of thin booklets held together by wire staples or plastic spirals. They can be economical to produce but unfortunately are easily mislaid – tending to become invisible on open shelves, and forgotten when stored in box-files. It is therefore a better policy, if you can afford it, to give your publication a spine bearing the title (abbreviated if necessary). The spine should read *downwards* so that it can be readily scanned as one moves to the right along bookshelves. A titled spine calls for a minimum of about sixty pages, and can appear in two main forms. The first is so-called 'perfect binding' which is a kind of glueing normally used with a semi-stiff cover. In the past this sort of binding has often proved less than perfect because of a tendency to split and fall apart, but modern glues are certainly stronger. The second, more expensive method which is used for both hardbacks and softbacks involves the sewing together of pages in sections and their attachment to a cover.

- The existence of many local printing firms means that simpler publications can be produced quite cheaply in short print-runs. If however, you are

---

[15] See Ritter, *Oxford Style Manual*, ch. 16, pp. 577–94; *Writers' and Artists' Yearbook, 2006*, pp. 619–20. R. F. Hunnisett, *Indexing for Editors* (British Records Assoc., 1977) was meant largely for editors of historical texts. The Society of Indexers can supply the names and addresses of professional indexers; they also publish a number of guides and have other relevant information on their website, <www.indexers.org.uk>.

[16] In indexing Persons, one should distinguish, wherever possible, individuals bearing the same name. However, in medieval and early modern studies it often happens that people of the same name cannot be separated.

aiming at a sizeable book, the printer's bill alone will run into several thousands of pounds. Money-raising is best done by a team because it requires time, planning and persistence. The normal methods include pre-publication subscriptions or loans, the finding of private or commercial sponsors and of advertisers, and grants from local authorities and trusts.[17] The amount of money needed depends of course on the length of the book and the number of copies you want to print (calculated against expected sales, at a particular price). The more copies you order, the lower the unit cost but the more you will have to sell. Your pricing should allow for the giving away of review and complimentary copies. You also have to decide whether to budget for a profit (perhaps to invest in the next publication) or just to break even.

• The great advantage of DTP, using a domestic computer or laptop, is that it reduces costs. You can, if you want, take responsibility for everything – including illustrations, cover and binding. You can also print a relatively small number to test the market, and print more as needed. This method is ideal for relatively short publications.

• When individuals or groups publish for themselves, the final problem (and a big one) is marketing. It is increasingly difficult to get local books into national chain stores, and independent booksellers are a threatened species. If a bookshop does agree to stock your book, it will normally demand between 33% and 50% of the cover price. The best chance of commercial success, therefore, is to find your own customers and sell direct to them. It will probably be worth throwing a launch party for invited guests and the media. The cost of wine and nibbles can be offset by immediate sales of copies suitably signed or dedicated. If the launch is made to coincide with an anniversary, a significant event such as a Local History Fair, or the pre-Christmas sales bonanza, so much the better. In approaching local newspapers, radio and TV, you are more likely to get mentioned if you go prepared with your own press release. A new or forthcoming publication can also be advertised by flyers and posters or mentioned in the newsletters, journals and websites of local societies. It can be sold in a variety of outlets (other than friendly bookshops) such as libraries, record offices, museums, churches and at local meetings and events. Marketing

---

[17] See *Directory of Grant Making Trusts* (19th edn in 2005–6), which lists trusts by geographical area. The Local History Initiative is a small-grants programme launched in 2000 'to help local communities bring their local heritage to life', though its main emphasis tends to be archaeological and architectural rather than documentary.

success seems best assured when a group of people tout the publication around. The effort has to be continued until all copies are sold, or at least the outlay is recouped.[18] Packages of unsold books are a nuisance and may be costly to store.

• To get your publication noticed by other historians, make sure that copies are deposited in appropriate record offices, local-studies libraries and university libraries. Also consider sending review copies to local radio, newspapers and journals, and to specialised national periodicals such as *The Local Historian* and *Local Population Studies*.[19] The danger of small-scale, private publishing is that good research may remain largely unknown outside the area studied. This is as regrettable as the opposite danger, that good academic research in specialised journals can remain unknown to local historians who would benefit from reading it.[20] Both these problems underline the importance in disseminating new titles by means of bibliographies, reviews and internet searches. Finally, do not forget the legal obligation to deposit a copy at the Legal Deposit Office of the British Library, Boston Spa, Wetherby, West Yorkshire, LS23 7BY.[21] This may lead to demands from the agents of the other five copyright libraries in Britain. Copies must be supplied if they are demanded.

---

[18]   See *Writers' and Artists' Yearbook, 2006*, pp. 255–7.

[19]   When editors are unable to review publications, they may merely list them. This can still be a useful form of publicity.

[20]   For example, local historians working on nineteenth-century migration need to know of key articles such as G. Nair and D. Poyner, 'The Flight from the Land? Rural Migration in South-east Shropshire in the late nineteenth century', *Rural History* (2006), 17, 2, 167–86.

[21]   For a discussion of copyright and the six national copyright libraries, a subject which causes mystification and resentment, see Alan Crosby, 'Copyright burdens on local history', *TLH*, 48 (Autumn 1998), 2; also *Writers' and Artists' Yearbook, 2006*, p. 256. Ritter, *Oxford Style Manual*, ch.14, pp. 490–501 discusses legal copyright in general.

11

Final reminders

- If you feel tempted to write, give in.
- But take writing very seriously. It will outlive you.
- Do not keep postponing the start of writing.
- Construct your writing around questions and problems, so that it reads as a logical argument or debate.
- Make a preliminary plan to decide the order of your argument, and be prepared to modify it as you write.
- Make sure that each paragraph is constructed around a single idea, and is neither too long nor too short. As a general rule, no paragraph should be longer than a single page.
- Control the length of your sentences. A short sentence can be very powerful.
- Do not let sources and their contents dictate your writing: *you* are in charge.
- Limit the use of quotations to those which are relevant, telling and not too long.
- Include as much detail as is necessary to sustain your argument, and no more.
- Do not necessarily expect to write the text from A to Z: parts can be written out of order and fitted together at a later stage, with adjustments.
- Never cease reading the work of other historians, in and around your subject.
- Revise your writing as many times as it takes.
- Invite the criticism of others.

12

Further reading

Writing, general

Inst. of Historical Research, Guides for Historians: *How to Get Published: A Guide for Historians* (pdf file, 133KB; accessed Jan. 2008)
Ritter, M. (ed.), *The Oxford Style Manual* (2003)
Writers' and Artists' Yearbook, vol. 102 (2009)

Local history

Beckett, John, *Writing Local History* (Manchester UP, 2007)
Carter, P. and Thompson, K., *Sources for Local Historians* (Phillimore, 2005)
Drake, M., 'Inside-out or outside-in? The case of family and local history' in Finnegan, R. (ed.), *Participating in the Knowledge Society: Researchers beyond the University Walls* (Basingstoke, 2005), 110–23.
Finberg, H. P. R., 'How not to write local history' in H. P. R. Finberg and V. H. T. Skipp, *Local History: Objective and Pursuit* (David and Charles, 1967), 71–86
Hey, David, *The Oxford Companion to Local and Family History* (OUP, 1996, 2nd edn, 2008)
Hindle, S., *On the Parish? The Micropolitics of Poor Relief in Rural England, c.1550–1750* (Oxford, 2004)
Lancaster, B., Newton, D. and Vall, N. (eds), *An Agenda for Regional History* (Northumbria UP, 2007)
Lewis, C. P., *Particular Places: An Introduction to English Local History* (British Library, 1989)
Lord, E., *Investigating the Twentieth Century: Sources for Local Historians* (Tempus, 1999)
Marshall, J. D., 'The antiquarian heresy', *Jour. of Regional and Local Studies*, 15, 2 (1995), 49–54;
—, *The Tyranny of the Discrete: a Discussion of the Problems of Local History in England* (Aldershot, 1997)
Phythian-Adams, C., *Re-Thinking English Local History* (Leicester UP, 1987)
Richardson, R. C., *The Changing face of English Local History* (Ashgate, 2000)
Riden, P., *Record Sources for Local History* (Batsford, 1987)
Royle, E., *Issues of Regional Identity: In Honour of John Marshall* (Manchester UP, 1998)

—, *Need Local History be Parochial History?* (Univ. of Cambridge Inst. of Continuing Education, Occ. Paper 4, 2001)

Sheeran, G. and Y., 'Reconstructing Local History', *TLH*, 29, 4 (Nov. 1999), 256–62

Snell, K. D. M., *Parish and Belonging: Community, Identity and Welfare in England and Wales, 1700–1950* (CUP, 2006)

Tiller, K., *English Local History: An Introduction* (Sutton, 2002)

—, *English Local History: The State of the Art* (Univ. of Cambridge Inst. of Continuing Education, Occ. Paper 1, 1998)

Selected local studies

Beckett, J. V., *A History of Laxton, England's Last Open-field Village* (Blackwell, 1989)

Borsay, Peter, *The Image of Georgian Bath, 1700–2000: Towns, Heritage and History* (OUP, 2000)

Broad, John, *Transforming English Rural Society: The Verneys and the Claydons, 1600–1820* (CUP, 2004)

Dresser, Madge and Fleming, Peter, *Bristol: Ethnic Minorities and the City, 1000–2001* (Phillimore, 2007)

Dyer, Christopher (ed.), *The Self-contained Village? The Social History of Rural Communities, 1250–1900* (Univ. of Hertfordshire Press, 2007).

Fox, Harold, *The Evolution of the Fishing Village: Landscape and Society along the South Devon Coast* (Leopard's Head, 2001)

French, H. R. and Hoyle, R. W., *The Character of Rural Society: Earl's Colne 1550–1750* (Manchester UP, 2007)

Goodacre, John, *The Transformation of a Peasant Economy: Townspeople and Villagers in the Lutterworth Area 1500–1700* (Scolar Press, 1994)

Hey, David G., *An English Rural Community: Myddle under the Tudors and Stuarts* (Leicester UP, 1974)

Hoskins, W. G., *The Midland Peasant: The Economic and Social History of a Leicestershire Village* (Macmillan, 1965)

Howell, Cicely, *Land, Family and Inheritance in Transition: Kibworth Harcourt 1280–1700* (CUP, 1983)

Levine, D. and Wrightson, K., *The Making of an Industrial society: Whickham 1560–1765* (Clarendon, 1991)

Marcombe, D., *English Small Town Life: Retford 1520–1642* (Univ. of Nottingham, 1993)

Reay, B., *Microhistories: Demography, Society and Culture in Rural England, 1800–1930* (CUP, 1996)

Reay, B., *Rural Englands* (Palgrave Macmillan, 2004)

Roberts, Elizabeth, *A Woman's Place: An Oral History of Working-Class Women, 1890–1940* (Basil Blackwell, 1984)

Robin, Jean, *Elmdon: Continuity and Change in a North-west Essex Village, 1861–1964* (CUP, 1980)

Sharpe, Pamela, *Population and Society in an East Devon Parish: Reproducing Colyton, 1540–1840* (Univ. of Exeter Press, 2002)

Underdown, D., *Fire from Heaven: Life in an English Town in the Seventeenth Century* (Harper Collins, 1992)

Walter, John, *Understanding Popular Violence in the English Revolution: The Colchester Plunderers* (CUP, 1999)

Walton, J. K., *The British Seaside: Holidays and Resorts in the Twentieth Century* (Manchester UP, 2000)

Wrightson, K. and Levine, D., *Poverty and Piety in an English Village: Terling, 1525–1700* (OUP, 1999)

Journals relevant to local and regional history

Archives (journal of the British Records Association, twice yearly)

The Local Historian (British Association for Local History, quarterly)

Local Population Studies (Local Population Studies Society, twice yearly)

Family and Community History (Family and Community Historical Research Society, twice yearly)

Midland History (University of Birmingham, once a year)

Northern History (University of Leeds, twice yearly)

Rural History (Cambridge University Press, twice a year)

Southern History (University of Winchester, once a year)

Urban History (Cambridge University Press, three times a year)

[*NB Almost every county has an historical-cum-archaeological journal, published annually.*]

Historical methods

S. Cameron and S. Richardson, *Using Computers in History* (Palgrave Macmillan, 2005)

Cheney, C. R. and Jones, M., *A Handbook of Dates for Students of British History* (CUP, 2000)

Fillmore, J., 'Local History Internet Sites: A Handlist', *TLH*, 37, 3 (Aug. 2007), 193–203

Finnegan, R. (ed.), *Participating in the Knowledge Society: Researchers Beyond the University Walls* (Palgrave Macmillan, 2005)

Gooder, Eileen, *Latin for Local Historians: An Introduction* (Longmans, 1961)

Harvey, P. D. A., *Editing Historical Records* (British Library, 2001)

Hudson, Pat, *History by Numbers: an Introduction to Quantitative Approaches* (Arnold, 2000)

Johnson C. and Jenkinson, H., *English Court Hand, AD 1066 to 1500* (Clarendon Press, 1915)

Martin, C. T., *The Record Interpreter* (reprinted, Hildesheim, 1969)

Appendices

'I say this only, next to the immediate discharge of my Holy Office, I know not how in any course of studies I could have better served my patron, my people and my successors, than by preserving the memoirs of this parish and the adjacent parts, which before lay remote from common notice, and in a few years time had been buried in unsearchable oblivion. If this present age be too immers'd in cares or pleasures, to take any relish or to make any use of these discoveries, I then appeal to posterity. For I believe the times will come when persons of better inclination will arise, who will be glad to find any collection of this nature, and will be ready to supply the defects, and carry on the continuation of it.'

White Kennett, vicar of Ambrosden, Oxfordshire, wrote these timeless words in the earliest published history of an English parish, *Parochial Antiquities of Ambrosden, Burcester and Other Adjacent Parts* (1695), pp. v–vi. (See Pl. 1 between pp. 80–1.)

Appendix 1

Published resources

The purpose of this section is to highlight various kinds of publication which are of value to the local historian. Until recent decades they of course took the form of printed books and journals, as normally found in major libraries or on the shelves of record offices. These still pour from academic and commercial presses, but a powerful alternative is now provided by the internet, sometimes duplicating books and journals but also carrying increasing amounts of entirely original material. Whether on paper or online, or both, the historian's published resources can be divided into three broad categories:

a)   all those historical texts or 'primary sources' from the past which have been transcribed, translated, summarised (calendared) or made available as facsimiles.

b)   various guides, lists and indexes which point the way to original manuscripts.

c)   the interpretative writings of historians, past and present, normally described as 'secondary sources' or 'historiography'.

A   Transcripts, translations, calendars and facsimiles

Over more than two centuries, a large amount of original evidence referring to local communities has appeared as printed transcriptions, translations, calendars and facsimiles. Indeed, in some cases the original has since disappeared and the published version is the only one left. For a general introduction to this kind of evidence, see E.L.C. Mullins, *Texts and Calendars* (last reprinted 1983; now supplemented online by the Royal Historical Soc.) which lists the publications of the Record Commissioners, of the Public Record Office (now The National Archives), of major record societies with national scope (for example Camden, Selden and Harleian), and of more localised record societies (for example Norfolk, Bristol and Surtees).

In general local historians will find value in the following publications:

- The text of Domesday Book is available in several forms: in general volumes published for each county by the *VCH*; in a county series edited by John Morris and published by Phillimore; in an edition edited by E.M. Hallam and D. Bates published in 2001 by Tempus in association with PRO Publications; in a translation by G. Martin and A. Williams, which Alecto published in elaborate county volumes in 1992 and which then in 2002 became a single-volume Penguin Classic; and online on TNA's website and on Hull University's 'Domesday Explorer'.

- Set up in 1800, the Record Commissioners published transcripts of many important early documents with wide geographical coverage (for example the Hundred Rolls of the late thirteenth century, the Ecclesiastical Taxation of 1291 (Pl. 5) and the *Valor Ecclesiasticus* of 1535).
- 'Access to Archives' (A2A) is an expanding electronic database, hosted by TNA, of the catalogues and calendars of record offices and other repositories in the United Kingdom. In December 2007 it held 10.1 million searchable records, ranging in date from the eighth century to the present, stored in 414 repositories.
- 'Newsplan' is an ambitious long-term programme for the preservation and microfilming of local and regional newspapers. It is organised by the national libraries of Gt Britain and the regional newspaper industry. In the period 2000–05 Newsplan saved for posterity 12.9 million pages of newsprint from 1325 different titles.
- A local historian should always be prepared to search through official calendars (for example, of the *Patent Rolls*, *Inquisitions Post Mortem*, *Acts of the Privy Council*, and *Letters and Papers of the Reign of Henry VIII*). Such volumes are usually indexed, though not always adequately by modern standards. A booklet called *British National Archives, Sectional List No. 24* (last printed in 1984) was traditionally useful because it listed all the officially published indexes, transcripts or calendars of documents in the national archives. From 2008 all these official calendars will be available online.
- Another great series of calendars, amounting to 239 volumes in 2007, has been produced by the Historical Manuscripts Commission (HMC, set up in 1869 and now merged with TNA). The purpose is to list and abstract major collections belonging to individuals, landed estates, urban corporations, dioceses, etc. Currently the commission is working, *inter alia*, on the manuscripts of the Marquesses of Salisbury and Bath.
- Many riches lie in a series called *Records of Early English Drama (REED)*, published since 1979 by the University of Toronto Press. The aim is 'to find, transcribe and publish external evidence of dramatic, ceremonial and minstrel activity in Gt Britain before 1642'. Volumes deal with individual counties and major cities, but the twenty-fifth in 2005 was devoted to the principality of Wales.
- Local historians working in the north of England should certainly be aware of *Borthwick Texts and Calendars: Records of the Northern Province*, published by the University of York. No.30 in this series appeared in 2003.
- An astonishing amount of primary material has appeared for generations in the form of antiquarian miscellanies, and in some cases is still appearing (for example *Devon and Cornwall Notes and Queries* from 1901).
- It should not be forgotten that individual historians and antiquaries have published and edited texts, sometimes singly and sometimes in series (for example Sydenham Hervey published twenty-two of his 'Suffolk Green Books' in the period 1894–1915; they included subsidy returns, hearth tax returns, parish registers, diaries and letters).

- County historical and archaeological journals contain many transcripts and translations of original documents, usually embedded in articles.

B Indexes and guides to primary sources

- For an introduction to the array of record offices, libraries and other specialist institutions, large and small, which keep original archives of any kind, see J. Foster & J. Sheppard (eds), *British Archives: A Guide to Archive Resources in the United Kingdom* (4th edn, Palgrave, 2002). The online directory known as ARCHON gives contact details for all kinds of record repository in the UK and elsewhere.
- M.S. Giuseppi, *Guide to the Contents of the Public Records Office* (three vols, 1963–8) gives general guidance on the national archives at Kew. For example it will tell you that lists of church goods compiled in the reigns of Edward VI and Mary are to be found under E 117, and that the Corn Returns of 1799 to 1949 are under MAF 10. Giuseppi is now out of print, but a later *Current Guide* (latest edition, 1995) can still be found on microfiche in major libraries and record offices. Another good general introduction to TNA is Philip Riden's *Local History: a Handbook for Beginners* (revised 1998).
- The *PRO Lists and Indexes* (begun in 1892) and the parallel productions of the List and Index Society (begun in 1965) give references to individual documents with brief details of contents, places and personal names. The hundreds of volumes already printed cover, for example, many manorial documents kept in TNA (court rolls, accounts and surveys), proceedings of the Star Chamber, port-books, and registers of the Society of Friends.
- Some county record offices publish broad guides to their own sources, for example K. Collis, *The West Glamorgan Archive Service, a Guide to the Collections* and *Handlist of the Contents of the Gloucestershire Record Office* (both 1998). Newsletters, lists of accessions and handouts are also produced to help searchers.
- Early printed books and lesser publications, from the fifteenth to nineteenth centuries, are listed in *Short-title catalogues* (*STC*): 3 volumes for the period 1475–1640; 3 volumes for 1641–1700; 5 volumes for the eighteenth century; 6 volumes for 1801–15; 56 volumes for 1816–70. This is a major source which local historians often neglect.
- An enormous amount of original evidence for local communities lies buried in *British Parliamentary Papers* (*BPP*). A helpful introduction can be found in P. Cockton, *Subject Catalogue to the House of Commons Parliamentary Papers, 1801– 1900* (5 volumes, Chadwyck-Healey, 1988). Alternatively, Southampton University's website BOPCRIS offers detailed abstracts of over 39,000 official publications from 1688 to 1995; over 1 million pages were fully searchable in 2007.
- Guides are also available for specific types of document and for particular historical themes. Good examples are P.D.A. Harvey, *Manorial Records* (reprinted 1999) and N.W. Alcock, *Documenting the History of Houses* (2003). Numerous guides to original sources have been produced for family historians, and often

published by the Federation of Family History Societies. Recent examples include J. Gibson & C. Rogers, *Poor Law Union Records: 3, South-west England, the Marches and Wales* (2nd edn, 2000) and J. Gibson & E. Churchill, *Probate Jurisdictions: Where to Look for Wills* (5th edn, 2002).

- The Historical Manuscripts Commission, previously mentioned for its calendaring, incorporates two other resources of value. The National Register of Archives (NRA), created in 1945, contains over 44,000 unpublished lists and catalogues of manuscript collections relating to individuals, families, businesses and organisations. The Manorial Documents Register (MDR), now partly available online, records the nature and location of all manorial documents which are known to survive.

C Secondary sources

- The historian's principal route to secondary sources (that is, the published work of other historians, living and dead) is by means of references, bibliographies, reviews and abstracts of articles (see pp. 57–60, above). Increasingly we are able to find helpful references by searching the online catalogues of major libraries (such as COPAC which now covers more than fifty leading libraries in the UK, and SUNCAT which opens up the contents of serial publications).
- Regional and county bibliographies listing all kinds of published history are valuable, where they exist. See for example J.D. Bennett, *Rutland in Print: a Bibliography of England's Smallest County* (2006).
- Of all printed sources, the most obvious for the local historian are the large red tomes of the *VCH*. Though this project to provide a detailed history for every English county is incomplete, over 200 volumes are currently available. They are of two kinds. 'General volumes' have valuable chapters on subjects such as religious history and agriculture, while 'topographical volumes' contain the histories of individual towns and parishes. Local historians working in counties *without* topographical coverage will still learn a lot from the *VCH* of other counties – about basic sources and about the infinite variety of human communities. Work on this scholarly enterprise still continues in about a dozen counties.
- Another detailed survey can be found in inventories of the three Royal Commissions on Historical/Ancient Monuments, recording the buildings, monuments and archaeological sites of England, Wales and Scotland. Coverage, however, is still incomplete. The English commission has merged with English Heritage, and is now concentrating on thematic publications.
- For basic architectural comment, at parish level, see the indispensable Penguin series, *The Buildings of England/Scotland/Wales/Ireland*, still affectionately known as 'Pevsner', which is undergoing constant revision by Yale University Press.
- For archaeological background the local historian should scan titles in two long series: *Research Reports* of the Council for British Archaeology (CBA), and *British Archaeological Reports, British Series (BAR)*.

- Obvious sources of comparative information include parish, town and county histories of any date, the journals of local historical and archaeological societies, and the more emphemeral bulletins and newsletters also published by many local groups. It hardly needs saying that the local historian should not search merely for the name of his or her own 'place', but should be prepared to undertake wider trawling geographically and thematically (see pp. 33–40).

- Of great value is the *Annual Bulletin of Historical Literature: a Critical Review of New Publications*, published by the Historical Association from 1911 and since 1997 in electronic form. This provides 'a selective and critical review of recent historical books, journals and articles covering all periods of history'. Sections deal primarily with periods (for example 'Later Middle Ages' and 'Nineteenth century') and are subdivided by subjects (for example 'Political and religious history' and 'Economic and social history'), and by national areas (England, Scotland, Wales and Ireland). This review makes frequent reference to localised work including examples published in regional journals, record series and occasionally in county journals.

- Bibliographies of a more narrowly thematic kind are also worth searching. For example: A.T. Hall, *English Local History Handlist, a Select Bibliography and Guide to Sources* (Hist. Association, up to 1979); Owen Chadwick, *The History of the Church, a Select Bibliography* (1966), and *A Bibliography of Vernacular Architecture* (up to 1999). It is sad that numerous bibliographies which academics prepare for their students are not regularly collected and published for wider consumption: this is a service which could now be done, and updated as necessary, on the internet.

- Although we as local historians would never call ourselves biographers, let alone autobiographers, we should be prepared to search biographical writings which have many references to local communities and places. Rich pickings will be found, for example, in the sixty volumes of the *Oxford Dictionary of National Biography* (2004) which is searchable online by place as well as by person, in the *History of Parliament* (twenty-eight volumes in 2007) and equivalent parliamentary volumes for Scotland and Ireland.

- Because local history has imprecise boundaries, we must keep an eye on journals and new books in several other historical specialisations. Obviously relevant periodicals include *Landscape History, Local Population Studies, Economic History Review, Agricultural History Review, Rural History, Urban History, Journal of Ecclesiastical History* and *Archives*.

Appendix 2

Recording the present and recent past

The best-known examples of this historical approach in Great Britain are undoubtedly the *Statistical Accounts of Scotland*. Three sets of these *Accounts* were published for the whole country, in 1791–9 (21 volumes), 1845 (15 volumes) and 1951–92 (28 volumes). For every Scottish parish these remarkable books contain a mixture of observations, statistics and illustrative material on matters such as agriculture, industry, trade, housing, communications and social trends. In other words, they record detail about local communities which could easily have been forgotten by contemporaries and not otherwise systematically recorded.

Since 1997, in acknowledgement of the pace of change and to mark the millennium, a fourth survey has been initiated by a consortium of eleven local history societies in the county of East Lothian. The resultant East Lothian Fourth Statistical Account Society, with the support of the county's library service, is committed to publishing a total of seven volumes. Two will deal with the county as a whole and five with the constituent parishes, and the books are backed by a fuller version in CD-ROM. Produced by different groups of people the parish accounts vary in length and style, and frequently include transcriptions of oral evidence. They look back to 1945 and sometimes refer to the earlier published *Accounts*, which means that contemporary description is consciously leavened by an historical dimension. On the following pages are brief extracts drawn from the fourth of the seven volumes, which was published in 2006 and covers five parishes in the north of the county against the Firth of Forth.[1]

Inevitably records of this kind contain personal judgements, inaccuracies and even prejudices, but that does not invalidate them. Here local residents take on the role of the contemporary historian, akin to that of a medieval chronicler, by ensuring that the trends of contemporary and recent life are described by people who have experienced them. Such records, preferably updated at regular intervals, could be of great value in all communities, not because they represent definitive or complete history in themselves but because they feed communal memory and stockpile evidence for historians of the future.

In some English counties, so-called 'parish recorders' carry out similar work on a continuous basis, ensuring that contemporary life, events and trends are recorded in words and images *as they happen*. This important task is best coordinated by an

---

[1] Sonia Baker (ed.), *East Lothian Fourth Statistical Account, 1945–2000, vol 4* (East Lothian Council Library Service, 2006). Four of the seven volumes are in print at the end of 2007.

umbrella organisation which can insist on basic standards and consistent presentation, and ensure that the record is systematically kept for posterity (see pp. 45–6).

Extracts from *East Lothian 1945–2000* (The East Lothian Fourth Statistical Account, vol. 4, 2006)

Parish of Dirleton

p. 43
'... Groups of new houses were built at Gylers Road in the 1940s and 1950s and by the East Lothian Housing Association at Castlemains Place in the 1990s. The latter has two associated workshops to encourage the establishment of small businesses in the village. Cottages in Chapelhill were demolished to make way for houses for the elderly. Major developments were latterly curtailed by the limited capacity of the sewer although this was rectified at the end of the century. This paved the way for a development of five houses at the paddock beside the Open Arms Hotel. Some council houses have been sold to the tenants leaving 73 council houses today compared to 94 in 1985.'

p. 45
'... Shopping patterns have changed generally in recent years, greatly influenced by increased car use. From the 1980s many people have made use of supermarkets in North Berwick, Haddington and the outskirts of Edinburgh where once they would have shopped locally. Despite this, Gullane has done better than many villages in retaining its local shops. Nevertheless changes have taken place. The 1953 Third Statistical Account gives around 30 shops in Gullane, reduced to 21 in 1977. In 2000 there were still 21. These include three grocery stores plus butchers, bakery, greengrocers, newsagent with confectionery, men's outfitters and ladies' dress shop. However there is now no ironmonger, fish shop, general draper nor dairy. Other types of businesses, such as a travel agency, antiques, interior design and curtain shops and a health and beauty salon, have moved in. There are, besides, two hairdressers, a solicitor/estate agent, chemist, charity shop, post office and bank. The original four Co-operative shops (bakery, grocery, drapery and butcher) were gradually reduced until, at the end of the century, only a grocery store remains.'

p. 46
'... In the Third Statistical Account of 1953 Gullane is credited with eight hotels along with three restaurants or cafés, with three hotels in Dirleton and a teashop attached to a shop. In 1977 the hotels in Gullane numbered six and restaurants/cafés four. At the end of the century Gullane has five hotels, four restaurant/cafés and one bar providing food. Of the eating establishments, La Potinière has a national reputation. Dirleton's two hotels are the Castle Inn, a 19th century coaching inn, and The Open Arms. The latter was converted from a guesthouse to a tearoom in 1947 and shortly

afterwards became an hotel. During the summer a marquee erected in the garden is used for wedding receptions (15 in 1999) and other functions. Throughout the parish a small number of homes offer bed and breakfast facilities.'

p. 56

'... The Gullane & Dirleton History Society genuinely involves both communities. It was inaugurated on 1 March 1995, following the amalgamation of the Gullane Local History Society, formed in 1985, and the Dirleton Local History Group, launched in 1982. A programme of illustrated talks alternates between the two villages. There has been an annual membership of well over 100 people throughout the 1990s. Members have been encouraged to undertake research projects, which add to knowledge of the history of the parish. Members of the societies have contributed to ten books published by the societies, two books published jointly with the former East Lothian District Council, and a number published by others. Its programme goes some way to plugging the gap left by the demise of the extra-mural lectures.'

Appendix 3

Transcribing documents:
basic rules with examples

These rules apply to the process of making one's first painstakingly accurate transcriptions direct from historical documents. Although increasing numbers of searchers in record offices or libraries prefer to use a laptop for this purpose, the majority still seem to transcribe by hand. It should be remembered that the equivalent of <u>underlining</u> (manuscript) is *italics* (printed). Note also, that when one prepares documents for publication, different conventions are often brought into play (see below, p. 136).

1. Each transcript should be headed with a reference to both repository and document. For example, TNA, E179/260/5.
2. The numbers of pages, folios or membranes should be shown at the appropriate points in the text. For front and back faces of each folio, use 'r' (*recto*) and 'v' (*verso*); for the back of a membrane use 'd' (*dorso*).
3. The aim is to reproduce the text as accurately as possible: nothing is to be added or omitted without acknowledgement in a heading or footnote.
4. If transcribing manually, underline any editorial insertions within square brackets, for example [<u>in another hand</u>] or [<u>illeg.</u>] for 'illegible'. If however transcribing directly into a computer, *italics* should take the place of underlinings.
5. A forward slash can be used to show where each line of the original document ends. In the case of a complicated manuscript with sub-headings and marginal notes, however, it is probably best to replicate the original layout as closely as possible.
6. Retain the original spelling, however idiosyncratic or inconsistent. Also retain the original punctuation (if it exists), marginal headings, paragraphing, capital letters (however odd their distribution) and use of the ampersand (&). Do not at this stage add your own punctuation or 'correct' the spelling.
7. However, the Anglo-Saxon 'thorn' (Þ, þ) should be transcribed as 'th' which is what was intended, and not as 'y'. Thus, 'the chirche', not 'ye chirche'.[1] Similarly, it is better to use 'u', 'v' and 'n' as pronounced, not as written. Thus, 'havyng' rather than 'hauyng'.

---

[1] However, the Anglo-Saxon 'yogh' (ȝ, 3) should be noted as such, because it represents a soft 'g' which cannot be translated exactly into modern orthography. For example, 'ȝeven' which stands for the modern 'given'.

8. Numbers should be given as in the original (whether Roman, Arabic or a mixture of the two).
9. Insertions should be distinguished (see conventions below).
10. Deletions should be noted, and transcribed if legible (see conventions below).
11. Abbreviations which are readily understood should be extended and acknowledged (see conventions below).
12. To show that an error is in the manuscript itself, and is not the fault of the transcriber, use [*sic*] meaning 'thus'.
13. Always re-check your transcript against the original. And check it again before publication.

Conventions recommended for transcribing

For insertions	\ /
For deletions	< >
For items illegible or damaged	[*illeg.*] or <*illeg.*> if deleted; [*damaged*]
For unfilled spaces in text	[*blank*]
For doubtful readings	[?] immediately preceding word or number in question, without a space
For abbreviations	Underline restored letters, thus 'parishioners', or put them in square brackets, thus 'app[ur]tena[u]nc[es]'. If you are uncertain about the spelling (for example, about a Latin case-ending), it is safer to put an apostrophe for the part omitted, thus *messuag'*.

Publishing transcripts

When a transcript is published, it is legitimate to help readers by making certain changes to the text. For example, one can extend obvious abbreviations without acknowledgement, convert Roman to Arabic figures, modernise the use of capital and lower-case letters, and introduce modern punctuation providing no contentious meaning is imposed. It is essential that any such changes are signalled in an explanatory note. For examples, see pp. 137–41 below.

Examples of transcription

In the two examples which follow, the original layout of lines has been retained, each numbered for ease of reference. Capital letters, punctuation and ampersands are given as in the original. Abbreviated words have been extended, with the restored letters underlined (they could equally well have appeared in italics or within square brackets).

1. A business letter from John Leake to Mr Antony Gell of Hopton, 1574. This concerns a survey of Mr Hutchingson's estate at Owthorpe in Nottinghamshire. Leake as steward of the estate has asked the tenants to cooperate, and is pressing Gell to sign the survey and not to put the valuations too high. See page 138 for facsimile.

TRANSCRIPTION

Derbyshire Record Office, D258/33/1/9

1.   Master Gell according to your appoyntment I have willed the
2.   Tenauntes to be redye to delyver you the Syrveye of the landes
3.   as Master Hutchingson latlye died seased of in the countrye.
4.   My requeste is you will delyver this bearer my servaunte the
5.   same surveye syned with your hande, soe as I maye <s> certyfie yt
6.   to the Courte of the wardes I ded perceyve by your laste answer
7.   that you ment to make the surveye to the uttermoste of the
8.   valewe, I hope you will not deale soe hardlye with me
9.   For in suche dealing you shall greatly hynder the warde
10. & dyspleasure me without eny profytt to yourself, I hearneste
11. -lye require your frendshipp' in this behalfe as not to rate
12. them in this your surveye to the uttermoste, Thus hoping
13. of your frendshipp' at this instant, I leave you from Owethrope
14. this xij^th of Aprill in Anno 1574.
15.   Yours moste assured
16.   John Leake

Notes

'Mr' has been restored as 'Master', although some transcribers might leave the original abbreviation because it is still familiar today (and pronounced 'Mister'). The original writer used meaningless space-fillers on lines 3 and 14, but these have not been noted in the transcription.

Line 2: the word 'tenants' contains four minims in a row. Some would transcribe it as 'tenanntes', but here a 'u' has been introduced to reflect the probable pronunciation.

Line 5: the writer has crossed out a long 's', so angle-brackets are used to show the deletion.

Lines 11 and 13: a flourish at the end of 'friendship' has been rendered by an apostrophe as an alternative to appending a final 'e'.

Line 16: The forename 'John' carries an abbreviation sign because the writer still had in mind the Latin 'Johannes'.

John Leake's letter of 1574

2. Probate inventory of Anne Ewbanke widow of Brough Sowerby in the parish of Brough, Westmorland, 1599. This document shows the usual introductory heading (though without naming her parish), followed by a detailed listing of the possessions of a recently deceased person. See page 140 for facsimile.

TRANSCRIPTION

Cumbria Record Office, Carlisle: P1599 Ewbanke, Anne of Brough Sowerby

1.	An Inventorie maide of all the	
2.	goodes and Cattells of Mistres Anne	
3.	Ewbanke wedow, moveable and unmove-	
4.	able, prized by those iiijᵒʳ sworne	
5.	men, viz Thomas Nicholson Roger	
6.	Waistell, Henry Ewbanke Willyam	
7.	Aiskell. Written this iiijᵗʰ day of	
8.	Apprile, 1599.	
9.	Inprimis vijᵒ kyne	xiijˡⁱ vjˢ viijᵈ
10.	Item one meare sold	iijˡⁱ iijˢ ijᵈ
11.	Item Another meare	iijˡⁱ vjˢ viijᵈ
12.	Item two whies	xlˢ
13.	Item one feather bed one bolster ijᵒ pillivers	xˢ
14.	Item thre Coverletes & one happen	xxvjˢ viijᵈ
15.	Item foure blankittes	xˢ
16.	Item two gownes one kirtell & one forekirtell	
17.	one cloke one safegarde one felt & one gorget	lˢ
18.	Item linnen in one trunke with one hatband one box	xlˢ
19.	Item one paire of Sathan sleves one velvet	
20.	hat one bonegrace & one litle cover	xijˢ
21.	Item two gownes	xˡⁱ
22.	Item more in linnen	xvˢ
23.	Item one velvet hoode one velvet gorget scarffes	
24.	two paire of gloves & one knife	xxxˢ
25.	Item one petticoote two forekirtels	iijˡⁱ vjˢ viijᵈ
26.	Item one glase one combe with braclettes	
27.	& one settinge sticke	iiijˢ
28.	Item in Ringes	iijˡⁱ
29.	Item two cupboord clothes & quishines	vjˢ
30.	Item in pude	xxˢ
31.	Item in fire vessell	xxxˢ
32.	Item in candlestickes	ijˢ vjᵈ
33.	Item in wood vessell	xijˢ
34.	Item in Iron geare	iijˢ
35.	Item pottes & pitchers	xijᵈ

An Inuentorie

maide of all the
goodes and cattells of mī Trib Anne
trubanke widow, moveable and vnmove-
able, prised by those mē svorne
waistell, Thomas nicholson, Roger
diskell, Henry trwbanke, william
Apprile / 1599 / written this iiij the day of

Inprimis viij kyne ——————————————

It one meare fole ———————————— xxvij s vj d

A nother meare ———————————— iij li iij s iiij d

It two whies ———————————— iij li xvj s viij d

It one fether bed one bolster ij pillibers ——— x s

It thre coverlets & one happen —————— xx s

It foure blankitt ———————————— xxvij s viij d

It two gownes one kirtoll & one forekirtoll
one clok one safeguarde one felt & one gorget

It linnen in one trunke with one hatband one box — vli s

It one paire of satean slevis one velvet
hat one bonygrace & one litle rower —— x xij s

It two gownes ————————————— x li

It more in linnen ———————————— x vi s

It one velvet hoode one velvet gorget starche

two paire of gloves & one knif ——————— xxx s

It one petticote two foot kirtolls ———— iij li iij s viij d

It one glas one rumbo with bracelet ——— x iij s
& one settinge stirke

It in pewter ————————————— iij li

It two cupboordclotheb & queshins ——— vij s

It in puder ————————————— xx s

It in fier vessell ————————————— xxx

It in brandelstirke ————————— ij s vij d

It in wood vessell ————————————— xvij s

It in iron geare ————————————— iiij s

It potte & pitcheors ————————— xvij s

It in thraft ——————————————— xvij s

It one ambre ——————————————— iiij s

It chaires & two litle tables ——————— iiij s

It a meate boord formes & bed stockes
two cloakes

It in husbandry geare ———————————— iiij s

It owinge to hir of Robet Emmisen of —— xxvij s
barnardcastle

It owinge to hir of Jamob hanmbie ——— vi s

It owinge to hir of michaell brinstoll — xlvij s

36.	Item in cheastes	viij^s
37.	Item one aumbre	iiij^s
38.	Item chaires & two litle tables	iiij^s
39.	Item A meate boord formes & bed stocks	⎰
40.	two fleakes	⎱ iij^s
41.	Item in husbandry geare	iiij^s
42.	Item owinge to hir of Robert Emmerson of	
43.	barnardcastle	xvij^s
44.	Item owinge to hir of James haumbie	vj^s
45.	Item owinge to hir of michaell brunskell	xvi^s
46.	Somma bonorum	liiij^{li} xvj^s iiij^d

Notes

This document, like many others in local collections, contains unorthodox spelling, dialect words and Roman numerals.

Lines 2 and 3: the words 'Mistres' and 'moveable' have abbreviation signs above them but, as is often the case, they are meaningless.

Lines 3, 7 and 8: note the occasional punctuation in the form of comma, full-stop and forward slash.

Lines 4, 9 and 13: Roman numerals end with superscript letters harking back to their Latin forms: *quatuor*, *septimo* and *duo*.

Line 5: 'vz' or 'viz' is not an word in its own right, but an abbreviation for the Latin *videlicet*, meaning 'namely' or 'that is to say'.

Line 21: note that Anne's two gowns are the second most expensive item in the inventory, after her seven cattle.

Line 42: debts owing to Anne Ewbanke are counted among her possessions.

Line 46: 'the sum of goods'. On the original document there follows a list of debts owed *by* Anne Ewbanke, totalling £11 4s 8d. A final line reads 'somma de claro xliij^{li} x^s viij$^{d'}$', meaning 'the sum remaining clear £44 10s 8d'. As is not unusual when Roman numerals are used, the subtraction is faulty!

Appendix 4

Making an abstract, with example

Abstracting is a way of 'gutting' an historical document, and recording it in a compact and modernised form. In a 'full abstract' every significant statement is retained, but without transcribing every word or keeping to the original spelling. Many historians handle their documents in this way, and record societies frequently publish abstracts because they save space and are more readily usable in historical debate and writing.[1] This important historical technique is illustrated below: a late-medieval will from the city of York is given first as an exact verbatim transcript and then as a full abstract.

1. Verbatim transcript

[from Claire Cross, *York Clergy Wills, 1520–1600: II City Clergy*, Borthwick Texts & Calendars 15, 1989, 10]

Will of John Smyth, chaplain of York, 10 August 1529

(York Minster Library, D & C Prob. Reg. 2, fol. 154r)
In dei nomine, Amen. The xth day of August in the yere of our Lord God Mv^cxxix. I, John Smyth, preist in Sanct William chappell of Ouse briege in the citie of York of hooll mynde and good memorie dooith ordane and maik my testament and last will in this forme folowing. Furst I gyve and bequeith my saull to Almyghtie God, to our blissed Ladie Sanct Marie and to all the celestiall cowrt of heven, and my bodie to be buried in the church erth of Sanct John Apposlte and Evangelist at thend of Ouse breige aforeseid. Item I bequeith to the church warkes their xxd. Item I bequeith to my broder Steven Smyth xiid. Item to Margaret my suster xiid. Item to my cosyne Christofer Magham viiid. Item to my kynswoman Malde Mawgham viiid. Item I bequeith to Sir John Stapleton a jaket of chamelet. Item I bequeith to Sir Henry Cookeson a dublet of chamelet with sarsenyt slevis. Item I will that all my brether in the said chappell of Ousebriege be at my derige and beriall and also all the preistes of Sanct John church aforseid. The reist of my goodes not bequeithide, my dettes paid and my funerall expenses done, I gyve to William Smyth my brother, whome I make executor of this my present will and testament. And my cosyne Sir Adame, vicar of Acome, the seid Sir Henrie Cookson and Sir John Stapleton to be

---

[1]   For example, P. Northeast (ed.), *Wills of the Archdeaconry of Sudbury, 1439–74* (Suffolk Records Soc., XLIV, 2001)

supervisoures hereof. Item I will that my brother Steven have the iii oxgange lande and the litle howse which was geven by the arbitrous. And I bequeith to the seid Sir Adame a silver spone. Theis witnes Sir Henrie Cookeson and Sir John Stapleton, preistes, with other.

 Prob. 9 November 1529

2. Full abstract

Here the same will is abstracted in 167 words instead of the original 289. Notice that some words and phrases of special interest, or of uncertain significance, are given in their original spellings and in inverted commas. These could be used later as direct quotations in writing. Place-names and forenames are modernised, unless they are in some way doubtful, but for safety's sake surnames are left in their original spellings (with variations such as 'Cookeson' and 'Cookson').

Will of JOHN SMYTH, priest of St William's chapel on Ouse Bridge, York, 10 August 1529

(York Minster Library, D & C Prob. Reg. 2, fol. 154r)
Soul to Almighty God, St Mary and 'all the celestial cowrt of heven'.
To be buried in St John's church at the end of Ouse Bridge ('in the church erth').
To repair ('church warkes') of St John's 20d.
To my brother Steven Smyth 12d.
To my sister Margaret 12d.
To my cousin Christopher Magham 8d.
To my kinswoman Maud Mawgham 8d.
To Sir John Stapleton a jacket of camlet ('chamelet').
To Sir Henry Cookeson a doublet of camlet with sarsenet ('sarsenyt') sleeves.
All my brethren in St William's chapel, and all the priests of St John's church, to attend my dirge and burial.
Residue, after payment of my debts and funeral expenses, to my brother William Smyth: executor.
Supervisors: my cousin Sir Adam, vicar of Acomb, Sir Henry Cookson and Sir John Stapleton.
To my brother Steven three oxgangs of land and 'the litle howse', given by the arbiters ('arbitrous').
To Sir Adam a silver spoon.
Witnesses: Sir Henry Cookeson and Sir John Stapleton, priests, and others.
Proved 9 November 1529

Appendix 5

Historical dating, with exercises

Medieval dates, and some later ones, are based on religious feasts and the regnal years of successive monarchs. To convert them to modern style, the following procedure should be followed. Using C.R. Cheney's *Handbook of Dates for Students of English History* (latest edition, revised by M. Jones, CUP, 2000):

1. Identify the date of the relevant feast (pp. 59–93).
2. Convert the regnal year into calendar years (pp. 32–45). In the vast majority of cases, this brings into play *two* calendar years (each of which has a reference number shown on the right-hand side of the page).
3. If, as is usually the case, your date does not fall exactly on the feast day but on, say, 'the Thursday before' or 'the Monday after', note the number given opposite the relevant calendar year on pp. 32–45. This is turn refers you to one of thirty-five tables between pp. 156 and 225.
4. Turn to the relevant table, and identify the precise day of the month.

NB: if the day falls in January or February, be careful to note whether you are, or are not, in a leap year (each table identifies leap years in bold print in its heading). If yours is indeed a leap year, use the two columns for January and February which are on the extreme left of the table.

Exercise

Using the methods described above, convert the following into modern-style dates (day of the month and/or year):

1. Feast of St George

2. Feast of St Etheldreda

3. Feast of the Eleven Thousand Virgins (*undecim millia virgines*)

4. Feast of the Second Translation of Edward King and Martyr

5. Feast of *Corpus Christi*

6. 4 Edward I

7. 21 Richard II

8.   38 Henry VIII

9.   12 Charles II

10. Saturday after the Feast of St Ambrose, 2 Edward II

11. Friday before the Nativity of the Blessed Virgin Mary, 10 Edward III

12. Saturday after the feast of St Luke the Evangelist, 21 Richard II

13. Wednesday before the Decollation of St John the Baptist, 38 Henry VI

14. Thursday before Candlemas, 50 Edward III

15. 9th January 1704/5

16. 56 Elizabeth II

(*Answers are given on p. 196.*)

Appendix 6

Analysis of documents

When using primary sources, we have several responsibilities to observe. First, the contents have to be read with great attention to detail to make sure that we understand, as fully as possible, what the writer intended to convey. Nevertheless, even after much speculation, some meanings will always remain elusive: in such cases our writing will have to express doubts and indecisions. Secondly, while reading our sources we naturally look out for words, phrases and perhaps larger chunks of prose worthy of direct quotation, in the belief that they will later enliven our writing (see pp. 95–6). Thirdly, we must be prepared to undertake careful analysis of the contents of documents, to extract meanings and construct interpretations which are not overtly stated in the original format.

The three examples of analysis which follow vary in complexity.[1] The first shows the extra value that can be extracted from a single source, in this case a printed trade directory of the late nineteenth century. By classifying, tabulating, counting and converting into percentages, a lot can be achieved without necessarily resorting to computers and elaborate software. Of course the documents most suitable for this type of analysis are those which have a consistent format. Other examples might include tax returns, census enumerations and probate inventories which list names, occupations, sums of money and other repetitive details. The process becomes more difficult or impossible with documents of highly variable and unpredictable form, such as personal letters and diaries.

In this context it should be recognised that one can analyse multiple examples of the same kind of source, such as all the surviving settlement certificates for a particular area or period. Alternatively one can correlate two or more different classes of evidence, such as wills, inventories and probate accounts. This latter approach is impossible without the overlap of clearly indentifiable personal names ('multi-source nominal record linkage' to use the jargon), and other internal details which need to be directly comparable. Sometimes, unfortunately, documents contain details which look comparable superficially, but which later turn out to be significantly different.

The second and third examples below indicate that, by using modern computers and appropriate software, it is possible to undertake much more elaborate types of analysis. This technology demands considerably greater inputs of time and effort, but is capable of sorting and cross-relating enormous quantities of data in response

---

[1] For permission to use these examples I am highly indebted to Dennis Mills, Peter Bysouth, Ken Sneath and the editorial board of LPSS.

to the historian's probing. Note that the second example below draws from more than one class of document, by associating nineteenth-century census returns with trade directories. By comparison the third example is based on the reading of over 1500 examples of one kind of source, early-modern probate inventories. This highly technical, computerised approach is characteristic of much modern professional and postgraduate research, which often covers more than a single community and can therefore be regional or sub-regional in scope.

Example 1: Analysis based on a single trade directory, from Dennis R. Mills, *Rural Community History from Trade Directories* (LPS Supp., 2001).

Table 7.2   Village interdependence: Ashby Folville (Leics) and neighbours, 1863

Village & Population Service	Ashby 160	Gaddesby 341	Thorpe Satchville 171	Twyford 372	Bars 29
Baker		X		X	X
Beerhouse			X	X	
Blacksmith			X	X	X
Bootmaker		X		X	X
Bricklayer		X		X	
Butcher		X	X	X	X
Carpenter/Joiner	X	X	X		X
C of E church	X	X	X	X	
Cooper		X			
Grocer		X			
Miller	X			X	
Nonconformist Chapel (Wesleyan)		X		X	X
Plumber					X
Public House	X	X		X	X
Saddler				X	
School		X	X	X	X
School (Wesleyan)				X	
Shopkeeper	X		X	X	X
Tailor		X	X	X	X
Wheelwright		X		X	

Source: White's *Directory of Leicestershire and Rutland*, 1863.

Many sources available to local historians, including directories, are of a comparatively simple form listing names, occupations and other details for individual parishes. At first sight they may appear of only limited value, but in fact they can be systematically analysed to reveal important social and economic differences within and between parishes. Here Dr Mills' purpose is to show services available in five Leicestershire villages in the early 1860s, and how smaller communities depended on larger ones for certain services and institutions – but with interesting aberrations such as the lack of a plumber, grocer, cooper and carpenter/joiner in Twyford, the biggest village.

Example 2: Analysis by Peter Bysouth of tradesmen and professionals in the small town of Buntingford (Herts), based on trade directories of 1870 and 1882 and the census enumerations of 1871 and 1881.

Using the software program Excel, Peter Bysouth has constructed a spreadsheet which combines four sources of two quite different types. Recognisable personal names provide the essential link between the documents. Colours are used to assist in the original analysis: yellow indicates where the data show 'differences' or breaks in continuity; purple indicates individuals who feature in a directory but not in the corresponding census; green indicates continuity across all four sources; pale blue indicates business women. In order to retain the colours of this table it has been reproduced as the centre spread of the plate section between pages 80 and 81.

Example 3: Analysis by Ken Sneath to investigate the social, geographical and chronological spread of expensive consumer goods. The four tables below plot the ownership of clocks in three Yorkshire deaneries, based on the reading of 1,523 probate inventories dating from 1690 to 1800.

Case Processing Summary

	Cases					
	Valid		Missing		Total	
	N	Percent	N	Percent	N	Percent
CLOCK * DEANERY	1523	100.0%	0	.0%	1523	100.0%

CLOCK * DEANERY Crosstabulation

Count

		DEANERY			Total
		Pontefract	Rydall	Holderness	
CLOCK	0	634	167	285	1086
	1	355	31	42	428
	2	7	0	0	7
	3	2	0	0	2
Total		998	198	327	1523

Case Processing Summary

	Cases					
	Valid		Missing		Total	
	N	Percent	N	Percent	N	Percent
CLOCK * PERIOD	1523	100.0%	0	.0%	1523	100.0%

CLOCK * PERIOD Crosstabulation

Count

		PERIOD			Total
		1690-1719	1720-1749	1750-1800	
CLOCK	0	397	417	272	1086
	1	76	150	202	428
	2	1	5	1	7
	3	0	0	2	2
Total		474	572	477	1523

The software used here is the Statistical Package for Social Scientists (SPSS), which Dr Sneath describes as 'an extremely effective tool for manipulating large amounts of data'. Once the data have been entered, a long process, they can be manipulated at the touch of a button. The tables above reveal that 428 inventories recorded the ownership of one clock, seven inventories recorded two clocks, and two inventories recorded three. The cross-tabulations show the distribution of clocks by deanery and by period. At a further touch of a button, other cross-tabulations can be produced such as the number of clocks by occupation or by urban parishes as opposed to rural. The software could then produce the median value of clocks by period or by occupational group, in less than a second.

Appendix 7

Producing an outline plan for writing

However much time they have spent on pondering their evidence, most writers find that they cannot plunge with confidence into a first draft without creating some sort of plan or skeleton of ideas. This exercise is a way of sketching the main outlines of one's historical argument, deliberately concentrating on broad generalisation rather than fine detail. The length and elaboration of such a plan will vary from individual to individual, though most people will probably want to mention the principal idea behind each successive paragraph. Opposite is an example from the author's own work: a manuscript sketch made for the introduction to a piece of historical editing.[1] Notice that the notes were not sacrosanct, and that they were modified and expanded as the first draft took shape. Items were ticked off as the writing progressed.

---

[1]   D. Dymond (ed.), *The Register of Thetford Priory* (British Academy and Norfolk Record Soc., 2 vols, 1995–6).

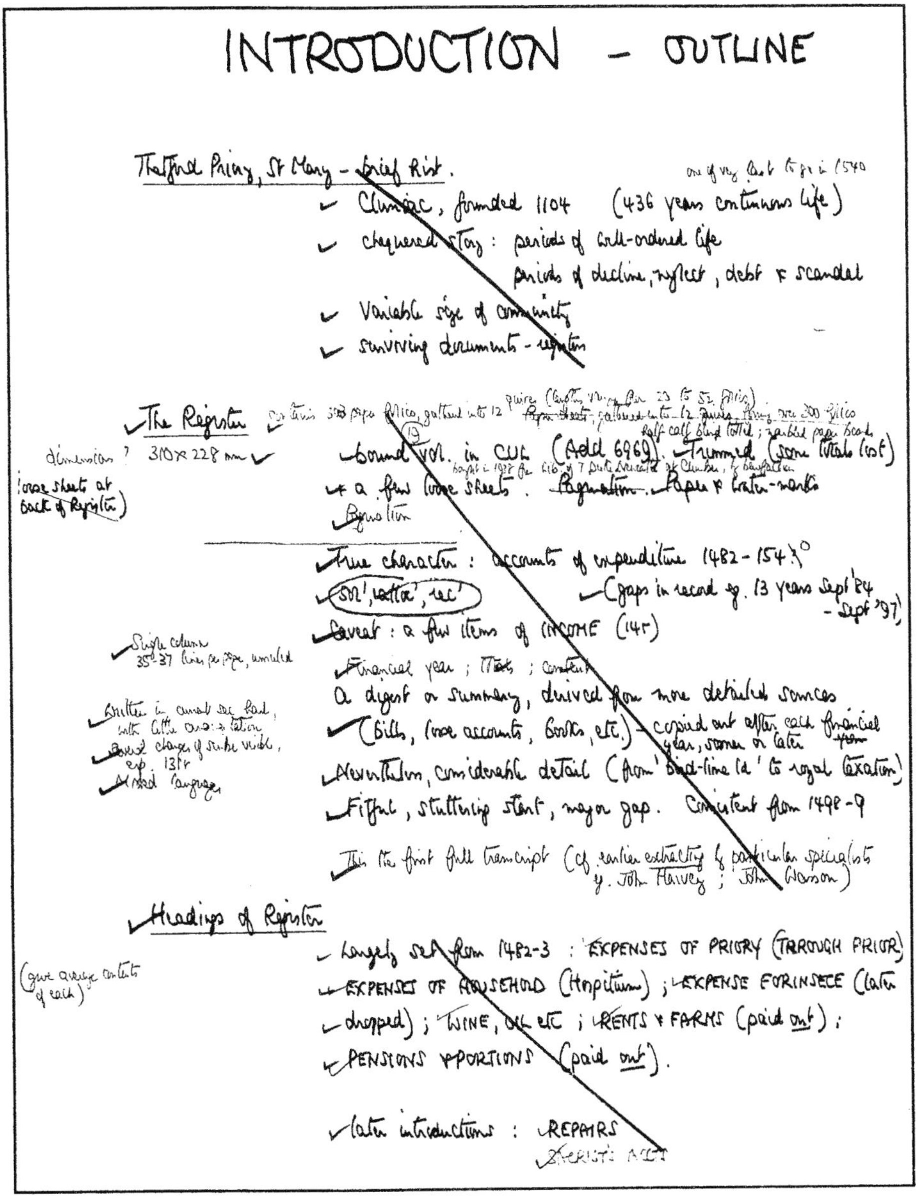
INTRODUCTION – OUTLINE

Thetford Priory, St Mary – brief hist.

✓ Cluniac, founded 1104 (436 years continuous life)

✓ chequered story: periods of well-ordered life

periods of decline, neglect, debt & scandal

✓ Variable size of community

✓ surviving documents – register

✓ The Register

dimensions? 310 × 228 mm ✓

bound vol. in CUL (Add 6969). Trimmed (some totals lost)

& a few loose sheets. Pagination. Paper & water-marks

(loose sheets at back of Register)

Pagination

True character: accounts of expenditure 1482–1540

(gaps in record eg. 13 years Sept '84 – Sept '97)

Caveat: a few items of INCOME (145)

✓ Single column 35–37 lines per page, unruled

Financial year; Totals; Content

A digest or summary, derived from more detailed sources

(Bills, loose accounts, books, etc.) – copied out after each financial year, sooner or later

Nevertheless, considerable detail (from 'bed-line la' to royal taxation)

Fitful, stuttering start, major gap. Consistent from 1498–9

This the first full transcript (cf earlier extracting of particular specialists eg. John Harvey; John Wasson)

✓ Headings of Register

(give average contents of each)

✓ Largely set from 1482–3: EXPENSES OF PRIORY (THROUGH PRIOR)

✓ EXPENSES OF HOUSEHOLD (Hospitium); EXPENSE FORINSECE (later dropped); WINE, OIL etc; RENTS & FARMS (paid out);

✓ PENSIONS & PORTIONS (paid out).

✓ later introductions: REPAIRS

Outline plan for writing.

Appendix 8

Shape in writing: an analysis

The purpose of this appendix is to show how written history has to be constructed around a basic framework of ideas. It makes use of an article published in August 2007 entitled 'A time of Change: Land Sales in the East Riding of Yorkshire in the Early Twentieth Century'.[1] The author is an agricultural historian who has a particular interest in the landed estates of the Yorkshire Wolds. She exposes a major shift in the economic and investment policies of landed families, which will undoubtedly have resonance in other parts of the country. The text is supported by endnotes which show wide reading of secondary literature, five tables and a map.

After an introduction, the article has been divided by the author into three sub-titled sections, which immediately give a broad thematic structure. They are:

[Introduction]

Reorganisation of estates

Disposal of land

Reinvestment of capital

What follows here is not a critique of the author's research or writing, but an attempt to summarise how she planned her text, drawing attention to the principal ideas and questions which appear to lie inside the article. This is the kind of deliberate design that should lie within any piece of historical writing, and which is essentially similar to the skeleton plan which is recommended in Appendix 7 (see pp. 150–1).

[Introduction]

- Background of agricultural prosperity in the mid-nineteenth century. The high price of wheat and rents had enabled landowners to build 'intricate webs of indebtedness'.
- The dramatic fall in the price of wheat 1879–1894 brought pressure to reduce rents, and jeopardised repayment of loans and mortgages.
- These troubles undermined the confidence and power of landowners. At this point summarise historians' views of the decline of the aristocracy, for example

---

[1]   Susan Parrott, 'A time of change: land sales in the East Riding of Yorkshire in the early twentieth century', *TLH*, 37, 3 (Aug. 2007), 146–55. This article was originally published in *East Yorkshire Historian*, 6 (2005).

D. Cannadine, J. Beckett and F.M.L. Thompson. Landowners in East Riding were forced to reorganise and restructure their estates and remaining wealth.

- Resumée (with map and two tables) of the six principal landowners of the Wolds, with acreages and gross values. Four of them also had smaller outlying estates in more fertile, low-lying Holderness.
- Origins of their wealth; mostly by inheritance and in one case by a leap from the merchant class.
- Golden Age of these estates in late-eighteenth and nineteenth centuries, peaking in 1860s and '70s: this prosperity was based on the purchase of cheap, light land; on intensive arable farming supported by new experimental techniques (marling, fertilising, cattle-breeding, crop rotation); and on large tenant farmers noted for their business skills.
- The crisis after 1879 stimulated a threefold reaction from landowners.

Reorganisation of estates

- Settled Land Act (1882) give greater flexibility in selling entailed estates, but anxieties increased with advent of death duties in 1894: Beckett suggests this was a watershed.
- Landowners began to sell in various parts of England. But with exception of Harrison Broadley estate, little changed at first on Wold estates.
- Main sales here, particularly of poor and outlying land, began between 1906 and 1913, stimulated by deaths of owners (Table).

Disposal of land

- At first the demand for land was weak; at its lowest in 1880s and '90s. But nationally landowners rushed to sell between 1910 and 1914. Among perceived threats in Lancashire was the growth of farmers' organisations.
- Beckett suggests that larger estates over 10,000 acres had the best chance of restructuring; sales could lead to reinvestment in securities paying twice the return from land.
- Strategy of selling to sitting tenants could bring advantages, but farmers were often reluctant to buy.
- However, some farmers, like David Holtby, got good bargains.
- Danger of saturated market. Some projected sales failed. Balance of power shifting towards tenants.
- Landowners normally clung to the core of their estates which, if well managed, might survive the depression.
- Mixed reactions on Londesborough and Hotham estates; movement was slow. Best prospects for sale lay with better-quality land in Low Wolds (Table).

Reinvestment of capital

- Strategies included paying off mortages and debts; reinvestment of surplus capital; trimming costs of social events; letting houses.
- Money released by sales on the Londesborough estate was used to buy railway shares, colonial shares and Consols (Table).
- Landowners on Wolds only differed from general trends by deferring sales until early twentieth century. Wrong to argue that their way of life was on the verge of disintegration (though the Londesborough estate was completely broken up). They were undergoing necessary reorganisation and rationalisation in the face of strong economic pressures.

Appendix 9

The opening words of paragraphs

The last two appendices emphasised the value of preparing a strong plan or skeleton of ideas, before beginning a first draft. Time spent in that way shows strongly in subsequent writing, and nowhere more so than in the opening words of each successive paragraph. Here, in the first sentence or two, one must state the principal idea lying inside the paragraph and awaiting development. So important is this principal that readers should be able to follow the gist of a piece of writing simply by reading the opening words of each paragraph on their own. This is here tested by using an article entitled 'Eighteenth-century child health care in a Northampton infirmary: A provincial English hospital' which was published in November 2007.[1] The author is a consultant paediatrician who has a strong interest in local medical history. Each sub-heading of the article is given, and a quotation made from the opening words of each successive paragraph. The end-result is a scheme which is in essence little different from the plan recommended in Appendices 7 and 8.

Introduction

'In 1700, there were very few hospitals in England ...'

'These hospitals were created by and dependent upon public subscription ...'

The Northampton General Infirmary

'Northampton is one of the oldest towns in England. Its first hospital, St John's Hospital, an almshouse, was founded in 1138 ...'

Admissions

'Ten patients were admitted on the day of opening ...'

'In the 18th century, admission to a Voluntary Hospital required a signed recommendation from a subscriber or a Governor ...'

---

[1]   A. N. Williams, 'Eighteenth-century child health care in a Northampton infirmary: a provincial English hospital', *Family and Community History*, 10, 2 (Nov. 2007), 153–66.

Ward Environment and Staff

'The wards were very basic in the 1740s …'

'The medical staff were two physicians, a surgeon extraordinary, a house surgeon …'

'The ward regime was very different from today. Patients could only leave the hospital with the signed permission …'

'Ward diets, much as today, were of real importance. Indeed, the Infirmary took great care to ensure that the food dispensed was of generous quantity, …'

'This emphasis on food and cleanliness is seen in looking at the expenditure …'

'It is interesting that the meat requirement was approximately ½ lb per person per day …'

Paedriatric In- and Out-Patients

'The regulations for children were explicit as to age of admission …'

'Within the first year of opening, for children of 10 years and under, there were 8 child in-patient admissions and a further 18 children were treated as out-patients …'

'Detailed case studies of five children provide a prism through which we can investigate the variety and effectiveness of treatment …'

'The first case is that of Thomasin Grace, 13 years old, admitted 29 March 1744 as an in-patient with scald head …'

'The second case was that of Elizabeth Ager, 8 years old, admitted 13 April 1745 with a one-month history of fever …'

'Our third case does much to support this view. Jos Furness, a 13-year-old boy, was first seen in out-patients on 25 August 1744 …'

'A fourth case is that of Mary Connor, a 2-year-old out-patient first seen 2 February 1745 as an 'asthmatick' …'

'Our final case is that of Ann Cox, 13 years of age with a three-year history of leprosy.'

'What these cases show us is that childhood in particular was an uncertain time in health terms.'

Conclusion

'In its first year (1744) Northampton General Infirmary treated children as young as 2 years of age as out-patients and from 8 years as in-patients.'

'Medical conditions in the United Kingdom today are very different from those of the 18th century, with infant mortality then breathtakingly high …'

'So how were children managed in the 18th-century English Voluntary Hospital?'

Appendix 10

Choosing words and framing sentences

The same thought can be expressed in many different ways, and the challenge of writing is to find a form which is clear, concise and elegant. As an example a single sentence has been chosen from an article published in a national journal in 1992. The place-name has been altered for diplomatic reasons:

> It would appear that the age at marriage of the Borchester nonconformists was not markedly different from their Anglican-marrying counterparts.

Wordy and lumpy in style, this is a fairly typical example of how some modern academics write. Notice the oblique impersonal opening and the use of a place-name as an adjective. The worst feature is the phrase 'Anglican-marrying counterparts' which is not only ungainly but actually ambiguous. It could imply, though unlikely, that the so-called 'counterparts' were people of *other* religious persuasions who were marrying Anglicans. By re-thinking the essence of this sentence, we can soon improve it. Each variant given below is better than the original, but the fourth, with a strong verb and simple directness, is the shortest, omits nothing and is probably the best.

Alternative versions:

1. 'The age of marriage for Borchester's nonconformists was roughly the same as for its Anglicans.'
2. 'In Borchester nonconformists married at approximately the same age as their Anglican neighbours.' [*The verb 'married' is stronger than the original 'was'.*]
3. 'The age at which nonconformists married in Borchester did not differ markedly from that of Anglicans.' [*This introduces a new verbal emphasis.*]
4. 'Borchester's nonconformists married at roughly the same age as did its Anglicans.' [*The word 'roughly' carries the element of doubt which appeared in two places in the original.*]

Note: Later revision, which all writers must be prepared to do, often necessitates this kind of fundamental re-thinking and re-working of individual sentences.

Appendix 11

Characteristics of historical language

The following is a tongue-in-cheek attempt to list some of the words and phrases which seem commonplace in historical writing. In all seriousness one can neither recommend nor condemn this kind of language: it results from the historian's expression of complicated thoughts and judgements by a scrupulous choice of words – even at the risk of being thought fussy, pedantic and indecisive.

Adverbs: perhaps ... possibly ... presumably ... conceivably ... arguably ... apparently ... admittedly ... nearly ... almost ... partly ...

Adjectives: questionable ... plausible ... unproven ... hypothetical ... likely ... reasonable ... misleading ...

Conjunctions: but ... if ... although ... whereas ... yet ... notwithstanding ... [1]

Double negatives: not improbable ... not a few ... not infrequently ...

Words of emphasis: indeed ... in fact ... furthermore ... moreover ... especially ...

Phrases: It seems that ... it may be ... suggests (implies) that ... one is tempted to say that ... it is a reasonable assumption (hypothesis, interpretation) that ... on balance it would seem that ... the balance of opinion probably favours ... the evidence so far as it goes ... the meaning is not altogether clear ... regrettably we are not told ... fragmentary though the evidence is ... there is no way of telling ... caution forbids ... it would be hazardous ... our best evidence lies in ... on the one (other) hand ...

The language of reviews: antiquarian ... heap of facts ... (un)controlled imagination ... (un)critical ... (un)scholarly ... respect for the truth ... rooted in the evidence ... keen judgement ... ill-judged ... axe to grind ... politically prejudiced ... persuasive argument ... masterly ...

Of course language of this kind can be overused, and often needs pruning at a later stage. In other words, writing can be weakened or paralysed by excessive caution. Indeed, when we have firmly held opinions for which the evidence seems reasonable, we should have the confidence to state them boldly – with the minimum of qualification – and invite the response of others.

---

[1]   For the frequent misuse of 'however' as a conjunction, see p. 107, footnote 25.

Appendix 12

The historian's use of sources

This section gives three examples of the use of sources in creative writing. Each is introduced separately. Note that asterisks mark footnotes or figures in the original text.

Example 1: K.D.M. Snell, *Parish and Belonging: Community, Identity and Welfare in England and Wales, 1700–1950* (2006), pp. 458–9

An historian in his writing does not normally summarise the strengths and weaknesses of every document he has used. That would be tedious, and could be an excuse for not writing at a higher, more creative level. Generally, the sources are pushed into the background, and into references, as the historical argument is unfolded. However, if a document (or group of documents) is of really central importance in research, and poses interesting problems of interpretation, the historian can with effect include a deliberate assessment. In the extract below we see the presentation of a 'completely untouched' form of historical evidence – the significance of those inscribed gravestones which mention place of residence. (Gravestones are, after all, just another kind of historical document.) Snell's argument is expounded at some length in a special chapter, of which this long paragraph is part, and is based on a survey of 1,000 gravestones in eighty-seven graveyards scattered across ten counties. To shorten this extract, five sentences have been omitted.

However, when we read gravestones which say 'of this parish', we are surely receiving a stronger message: for this seems to indicate greater rootedness to locality than underlay some parish-register usage of the term. Nobody dying and being buried in a parish in which s/he was a temporary resident would have any obvious motive to have 'of this parish' inscribed on a monumental stone, nor would their relatives. A very certain, enduring and meaningful attachment to place was being chipped into stone and inscribed to posterity by such a memorial statement. The phrase usually had varying subjective rather than legal meanings; although it may have been buttressed in a family's thoughts by formal considerations such as legal settlement, or at least by economic and social criteria (property ownership, renting for £10 per annum, serving local offices, etc.) underpinning legal settlement. The latter was something that could usually be taken for granted by the classes that concern us here, for it was legally contingent upon their propertied status ... * ... As for rights to burial, to be 'of this parish' was not a strict requirement for burial in the churchyard. All inhabitants had a right to be buried in the parochial churchyard. Furthermore, one could be buried there even though one came from elsewhere. There was also a necessity to bury the dead speedily in the interests of hygiene. Having obtained burial, there was little further need to have a stone inscribed to display one's entitlement to that grave.* Nor in English culture would there appear to have been a strong requirement of a superstitious nature to 'fix' the dead in their place – to ensure 'the grateful corpse', or the non-malevolent spirit that would not trouble the living – that might have inclined people to use a terminology of local attachment as a spiritual means to this end: a stony *aide-mémoire* for the dead.* In all periods there were always plenty of burials of people with no such claim on their gravestones; and a majority of burials in the eighteenth and nineteenth centuries were unmarked by any long-lasting stone memorial, or even perhaps by a significant wooden memorial.* Many other stones celebrated (if that is the right word) ties of the deceased to other places, which were sometimes far away. So while it could be argued that entries of local attachment in marriage registers had a formal and permissive aspect to them, legitimating the marriage, any such requirement seems to have been lacking in the case of burials and subsequent memorials to the dead.*

Example 2: A.J.L. Winchester, *The Harvest of the Hills: Rural Life in Northern England and the Scottish Borders, 1400–1700* (**2000**), p. 85

Even in the writing of a single paragraph, we as historians may have to wrestle with a dozen or more bits of evidence from original and secondary sources. If we are lucky, they are neatly complementary, but more often than not they present problems of interpretation. They have to be 'bounced' off each other in order to expose their respective strengths and weaknesses. This kind of accumulation, cross-fertilisation and squeezing out of meaning enables us to build up a more detailed and therefore more truthful picture of the past. If we do not appreciate such differences and nuances within our sources, and allow for them, we cannot hope to interweave the evidence to form an acceptable interpretation.

In this example scattered references are brought together for a wide geographical area, but are sufficient to portray a distinctive way of life. This paragraph also shows the value of quotations, one of moderate length but the rest quite brief. Note that the area concerned is illustrated with a map, not reproduced here.

Explicit evidence for the removal of stock to summer pastures and the seasonal occupation of shieling huts comes from a handful of manors along the Border and in the North Pennines in the late sixteenth and early seventeenth centuries.* The evidence from the Borders is the better-known, through Camden's description of transhumance in Gilsland and Redesdale, apparently written after he visited the area in 1599:

> Every way round about in the wasts … you may see as it were the ancient Nomades, a martiall kinde of men, who from the moneth of Aprill unto August, lye out scattering and summering (as they tearme it) with their cattell in little cottages here and there which they call Sheales and Shealings.*

Such 'summering' is recorded over much of the hill land in the heart of the dangerous reiving country hugging the Border. On the West March, there were shieling grounds in Bewcastle and Askerton North Moor in the early seventeenth century, the latter providing summer pasture for lowland manors in Gilsland barony, though this use appears to have declined to extinction between *c.*1590 and *c.*1630.* In the Northumberland hills there were shieling grounds in Wark, North Tynedale and Redesdale; in the 'hoopes and valleys' of Kidland in the upper reaches of Coquetdale, though few survived in 1604 because of the depredations of the Scots;* and in Cheviot Forest, where men from the surrounding townships had 'summer sheildes'.* Similar practices are recorded on the Scottish side of the Border in references to summer shielings at Kershopefoot on the West March in 1583, and to the people of the Scottish Middle March going 'in thir symmeryng' in the spring of 1584, for example.* Shieling practices appear to have disappeared in southern Scotland by the seventeenth century, though 'emptie sheels' were still a feature of the landscape of Jedburgh Forest, close by the Border, in the 1670s.* The shieling practices recorded in the Borders involved the wholesale removal of families and stock over several miles; the slow driving of livestock from home to summer pasture must often have taken a full day.

Example 3: Geoffrey Doye, 'Throw out your bread, throw out your tommy': the Torquay food riots of 1847', *Southern History*, 25 (2003), 67

This article is mainly concerned with printed primary sources which often predominate in nineteenth-century studies. When contentious subjects like political unrest and rioting are under investigation, we must positively expect sources to collide creatively.

Inevitably the recollections of any popular disturbance are confusing both to participants and observers; so it is not surprising that records of the events in 1847 are both confused and contradictory. One example derives from the two reports from separate observers which differed significantly, published on 22 May in the *Western Times*. This source of contradiction is further compounded by the later descriptions given by eye witnesses in the trials of rioters in July, and by other contemporary claims, among them those made in the open letter from Devon's Lord Leiutenant, Earl Fortescue to 'The Magistrates in the County' penned on 21 May. White's *The History of Torquay* published in 1878 fails to state whether his account is derived from memory, or contemporary sources, or – as is most likely – a mixture of both.* These reports, together with others from both the local and national press, together with contemporary maps of the local topography, have been used to reconstruct the events, to determine their origins and effects and the reactions of the local authorities.

Appendix 13

Two examples of writing, with detailed critique

Two short extracts from very different publications are here analysed in some detail. The first is taken from an A to Z village history written by a non-professional, whilst the second is a piece of academic, early-modern history dealing with a major town. In comments appended in square brackets, I have attempted to emphasise the importance of giving critical shape to our re-enactment of the past, and the responsibility of finding, if necessary by trial and error, the most effective language with which to express our thoughts.

Example 1

The extract below comes from a parish history published in 1933. For diplomatic reasons its title is not mentioned, for it contains most of the flaws which disfigure historical writing. To put the case bluntly, this is no more than an uncritical ragbag, often in the shape of overlong quotations (without references). Although the author consulted local and national sources, he made little attempt to use, shape or interpret his information. It is no good quoting an historical fact unless one explains or debates its significance.

This shapeless piece of prose is of little interest, even to a local resident. Yet such writing is frequently justified by authors and publishers on the grounds that it is designed for local consumption and not for 'academics'. This insults the intelligence of local people who need properly constructed history as much as anyone else.[1] Sadly, prose of this kind is probably more common today than in the 1930s because of the greater numbers of people now writing and publishing. Each separate chunk quoted below is a short paragraph in the original. Short paragraphs (often containing long sentences) are a sure sign of heaped uncritical history.

> The parish constable was elected annually, and occasionally the headborough was mentioned in the accounts. The first direct reference to a parish beadle appears in the Minutes of 17th November, 1770, when John Wicksteed was appointed at a salary of four pounds a year, 'time and extra expenses being extra'.

---

[1] But this descriptive or heaping approach to the past is not confined to the work of amateurs. It can also be found in postgraduate theses and even in academic journals.

What did the parish constable do? What is the significance of a headborough? We are not told. If it is important for us to know that Wicksteed was paid £4 a year, was it a good or bad wage by contemporary standards?

> The making of rates was not a popular task, as Mr John Fassett, overseer, found when he called a vestry meeting on 21st May, 1771. No one attended, and so no business could be done. But the money was wanted sadly, and so after waiting two hours, Mr Fassett called upon his brother overseers and churchwardens, and they took the law into their own hands, and levied a rate of one shilling in the pound – two pence for the church and ten pence for the poor.

The apathy of the vestry is noteworthy, but again nothing is questioned or explained. Why did the vestry have this attitude, and was it usual? How much money was raised by this rate, and how was it actually spent? Does expenditure vary much over the years?

> The churchwardens and constable were the only persons present at a vestry held 23rd September, 1771, and they nominated ten gentlemen as parish surveyors, including the parson, under a penalty of one guinea each if they refused.

To appoint as many as ten highway surveyors is not common, except in very large parishes. And were they all truly 'gentlemen'? What problem with local roads lay behind this interesting decision?

> At a vestry held at the Gymcrack, April 21st, 1772, six persons attending, it was ordered 'That Mr Harradine pay five shillings for a vestry held June 6th, 1771, six shillings for a vestry held September 23rd, 1771, ditto December 5th, 1771, fourteen shillings and three pence, and for this Easter Vestry One Pound three shillings and threepence, halfpence, making in the whole Four Orders £2 8s. 6½d'.

What a boring and muddled quotation! What does it amount to? Was Harradine fined for non-attendance, non-payment of rates, or for some other reason?

> In an Act of Parliament, passed in the reign of William III, 'for supplying some Defects in the Laws for the Relief of the Poor in this Kingdom' was made the following enactment. 'And to the end that the money was raised only for the relief of such as are as well impotent as poor, may not be misapplied and consumed by the idle, sturdy and disorderly beggars: Be it further enacted by the authority aforesaid ...'

The quotation continues for another 250 words and is grotesquely long. If relevant to the case, the whole extract could have been neatly paraphrased, with perhaps a short and really effective quotation from the original.

> 'This Act seems to have been a dead letter in [Ambridge] in this respect, for it was not put into operation until the vestry of 21st April, 1772, when the following

was entered on the Minutes:- 'It is agreed by this vestry that whoever receives any almens or pencion from this parish shall wear a badge on his or her right sleeve with a P cut in red or blue cloth and two letters for the name of the parish according to an Act of Parliament. Past *neme con.*'

It is interesting that the 1697 Act for badging the poor was still being invoked in 1772. Was there any particular reason? We are clearly meant to be amazed by the quaint spelling.

Example 2. Diana Ascott, Fiona Lewis & Michael Power, *Liverpool 1660– 1750: People, Prosperity and Power* (Liverpool Univ. Press, 2006), p. 147

Because of the sheer scale and complexity of the task, the history of towns is now frequently researched and written by groups of historians. This is particularly true of the early modern and modern periods. Individuals make their own specialist contributions, and then the group as a whole must agree on a final text. This is not an easy task, even when specific responsibilities are allotted, and the inevitable inclusion of a great deal of statistical analysis imposes another heavy responsibility. The extract below is concerned with the social and economic composition of Liverpool's corporation and ruling oligarchy in a formative period. This is without doubt a competent piece of professional history, but the actual writing displays a surprising number of basic flaws.

> The concentration of power was not simply a matter of authority being vested in fewer hands. There was an economic dimension to oligarchy which is revealed by analysis of the occupations of councillors and officials.

The last sentence which could have been made tighter and smoother by omitting the words 'There was' and 'which', and substituting 'analysing' for 'analysis of'.

> Only 251 (16 per cent) of the 1,587 individuals listed in the Town Books are described by occupation; a larger proportion, 28 per cent (438), are ascribed a status.

It is a perfectly acceptable ploy to quote absolute numbers and then immediately translate them into percentages (in brackets). However, in this sentence that form is first used and then reversed. One might have expected some explanation of 'status', such as 'Mr' and 'gent'. 'Given' would have been a better choice than the slightly pompous 'ascribed'.

> The occupations of more councillors and officials can be traced in wills and adult male burials.

An illogical mixing of sources and events. Instead of 'adult male burials', substitute 'burial registers'.

Some 214 (13.5 per cent) were linked to testators and 374 (23.6 per cent) to adult male burials.

Here the writing is surely too impersonal and telegraphic. A more humane version would be, 'In making their wills 214 men (13.5 per cent) gave their occupations, and ministers of religion mentioned similar details when burying 374 others (23.6 per cent)'.

> Such modest success casts an interesting light on the sources and on Liverpool society. It implies that less than one in seven town officers and councillors made a will which was proved in the period, a rather low ratio considering that this sample of the population contained the powerful and wealthy.

At this point one might have expected a comparison with the élite of other towns. 'Less' should have been 'fewer', which is correctly used at the start of the next sentence.

> Fewer than one in four were recorded as buried in the parish, which seems very low. St Mary's, Walton-on-the-Hill, the mother church of the town, remained a frequent place of interment even after St Nicholas was made parochial in 1699, and burials took place in other parishes too. The tantalising propensity of many Liverpool men to be buried elsewhere provokes thought about the notion of a Liverpool community and what it meant to those who were part of it.

In the light of the evidence quoted, the question of 'belonging' to the port is properly raised. However, the last sentence is curiously stiff, especially the phrase 'provokes thought about the notion'. The so-called 'propensity' was in fact a 'choice'.

> Such linkage boosts the number of councillors and officials who can be ascribed an occupation to 466, 29.4 per cent of the total.

'Ascribed' has reappeared. The number and percentage need more separation than a comma. It is better to avoid the juxtaposition of two different numbers, of whatever kind.

> Together with the status afforded to a further 28 per cent of the total there is supplementary information about the character of over half the group.

The word 'status' is easily missed and needs greater emphasis. As usual, 'there is' complicates and lengthens the sentence. A better version might be, 'By counting in a further 28 per cent whose social status is known, we now have extra information for more than half of the governing group'.

> It is good enough by the standard of knowledge of early modern town populations to encourage analysis and the results are suggestive of the balance of power and influence in the town.* The 466 individuals with a known occupation followed 112 distinct avocations, a reasonable spread for a town often assumed to

be monopolised by its port functions. They have been categorised into generic groups and the occupational profiles of officials and councillors together, of councillors, and of aldermen are displayed in Table 5.3.

The writers were forced to use the ponderous 'avocations' because they have already used the word 'occupation' in the same sentence. A better solution would have been to rethink the whole sentence to create something like, 'Among the 466 individuals whose work is known, we can distinguish 112 distinct occupations ...' The phrase 'categorised into generic groups' is tautological.

Appendix 14

An exercise in historical writing

A medieval pilgrimage at Stanton, Suffolk

This section gives ten pieces of evidence, all that could be found for a minor historical subject investigated during the writing of a church-guide. They are given in the order in which they were accidentally found or deliberately looked for, and consist of eight primary documentary sources, one secondary source and one architectural observation. I have then appended two paragraphs which are my attempt to write a piece of original history based on that evidence. Some readers might like to produce their own versions to compare with mine. At all events, we can be sure that no two accounts will be the same.

[Note: the following abbreviations have been used: BL – British Library; SROB – Suffolk Record Office, Bury St Edmunds; SROI – Suffolk Record Office, Ipswich.]

The evidence

1. Petition of Richard Sheparde, rector of Stanton, to the Lord High Treasurer, 1590: 'In tyme past the Church called Allsaintes had a Saint called St Parnell standinge in it, wherunto many resorted as Pilgrims and did offer, and therof great gayne was made, which in those daies much holpe the Minister of that Church, and now that lyvynge is much the lesser' (BL, Lansdowne 64, MS 12826).[1]
2. Inquisition of the Ninths, 1340/1: *Item de oblationibus capell' Sancte Petronille virginis vjs viijd*. Translation: 'Also in oblations to the chapel of St Petronilla the Virgin, 6s 8d.' (*Nonarum Inquisitiones*, Record Commissioners (1807), p. 72).
3. Will of John Pyke of Stanton, 1451: *Item lego ad ymaginis*[sic] *beate Petronille iiijd*. Translation: 'Also I leave to the image of the Blessed Petronilla 4d' (SROB, IC500/2/9, f. 135v).
4. Will of Margaret Glover, widow of Stanton, 1474: *Item lego summo alteri ecclesie*

---

[1]   Sheparde's petition was a chance discovery, based on a reference in W.A. Copinger, *Suffolk Records and Manuscripts*, V, 26. It immediately raised the question: where can I find more about this cult? Wills and ecclesiastical surveys were possible answers. Note that Parnell is a shortened version of Petronilla. D.H. Farmer's *Oxford Dictionary of Saints* reveals that Petronilla was an early Roman martyr, supposedly the daughter of St Peter, who fasted to death rather than marry a man she despised.

sancte Petronille in villa de Stanton predicta pro decimis et oblacionibus meis oblitis iijs iiijd. Translation: 'Also I leave to the high altar of the church of St Petronilla in the town of Stanton aforesaid, for my tithes and offerings forgotten 3s 4d' (SROB, IC500/2/10, f. 568v).

5. Will of Richard Spede of Stanton, 1449: *Item lego pro picturand' imaginis Beate Marie existentis in capella Beate Petronille iijs iiijd.* Translation: 'Also I leave for the painting of the image of the Blessed Mary in the chapel of the Blessed Petronilla 3s 4d' (SROI, IC/AA2/1/196).

6. Memorandum, 14th century, that certain feoffees intended to provide two wax candles every Sunday and feast day for a year in All Saints' church: *unum ante crucificum et alterum ante ymaginem Beate Marie Virginis.* Translation: 'one candle before the crucifix [rood] and the other before the image of the Blessed Virgin Mary' (SROB, 574/14).

7. Parish register of Stanton All Saints, 10 Jan. 1602: 'Parnell the wife of Climent Rainer buried' (SROB, FL629/4/1).

8. Among the 'vain and fictitious relics' which Drs Leyton and Legh noted at Bury Abbey in 1536 was the skull of St Petronilla, which 'simple folk put on their heads, hoping thereby to be delivered from fever' (*Letters and Papers of the Reign of Henry VIII*, 10, no. 364, 144).

9. Eamon Duffy describes minor pilgrimage cults in the later Middle Ages centred on images rather than relics (*The Stripping of the Altars: Traditional Religion in England, 1400–1580* (1992), pp. 167–9).

10. Architectural evidence: All Saints' church has three piscinae marking the positions of medieval altars; one is in the chancel, another in the cramped north-east corner of the nave where the pulpit now stands, and the third in the spacious and stylish south aisle. The whole church appears to have been rebuilt in the early fourteenth century.

A suggested draft

By Suffolk standards, All Saints in Stanton is an ordinary parish church of no special architectural distinction. One is therefore surprised to learn that it attracted pilgrims for at least 200 years before the Reformation. Richard Sheparde, an Elizabethan rector, revealed in a petition of 1590 that 'in tyme past the Church called Allsaintes had a Saint called St Parnell [Petronilla] standinge in it, wherunto many resorted as Pilgrims'.[2] So somewhere within this church had been a wooden or stone image of that saint, the supposed daughter of St Peter, which was revered not only by the people of Stanton but by others from further afield. In addition we know that a special chapel was dedicated to St Petronilla from at least 1340, soon after All Saints was rebuilt in its present form, and that it contained an image of the Virgin Mary as well

---

2   BL, Lansdowne 64, MS 12826.

as one of St Petronilla herself.[3] In support of the chapel, visitors gave offerings and local residents left bequests in their wills. To Margaret Glover, a widow of Stanton who made her will in 1474, St Petronilla was so important that she mistakenly named the whole church after her.[4] This kind of local piety is by no means unusual in the later Middle Ages. All over the country, minor cults sprang up not, as in earlier periods, around the shrines and relics of saints but around particular carved images of them. Their influence was usually quite localised, though in their piety some individual testators left bequests to several such cults in their home districts.[5]

But where, within All Saints' church, was St Petronilla's chapel? Three fourteenth-century piscinae betray the presence of medieval altars: one in the chancel, another in the cramped north-eastern corner of the nave, and the third in the south aisle. As the high altar was dedicated to All Saints and the nave altar could never have been within a screened chapel, St Petronilla's chapel can confidently be placed at the east end of the spacious and stylish south aisle. In all probability her image, condemned as idolatrous, was destroyed at some point in the 1540s or '50s. Her more famous skull which 'simple folk put on their heads, hoping thereby to be delivered from fever' was kept ten miles away at Bury Abbey, but must also have perished soon after the abbey was dissolved in 1539.[6] In spite of such losses, however, reminders of the old ways and 'superstitions' could linger on for generations in the new officially Protestant world. In January 1602 the register of All Saints records the burial of the wife of Clement Rainer: her Christian name was 'Parnell'.[7]

---

[3] *Nonarum Inquisitiones* (1807), p. 72; also the will of Richard Spede of Stanton, 1449 (SROI, IC/AA2/1/196).

[4] Will of John Pyke of Stanton, 1451 (SROB, IC500/2/9, f. 135v); will of Margaret Glover of Stanton, 1474 (SROB, IC500/2/10, f. 568v); memorandum for provision of wax candles, 14th century (SROB, 574/14).

[5] E. Duffy, *The Stripping of the Altars* (1992), pp. 167–9. Other testators from Suffolk such as Christopher Benytt of Debenham (died 1477) and John More of Gislingham (died 1493/4) left bequests not only to major, long-established cults like St Thomas of Canterbury and Our Lady of Walsingham but also to several more localised cult-images including Our Lady of Woolpit, St Mary of Grace in Ipswich, St Nicholas of Tibenham (Norfolk) and the roods of Gislingham and Beccles (SROI, IC/AA2/2/347).

[6] *Letters and Papers of the Reign of Henry VIII*, 10 [1536], no. 364, 144.

[7] SROB, FL629/4/1.

Appendix 15

Short extracts of written history

The following are all genuine quotations from published pieces of local history but, for diplomatic reasons, names and references are not given and place-names are disguised. If you had written these extracts in a first draft, would you be satisfied? If not, how would you re-write them? Some of the examples are wordy and repetitious; others are illogical; many were written carelessly or are misshapen. But not all are bad. My own reactions are sometimes given in square brackets after the quotation.[1]

1. Such evidence may well suggest that it would be unwise to conclude that ... [*Introductory waffle which begs to be pruned or entirely cut out.*]
2. These are the only remaining timber-framed buildings surviving in the street today. [*'Remaining' and 'surviving' say the same thing.*]
3. Borchester appraisers tended to neglect fuel, and in the 18th century often omitted to include poultry and bees.
4. During the 18th century there is no doubt that there was a massive increase in the provision of land carriage. [*The colloquial 'there is', 'there was', etc., is woefully overused, sometimes several times in a single sentence. Such language can always be tightened by finding sharper verbs.*]
5. There is evidence that there was a serious fire in the town in 1610.
6. Time seemed to stand still as every day was filled to the brim with adventures, bike rides, damn building. [*Spelling can be rather important!*]
7. Within the Church and Parish the Rector and his Churchwardens wielded considerable authority, though the Manor and its Court still survived. [*Many writers unnecessarily use capital letters for common nouns; this is a Victorian hangover.*]
8. The total population was 896 in 1861 excluding those working in the workhouse with an equal distribution of the sexes. [*A badly constructed sentence which could have been redeemed by some punctuation.*]
9. Although brick was used increasingly in Borchester for walling, roofs, floors and occasionally internal partitions were made of timber. [*Punctuation can confuse as well as clarify.*]
10. But the enduring resentment of the poor against the New Poor Law was shown by the threatening letters, the animal maiming and the arson which continued to

---

[1]   Here in the first edition of this book, I included the following sentence: 'Standards-wise it is to be hoped that this quotation series may have an ongoing benefit effect on the history writing situation'. Subsequently I received several critical letters from readers who had not seen the joke.

be directed against the local administrators of the poor law after the new system had been imposed in the region. [*The definite article 'the' occurs ten times in this sentence; five are unnecessary.*]

11. The potential of the study of faeces was first realised at the Lloyds Bank site where an object described in the academic report as 'a single elongate fusiform mass of organic debris, concreted by mineral deposition', and more commonly known as 'the Lloyds Bank turd', was found. [*This sentence pokes fun at academic pomposity but ends weakly with the words 'was found'; it should have ended with the climactic word 'turd'!*]

12. An identifiable region for most purposes of social and cultural investigation is one in which there exists a regional identity and regionalism. [*This sentence momentously concludes that a region is a region.*]

13. As you stand on the chancel steps looking around there are many things that you cannot see because they are no longer there.

14. Its semi-ruinous state is now happily being restored by a new owner. [*Illogicalities are not infrequent.*]

15. He died after 1637 or later.

16. [At a lecture] the true date of Magna Carta will be questioned.

17. Despite D. Worster's exclusion of the built environment from his agroecological perspective, a number of historians pursued the relationships between urban environment, technology, pollution and sanitation throughout the 1980s and 1990s. [*Thought must always be given to the correct placing of dates.*]

18. St Agatha's church stands on a downward slope overlooking the valley.

19. A property with a heavily disguised frontage …

20. In 1548, a Chantry Certificate covered an acre of land in Barchester.

21. Nothing is known of the past landscapes without their historical features, which explain records in maps and documents and are valuable for wildlife.

22. … outdoor space was not gendered at this date … [*Ugly jargon meaning that 'women were not restricted in their movements'.*]

23. The aim of this paper is to determine how socially excluded visitors to two museum exhibitions and two museum-based community development projects use that experience to construct individual and social identities.

24. Medieval guildhalls were spaces in which a salvation-orientated form of corporate charity exploited the spiritual labour of the poor. [*Academic gobbledegook devaluing and obscuring a deeply human issue.*]

25. The effect of offspring on the mobility of family heads was for persistency to increase with the number of resident offspring. [*Demographic history often attracts jargon and bad, noun-laden writing, as this and the next few examples indicate.*]

26. Recent medical research, on the other hand, has introduced the possibility that a sagging age-specific marital fertility curve might equally well be caused by undernourishment: which can both inhibit ovulation and increase the incidence of miscarriage. [*An excellent example of divorcing words which should be adjacent: 'sagging' refers to 'curve' which comes four words later.*]

27. Distance decay in marriage horizons was found, but not in a straightforward sense.

28. Householders not having gained legal settlement in Ambridge, or who could not prove their financial independence, out-migrated.

29. It was suggested that one of the reasons why fertility was concentrated into the earlier years of marriage had to do with the comparatively unfavourable mortality experience of first-born children.

30. Such a figure [of illegitimate births] might strike modern readers as rather high, accustomed as they are to present-day contraceptive devices and a view of the past coloured by Victorian prurience. [*Note the amazing use of the word 'prurience' when 'prudery' was surely intended.*]

31. In May Council approved the final report on the Churches Plans Index pilot project. [*Five nouns in a row!*]

32. … personal qualities such as people skills …

33. We are striving to attain student enrichment values and to avoid information overload anxiety. [*A classic example of transatlantic jargon and noun-clumping.*]

34. Having a ludic life probably did not mean that peasants were less involved in crime than thought heretofore.

35. Socio-economic change and the loss of spiritual incentives for parish harmony had reinforced existing internal polarization. [*An important observation spoilt by impersonal and de-humanised writing.*]

36. The peak of enlistment in Britain coincided with economic recession, mass unemployment and sharp price increases in autumn 1914, when the Army was the one economic 'growth sector' (French 1982: 63l; Ferguson 1998; Beckett in Turner 1988: 103; Waites 1987: 8; Lawrence in Winter and Robert 1997: 156; *Forward* 5 Dec 1914: 1; *Galashiels Border Standard* 8 Aug 1914: 34; 22 Aug 1914: 1, 8). [*An horrific example of the Harvard system of referencing.*]

37. The entry of key sources into databases, both flat file and relational, with text encoding, hypertext or similar, facilitates their use for multiple research purposes. [*Dull, ponderous language typical of the new computerised history. Such writers genuinely want to make converts, yet they often have the opposite effect.*]

38. The appreciable dilution of proprietorial control meant an increasing tempo in the numbers of directors.

39. Much nearer can be seen fine churches at Ambridge and Penny Hassett, whilst in Borchester we have St Julian's church, the oldest ecclesiastical site in the town, dating back to the 7th century the mother church of Borchester, much of it rebuilt by William of Borchester, the 30th Archbishop of Canterbury, founder of Borchester College whose head is preserved in the vestry. [*A sad piece of writing, jumbled and rambling. It could form the basis of at least three separate sentences.*]

40. The tower built of flint, stone and some brick, began to lean between the two World Wars.

41. A habit of twenty years or so could be convincingly designated 'immemorial custom'. [*How welcome is a touch of dry humour.*]

42. Our ignorance is always greater than our knowledge.

43. And when we are served statistics deliciously cooked we are wise to scatter over them the herbs and spices of imaginative literature very finely ground and sieved.

44. Like soft-bodied creatures of the Palaeozoic era that left little trace in the fossil record, the poor who did not come to the formal attention of the law left little or no evidence of their time on earth.

45. The surviving peasantry of Western Europe still shock us with their worn hands and faces, their immeasurable fatigue. [*A beautiful sentence: the slight pause demanded by the comma has an almost musical effect.*]

Appendix 16

Longer extracts of written history

All historical writing is in the last resort unique. Two people may use the same evidence, but the total blend of information and interpretation, and the precise words chosen to express an historical argument, can never be repeated – even by the same writer at a later date.

Given that writing reveals more about a person's mind than any other activity, and outlives its creator, it is astonishing that so much careless and uncritical work is published. To show the value of careful thought and style, this appendix gives extracts of one to three paragraphs from the work of eleven historians, both academic and non-professional. Before each extract, a few comments are given. Asterisks indicate where references were given in the original.

1. R.W. Ketton-Cremer, *A Norfolk Gallery* (London, 1948), p. 95

This extract was written by a landowner-scholar at the end of the second World War. It seems self-indulgent by modern standards, but has great literary quality and humanity. Here a physical landscape is truly 'peopled' by the historian's imagination.

When looking at these churches, scattered under the enormous Norfolk sky, and pondering all they represent, one thinks inevitably of the succession of incumbents who ministered in them; the tranquil and unperturbed careers of some, the struggles of conscience and conviction which were forced upon others in the recurrent storms of our ecclesiastical history. At any of the great crises of the church, who was tending his flock in the shadow of each soaring grey tower, who knelt at the altar, whose words were echoed by the sounding-board of the pulpit? Devotee, fanatic or time-server? Wycliffe, Reformer, Marian, Elizabethan, Puritan, Laudian, Non-Juror? What persecutions did he undergo, or what submissions did he make? Did he succumb to, or did he weather his particular storm?

2. Steven Runciman, *The Fall of Constinople, 1453* (CUP, 1965), p. 147

The following paragraph from a classic book describes an horrific human tragedy, how the great Byzantine church of Haghia Sophia was despoiled in 1453 by Turkish soldiers who had just smashed through the ancient defences of Constantinople. Written with economy and clarity, it is here offered as an example of narrative history at its best. Notice in particular the value of varying the length of sentences: the shorter ones are especially powerful.

The church was still thronged. The Holy Liturgy was ended, and the service of matins was being sung. At the sound of the tumult outside the huge bronze gates of the building were closed. Inside the congregation prayed for the miracle which alone could save them. They prayed in vain. It was not long before the doors were battered down. The worshippers were trapped. A few of the ancient and infirm were killed on the spot; but most of them were tied or chained together. Veils and scarves were torn off the women to serve as ropes. Many of the lovelier maidens and youths and many of the richer-clad nobles were almost torn to death as their captors quarrelled over them. Soon a long procession of ill-assorted little groups of men and women bound tightly together was being dragged to the soldiers' bivouacs, there to be fought over once again. The priests went on chanting at the altar till they too were taken. But at the last moment, so the faithful believed, a few of them snatched up the holiest vessels and moved to the southern wall of the sanctuary. It opened for them and closed behind them; and there they will remain until the sacred edifice becomes a church once more.*

3. W.G. Hoskins, *The Midland Peasant* (Macmillan, 1957), pp. 278–9

Hoskins's writing has an easy elegance which no doubt conceals a lot of hard work and preparation. The rise of nonconformity in Wigston Magna is demonstrated, first by the use of total figures and then by percentages. Throughout we are never in any doubt that statistics mean people. Notice the value of imaginative phrases like 'flourished obscurely', 'loud defiant singing' and 'empty Sunday streets'. Characteristically, too, this paragraph contains some of Hoskins's personal attitudes, for example his sympathy with underdogs and distrust of 'masters'.

The church was too closely linked with the masters in the nineteenth century: the wage-earners filled the chapels. Non-conformity had grown strong in Wigston all through the Georgian era. The return made to Parliament in 1829 revealed 520 Independents, 195 Wesleyan Methodists, 105 Primitive Methodists, and 30 General Baptists – a total of 850 nonconformists out of about 2100 inhabitants. In 1676 they had been about 4 per cent of the total population; by the 1720's about 16 per cent; and a hundred years later they were fully 40 per cent. Their strength had continued to increase in the mid-Victorian decades. The Wesleyans had put up a new chapel in 1839. Two years later the Independents had rebuilt and enlarged their attractive old Georgian meeting-place (first built in 1731), and in 1845 the Primitive Methodists blossomed forth in a new chapel. Here and there in odd corners behind the main streets, other little sects flourished obscurely, worshipping the Almighty in their own way in bare brick tabernacles as ugly as their own cottages. So in 1870 the empty Sunday streets would suddenly resound with the loud defiant singing of the chapels from one end of the village to the other, while from the parish church came the more subdued murumur of 'the Conservative Party at prayer'.

4. Richard Jones & Mark Page, *Medieval Villages in an English Landscape: Beginnings and Ends* (Macclesfield, 2006), p. 1

This extract is included to emphasise the great importance of a book's first paragraph. The writing is direct, clear and strong. It immediately captures our interest and imagination with the challenging notion that the English village is not as stable as many think it is. Anyone would have been proud to write these elegant opening lines. (Although this book was written by two authors, this extract reads as the creation of one mind.)

The village has a powerful hold on the English imagination. Generations of writers and artists have celebrated and idealised the visual charm and traditional social rhythms of village life. A common perception of the village, inspired by the apparent antiquity of its buildings, lanes and fields, is of an unchanging place, a constant and comforting presence in a rapidly changing world. This picture is not entirely false; elements of continuity can be identified in the countryside over long periods of time. But in recent years, the emphasis of much writing on the English village has been on change, even if the precise nature of that change is disputed. The study of villages and landscapes, especially in medieval England, offers ample scope for controversy and debate …

5. *RecordKeeping* (Spring 2007), 21

This piece is included as a contrast to the last. It was written by an 'Interim Records Manager' (the concept of 'interim records' is not explained). He is discussing the management of contemporary records as they accumulate in preparing for the Olympic Games of 2012. The language is thick with jargon, opaque wordiness and acronyms. (ODA stands for Olympic Delivery Authority, and EDRM for Electronic Document and Records Management.)

ODA has contracted the implementation of back office systems including EDRM to a third-party integrator. After an extensive review of ODA requirements and with due regard for TNA's guidance, an EDRM application has been selected and we are now planning a pilot within the ODA legal department. The pilot will test the core functionality of the product and will enable us to fine tune a file plan and access model that have been developed over the past few months. There are complex interfaces to manage between other collaborative tools for the design community and between finance and HR systems. The project as planned will run to October when all ODA staff will have access to the application.

6. Harold Fox, *The Evolution of the Fishing Village* (2001), pp. 136–7

This paragraph is taken from an important and pioneering study of early fishing communities in South Devon. 'Cellar settlements' were groups of storage huts built by fishermen on local beaches. Here a complicated historical argument is advanced, based on place-names, primary sources, the landscape and a secondary printed source. This is a good example of 'argued' history though the style tends to be rather wordy, jerky and repetitious.

Finally, a little further detail, about ecclesiastical provision, may be added through speculation raised by the names of the two former cellar settlements, later fishing villages, called Torcross and Starcross which share a second element 'cross'. The former is the easier. The editors of *Place-Names of Devon* give 1714 as the earliest recorded mention of the name, but we can now push this back to 1569 (*Torcrosse*) after inspection of court rolls which were still in private hands when that survey was published.* There is a very prominent cliff-top just to the south of the cellar settlement and later fishing village, clearly the tor of the first part of the name; the name quite unambiguously calls for the existence of a cross on this hill and there is some suggestion that a cross-shaft now situated in a lane leading to Widdicombe is the one which once stood above the village.* Starcross, the cellar settlement discussed at length in an earlier section of this chapter, is a more difficult name. The editors of *Place-Names of Devon* give *Star Crosse* (1689) as the earliest known mention but this can now be pushed back to a *Starcrosse* in about 1578; the editors of this volume confess that it is a difficult name but hazard the guess that the cross may have been shaped like a star.* Far more likely is 'cross by the stair', the latter word referring to a set of steps or stairs (O.E. *Staeger*) which took people down a small bluff to the beach at low tide. We can compare one definition of 'stairs' in the *Oxford English Dictionary*, 'a landing-stage, especially on the Thames', and the many named landing places of the Thames such as Billingsgate Stairs.* At Starcross, then, we have another cross at a fishing place and cellar settlement, this one being at the top of a flight of steps.

7. Frank Grace, *Rags and Bones: A Social History of a Working-Class Community in Nineteenth-Century Ipswich* (2005), pp. 234–6

Here a local historian evokes the life of a teeming slum district, putting the emphasis firmly on people and, where possible, on individuals. The main sources are oral evidence, newspaper reports and official records. In this particular extract, the author reveals the significance of a local philanthropic institution founded in 1896, measuring it against comparable institutions elsewhere.

In important ways civic and philanthropic action began to strengthen and enrich the social life of the community towards the end of the nineteenth century, especially for young people, and one institution more than any other came to play a role of central importance to the community in St Clement's – the Social Settlement.* Founded by Daniel Ford Goddard, a radical Congregationalist and a leading figure in the town's affairs, Goddard's Social Settlement on Fore Street was opened in 1896, appropriately, adjacent to two insanitary courts, Clark's and Ship Court, which were later demolished when a new Settlement building was erected. The Settlement idea, inspired by the work of Canon Barnett in the slums of the east end of London in the 1880s, stands at the watershed between the individually inspired good works of the Victorian era and the ideas on which the origins of state intervention in social welfare were to rest in the twentieth century. Social welfare was its prime mission, not the saving of souls. Its example and communitarian spirit are clear in Ford Goddard's choice of motto, 'For God and the People'. He appealed to the altruism of the better-off for 'gifts of sympathy and service from the rich surplus of [their] cultured lives' with the stated aim, non-sectarian and non-political, being 'to foster the spirit of brotherhood amongst all classes'. This was to be a People's Palace like that built some years earlier in the Mile End Road in the East End of London.

Over its lifetime the Settlement offered an astonishingly wide range of welfare and recreational facilities for working people, some run on self-help principles. It was not, of course, wholly secular. Religious work continued to be central with Bible classes, prayer meetings, a People's Sunday Class and Lantern Services for men during the winter months, the men contributing to the cost. Educational work too was integral to its life, consisting of Saturday lectures and Thursday debates and, in 1915, co-operation with the newly-founded Workers' Educational Association began. But it was the social and recreational dimension of the Settlement's activities that offered most to the community. Summer fetes, children's parties and Saturday concerts were conventional fare, but in addition clubs for billiards, bagatelle, parlour quoits and bowls were formed, and a gym class and a bicycle club, which had eighty members. In 1902, a Brass Band was formed and there was also a mixed choir that visited local towns. All of this offered leisure opportunities to ordinary working men that were impossible before. Some aspects of cultural provision were minuted in the Settlement's records with varying degrees of apprehension although they were eventually allowed. Dramatic performances, for instance, first given in 1909, were thought to have endangered the character of those who came and lowered the tone, and they were compared sniffily with the variety shows at the local Hippodrome. During the First World War for purposes of morale and because the Settlement was also a feeding centre for troops, cinema shows were held, but after 1918 it was argued that such things were 'not consonant with the Settlement's ideals' and in his address of 1919 Goddard declared that cinema would not 'fulfil the needs of working men'. Card playing, too, was not allowed by the council of the Settlement for ten years until they gave way in 1920. On the other hand, there was some tolerance for allowing drinks on the premises and, true to its word, neither the Teetotallers nor the Rechabites were allowed to proselytise.

8. Michael James, 'A Georgian gentleman: child care and the case of Harry Tremayne, 1814–23', *Family & Community History*, Vol. 9, No. 2 (Nov. 2006), 79–90

This article, written by a former chartered accountant who took up medical history in retirement, explores the experience of a wealthy family who lost a child after an illness of over two years. The tragic events revealed in personal correspondence are carefully weighed against the background of medical developments in the early nineteenth century.

London, not surprisingly as the metropolis, had substantially the highest doctor/patient ratio in the country and by 1800 one not dissimilar to that of two centuries later, about 1 to 950.* In the 1820s John Tremayne, as a wealthy MP in London, would have consulted the foremost physicians of the day over his son's debilitating and deteriorating medical condition. Those consulted included Dr Baillie, a nephew of Dr William Hunter, and Dr Maton, both at the time holding royal appointments. They visited the Tremayne household in London on a regular basis, usually weekly, often together. They discussed Harry's deteriorating condition and from the evidence came to common conclusions. Despite such erudite medical advice the London oculist, Alexander, was also consulted about Harry's squint.

The need for John Tremayne to travel on long journeys between his constituency in Cornwall and London before the railways would have required overnight accommodation in various towns and cities. While the need for medical consultation during such journeys may normally have been rare, travelling with a sick child necessitated calling on various practitioners across a wide and varied geographical medical market place. When Harry was first unwell in Honiton in January 1821, John Tremayne, conscious of the need to be aware of the location of medical advice, wrote, 'I was really unwilling to launch into the New Road where I knew of no Physicians, whereas I knew there was a good one here & at Salisbury'.* In the immediacy of his concerns for Harry, John Tremayne would probably not have appreciated that he was living in the midst of what Irvine Loudon referred to as 'The period of medical reform'.*

Be that as it may, during the 1820s medicine remained an immature science, a reality all too familiar to the Tremayne family from the case of their relative, William Davie, for 'though the Doctors know as before his Disorders, they are not sure of the Causes'.* It is doubtful whether at that time the curative powers of the medical practitioner had noticeably improved over the previous century.* Further, the medical profession became overcrowded during the early 19th century following the end of the Napoleonic Wars. Dr John Simpson wrote in 1825 that, 'As a young physician I cannot have practice to keep me fully employed. I read a great deal'.* A combination of over-supply and increasing demand for medical services encouraged medical specialization within evolving professionalization ... Growth in demand in what was still a consumer market was fuelled by an expanding and increasingly well-to-do middling class as well as from greater medical expenditure under the Old Poor Law. Within this changing environment the middling classes 'in particular became well informed and grasped the belief that illness could and should be cured rather than simply borne with resignation'.* An inevitable result was that 'By the 1820s, middling patients and the poor were spending more of their medical lives under supervision of the doctor than had been the case in 1750'.* Evidence of such changes between the late 18th and early 19th centuries may be glimpsed through the unwiting testimony, even if only recorded by John Tremayne, of a disagreement with his father.

9. Peter Borsay, *The Image of Georgian Bath, 1700–2000* (OUP, 2000), pp. 258–9

Here a professional historian discusses how Bath fostered its image as a fashionable resort in the eighteenth century. This is the kind of 'conceptual' history which non-professional writers normally find it very difficult to compose. What Borsay has done, to make sense of all the detailed evidence available, is to advance a powerful over-arching interpretation to show how the town was 'sold' to the outside world. Of course his vision could be questioned and further debated. For example, was not the reputation of Bath as much the result of thousands of conversations in drawing rooms and assemblies all over the country? The writing is powerful and clear, with considerable variety in the length of sentences. A new paragraph might have begun with the words, 'Beauty of landscape …'

Image played a role in the evolution of Bath's Georgian economy, that both reflected and influenced the process of change. In the early eighteenth century the city was concentrating its resources upon developing as a resort. The way the city was represented to the world became of vital importance. There was no formal promotion machine, no council committee or commercial agency to take on this task. But this does not mean that there was no publicity. With varying degrees of self-consciousness, a heterogeneous group of institutions and individuals adopted the role of image-maker: the corporation, charities, guidebook compilers, historians, medical writers, poets, novelists, mapmakers, and artists. The economic value of image lay in its capacity to invest the locality of Bath with the status of a marketable object, to commercialise the 'genius of the place'. The elements in the city's image – health, environment, sociability and status, consumerism, morality and respectability, and order – were all commodities, and highly valued ones in Georgian society. What the image-making process did was to fix these on Bath. There was nothing automatic about this. As the critics of the spa demonstrated, Bath was not an inherently healthy, beautiful, sociable, prestigious, moral, or orderly place. The case had to be made, and made continuously. That the springs were perceived to have medicinal qualities depended upon a mass of propaganda to that effect. Indeed, over the years it proved remarkably difficult to demonstrate that the waters possessed any endemic quality, other than their warmth, of benefit to those who used them. Beauty of landscape was also something which depended upon 'education' as Jane Austen pointed out in *Northanger Abbey*. When the naïve Catherine Morland went walking on the outskirts of Bath with the sophisticated Tilneys, she found them 'viewing the country with the eyes of persons accustomed to drawing', deciding 'on its capability of being formed into pictures, with all the eagerness of real taste. Here Catherine was quite lost.' However, after 'a lecture on the picturesque' from Henry, 'Catherine was so hopeful a scholar, that when they gained the top of Beechen Cliff', one of the most celebrated viewpoints in the spa, 'she voluntarily rejected the whole of the city of Bath, as unworthy to make part of the landscape'.* Fortunately there was a torrent of positive propaganda in the form of guidebooks and illustrations, to instruct visitors in a view – if a pun may be deployed – opposite to that of Catherine's.

10. Andy Wood, *The Politics of Social Conflict: the Peak Country, 1520–1770* (CUP, 1999), p.2

This extract comes from the opening pages of an impressive and engrossing study of north-west Derbyshire. It illustrates very well, in effective though not perfect prose, how a confident historian can paint the distinctiveness of a region and its industrial and agricultural society in a few hundred words. The writing is obviously very politically aware, but for most readers that will be more than justified when the hard and dangerous life of lead-miners is compared with that of a governing élite. It is arguable that some of the strongest writing nowadays is coming from specialists in the early modern period.

Although few of Defoe's literate, urban readers were likely to have visited the place, the Peak Country was not unknown to them. Tutored by Thomas Hobbes' and Charles Cotton's published accounts of the region, the middling sort of Augustan England knew the Peak to be a backward, barbarous place inhabited by unruly miners and illiterate peasants. Famously, its hills contained the finest lead ore in Britain, from which was manufactured the pewter vessels which sat upon their table and the shot which their armies used to dominate Europe and the New World. But the hills also appeared to succour a peculiar, dangerous local culture. The thin resources of the wide, barren moors seemed to be given over to common use by poor households. Within those hills, and down below in the valleys, the men of the villages laboured in mineworkings. Here educated readers understood the miners to dig for lead under a custom of free mining which overrode private property in land. The polite culture of the early eighteenth century followed its forbears of the seventeenth century in seeing in material environment the germs of popular culture. Moors, fens and forests were thought to breed a rebellious and independent culture amongst the lower orders. Like the East Anglian fens or the forests of western England, the Peak Country was perceived by upper-class outsiders as a dark corner of the land occupied by troublesome people whose local cultures were nourished by the black water of custom.* In all of these regions, local customary law gave wide freedoms to poor people. But the customary laws of the Peak Country enshrined a special, almost unique, right: that of free mining. In many manors within the Peak Country, any man (whether newcomer or settled inhabitant) enjoyed the right to dig for lead on any land, regardless of its ownership. This right of free mining was guaranteed by a body of laws which dated back to 1288. Unsurprisingly, the right had been the subject of intense dispute between lord and miner for generations before Defoe's visit to the region. In the Peak Country more than perhaps anywhere else, therefore, early modern élite perceptions of environment helped to reproduce a larger social conflict.

11. J.V. Beckett, *A History of Laxton: England's Last Open-Field Village* (Basil Blackwell, 1989), pp. 281, 322–3

In the tradition of parish histories this book carries the reader from the Middle Ages to the late twentieth century. It was written by an academic who particularly wished to explain Laxton's outstanding and famous characteristic – its surviving open-field system. Notice the double title which combines local and national. In the first paragraph below, John Beckett depicts conditions in the Victorian village, drawing on many sources but avoiding detail. It begins with short sentences and clauses to build the picture rapidly; thereafter sentences lengthen as more difficult issues are debated. (Some writers would have begun a new paragraph at 'Not that any of this meant ...')

The second paragraph jumps to the end of the whole book; it stresses the passage of time and successive generations in the same place, not forgetting its claim-to-fame in an English context. In an humane but not sentimental tone, it binds together past, present and future.

Victorian Laxton was a village in decline. Population fell steadily after 1831, and rapidly after 1861. House were pulled down and not replaced; public houses were closed. Work opportunities faltered, and domestic servants were in less demand. It was agricultural conditions which were the causes of these reverses. The prosperity of the middle decades, with rising rents and optimistic talk about enclosure (at Thoresby if nowhere else), was followed by deep depression, falling rents, bankrupt tenants, and a necessary change in the farming pattern. The remaining freeholders were bought out; tenancies changed hands and out went some long-standing village families; and finally the open fields were reorganized, although not enclosed. Not that any of this meant the village was a depressing place in which to live. Conditions could be hard, and for some the workhouse was the final destiny, but there was plenty of activity with hunt meets and feast weeks, jubilee celebrations and Sunday School parties. The church was partly rebuilt (and Moorhouse chapel almost entirely so), and Lord Manvers funded two school buildings and a schoolhouse. But he lived at Thoresby and exercised only limited influence in Laxton, which may explain why the villagers were not over-conscientious attenders at church worship. Agricultural depression may have plunged some families into financial problems – particularly, perhaps, the freeholders with no landlord to help them out – and forced young people to seek their fortunes elsewhere, but it did not destroy the community. The village was still largely self-contained in terms of the services on offer, and the farmers helped each other through difficulties. By the early years of the twentieth century, the depression had partially lifted, the farming cycle had been adjusted to cater for more livestock and the demand for animal feeds, and the open fields had been reorganized to improve efficiency. When the plough boys performed their play in January 1914, and the young girls danced round the maypole on May Day, few could have foreseen just how much the village was destined to change as the twentieth century unfolded.

...

Over time much has changed in Laxton but today's farmers walk the same paths and tracks, and follow the same agricultural routines as their predecessors of the seventeenth century and earlier. No one today remembers the wealthy Francis Green who died in 1712, or the formidable William Doncaster in the eighteenth century. The graveyard offers evidence of names now long gone, the Pinders and the Weatheralls among others, and today's families believe they have a heritage to carry into the future. The villagers are as concerned about the future as their predecessors in the 1620s and 1630s, when the lordship of the manor changed hands several times in a couple of decades, or in the nineteenth century when enclosure was so frequently under discussion. It is not easy to be optimistic, but Laxton has survived numerous attempts to enclose it, or to alter the way of farming, and it will doubtless resist a few more in the future. However attenuated, it remains as a monument to an agricultural system which can be seen nowhere else in England, and as such it is unique.

Appendix 17

Basic rules for referencing

Historical publications are frequently marred by inadequate, inconsistent and eccentric referencing. Yet the rudiments, which might at first sight seem complicated, are soon mastered with practice. Below is a résumé of the rules which are generally if not universally adopted, *and* of those details which vary according to personal choice or the system demanded by a particular journal or publisher. For the physical character and placing of footnotes and endnotes, see pp. 108–11.

Books

In a full reference, details should be given in the following order:
- The <u>name of the writer</u>, with initials or forename first. It is acceptable to use initials instead of forenames.
- The <u>full title</u>, however lengthy and sub-divided, in *italics* or <u>underlined</u> (the latter instructs a typesetter to use italics).

[*Then comes an awkward choice which divides historians.*]

EITHER
- The <u>place of publication</u>. This traditional practice, still used for example by the *VCH*, is still used by many scholars. It is, however, becoming less helpful for two reasons: some towns and cities, such as Oxford, contain several distinct imprints, and modern publishers often quote two or more places in utterly different parts of the world. In following this style, some writers omit London because so many books have originated from there.

OR
- The <u>name of the publisher</u>, which as a point of identification is more precise and therefore more directly meaningful to readers, librarians and bibliographers. This style, for example, is used in the review sections of *Local Population Studies* and *The Local Historian*.

[NB: *To reflect the two styles, this book gives some references with publishers' <u>names</u> and others with the <u>place</u> of publication (including London). One could of course quote both pieces of information (such as 'Boydell, Woodbridge') but that eats up more space.*]

- The <u>year of publication</u>, an essential piece of information which is best given in brackets, to avoid confusion with high page numbers; the brackets are often shared with the publisher and/or place of publication.
- Page(s) thus: p. 93 *or* pp. 93–5; chapter(s) thus: ch. 4 *or* chs 4–5.

EXAMPLES:
Richard Marks, *Image and Devotion in Late Medieval England* (Stroud, 2004), p. 59.

OR:
Richard Marks, *Image and Devotion in Late Medieval England* (Sutton Publishing, 2004), pp. 18–21.

Books in more than one volume

As with a single book except that:
- The number of the relevant volume and its sub-title (if it exists) come before the date of publication. This is because individual volumes often appear in different years.
- The abbreviations 'p.' and 'pp.' are dropped.

EXAMPLE:
VCH Somerset, VIII The Poldens and the Levels (Boydell, 2004), 109.

Articles in journals

For a full reference, give details in the following order:
- The name of the writer.
- The title of the article, in single quotation marks.
- The title of the journal, italicised. Some very familiar parts of titles can be abbreviated, for example *Trans.*, *Hist.* and *Soc.* (see Appendix 18, pp. 191–3)
- The number of the volume and, if necessary, the part. It is not necessary to use the words 'volume' or 'part', either fully or abbreviated; the relevant numbers will suffice. However, other details such as '4th series' or '4th ser.' must be retained. It is best to give the numbers of volumes in their original form, although Arabic numerals are often preferred to Roman because they are more readily intelligible to modern readers and take up less space. When Roman numerals are used, make sure that they are of a consistent size (either upper- or lower-case).
- The date, in brackets. A calendar year may have to be supplemented by a month or season.
- Page numbers, without the abbreviations 'p.' and 'pp.'

EXAMPLE:
Christopher Marsh, 'Order and place in England, 1580–1640: a view from the pew', *Jour. British Studies*, 44, 1 (Jan. 2005), 3–26. (This journal could have been given as *Jour. Brit. Stud.*, and the numbers for volume and part separated by a colon, thus: 44: 1)

Essays or chapters in edited volumes

As with an article in a journal, except that the title of the essay (in single quotation marks) is followed by 'in' and the name(s) of the editor(s) with 'ed.' or 'eds' in round brackets. There then follows the title of the book in italics, publisher or place, date and pages.

EXAMPLE:
Roger Thompson, 'The uprooted: East Anglian emigrants to New England, 1629–40' in David Postles (ed.), *Naming, Society and Regional Identity* (Leopard's Head, 2002), 49–68.

Manuscript sources

The following details are needed:
- A brief description of the source, with some indication of its date.
- The repository, often in abbreviated form (for example BL for British Library).
- The reference or call-number to the individual piece, usually a combination of letters and numbers.
- If necessary, the number of a particular page, folio or membrane.
  (NB some writers put the description *after* the reference.)

EXAMPLE:
Extent of the manor of Writtle, Essex, 1304: TNA, C 133/113(1).
If you have read a manuscript on microfilm, confess the fact and also give *its* reference.

Newspapers and other printed primary sources

Newspapers, parliamentary reports, commercial directories and many other printed sources should also be handled consistently. In the case of newspapers, one should assist the reader by mentioning the relevant column as well as page. Acts of Parliament have a particular form of reference, quoting the regnal year and chapter number. At the first mention of an Act one should again help the reader by quoting its title and translating its date into the modern equivalent.

EXAMPLES:
Ipswich Journal, 5 Nov. 1814, p. 3, col. 2.

Expense and Maintenance of the Poor, *BPP*, 1818, xix, 426–7.
   [Note: *BPP* stands for *British Parliamentary Papers*]

Act for Debarring of Unlawful Games, 2 Geo. II, c. xxviii (1728–9).

Unpublished theses and dissertations

Give details of author, title, degree, institution and date. Notice that titles are given within single inverted commas.

EXAMPLE:
T. O. Licence, 'English Hermits, 970–1220', unpublished PhD thesis, University of Cambridge, 2006.

Oral evidence

Where one relies on personal testimony, diplomacy is just as necessary. Give details of each informant (if permitted) with indication of gender, place of residence, occupation, age (if only approximate), the medium used, and date when interviewed.

EXAMPLE:
Personal communication from William Smith of Laburnum Rd, Borchester, retired postman, aged 70+ years, interviewed July 2006.

Electronic sources

For secondary sources, one should provide the following details: author or editor; title of the article or section used (if applicable); the title of the complete work, in italics; address of the electronic source; page or equivalent (if needed); and date when last accessed.[1]

EXAMPLE:
J. Corbett, *Ernest George Ravenstein: The Laws of Migration*, 1885, http://www.csiss. org/classics/content/90 (last accessed Jan. 2008)

For manuscript sources, a brief description with a date should precede the electronic source.

EXAMPLE:
Will of Jane Austen of Chawton (Hants), 27 Apr. 1817, http://www.nationalarchives. gov.uk/dol/images/examples/pdfs/JAusten.pdf (last accessed Jan. 2008)

---

[1] Ritter (ed.), *Oxford Style Manual* (2003), Ch. 15, 'Electronic data', pp. 545–53.

Other aspects of referencing

a) Using capital letters in titles of publications

In this respect we have two choices. The first, known as 'title case' has been used throughout this volume; it makes every grammatically important word begin with a capital.

EXAMPLE:

M. Aston & R. Horrox (eds), *Much Heaving and Shoving: Essays for Colin Richmond* (Lavenham, 2005).

The second option, known as 'sentence case' uses capitals only at the start and for proper nouns.

EXAMPLE:

M. Aston & R. Horrox (eds), *Much heaving and shoving: essays for Colin Richmond* (Lavenham, 2005).

The same choice applies to titles of articles within journals, and of essays within edited collections. In this volume, 'sentence case' has been the general rule.

b) Use of the ampersand (&)

Some writers and publishers use ampersands in references and bibliographies in order to save space. This is often done either to shorten titles, as in 'Bonfires & Bells', or to connect two or more authors or editors, as in 'Peter Clark & Paul Slack'. Others will have nothing to do with this practice.

c) The shortening of references

Once a reference has been given in its full form, its later re-occurrences can and should be shortened with adjustments of page-numbers as necessary. This convention enables one to save space and to avoid unnecessary repetition. Normally, abbreviated forms contain the surname of the writer and a few words of the title, such as 'Reay, *Rural Englands*, p. 124' or 'Reay (2004), p. 124'. One could even use 'Reay, p. 124' providing it created no ambiguity. Where several works of the same author have been quoted, one has to be particularly careful to distinguish them when in shortened form. Here the importance of dates is obvious. Other strategies for shortening repeated references are to use *ibid., op. cit.* and *loc. cit.* (see 'Latin terms used in references', p. 189), and to use accepted abbreviations for the titles of journals and other published series (see Appendix 18, pp. 191–3). The bibliography at the back of a book, gives the *full* details of all sources consulted and thus supports the shortened references (see 'Bibliographies', below, p. 190).

d) Punctuation in references

Generally, to make the printed page less spotty, it makes sense to minimise the number of full-stops (*OED* and TNA rather than *O.E.D.* and T.N.A.). Whether or not to put a full-stop at the end of each reference is a matter of personal choice. However, complete sentences within references should always end in full-stops. When words are abbreviated, use a full-stop only when the final letter is not the same as that of the whole word, thus: 'ed.' for one editor, but 'eds' for more than one.

The vital principle with punctuation is consistency. To check references, it is easier to bring them all together temporarily in the form of endnotes (see p. 111).

e) Page-numbers in references

Again, consistency is important. To save space it pays to use as few digits as possible, thus 34–7 (rather than 34–37). However, in the sequence 10–19, one should retain the penultimate figure, hence 12–14 and 113–18. After 'p.' or 'pp.', it is normal (as in this book) to leave a space, though you will find publications where the number directly follows the stop.

f) Latin terms used in references

These conventions are avoided by many writers unfamiliar with Latin, yet they (or some of them) still feature regularly in references and bibliographies. Where they are used, it must be with accuracy and attention to detail. For example:

- *ibid.* (for *ibidem*, 'in the same place') is applicable when a reference repeats the one immediately before. It is used without an author's or editor's name. This is the Latin term which is most likely to survive, but it must not be confused with *idem* ('the same person') sometimes used to avoid repeating the name of an author or editor.
- *op. cit.* (for *opere citato*, 'in the work quoted') is also used when a reference is repeated, but not necessarily immediately following. It follows an author's or editor's name. Sometimes this Latin term is used in a very irritating way, forcing the reader to look back through scores, even hundreds, of pages to find the original reference. In such cases, it is far better to repeat the information in abbreviated form.
- *loc. cit.* (for *loco citato*, 'at the place quoted') which is used to avoid repeating exactly the same reference, including the page number. Again, it follows an author's or editor's name. The physical gap between the two references should not be annoyingly lengthy.
- *passim* (for 'throughout') indicates that the whole of a particular book or article is relevant. It follows a normal reference, and appears instead of a page-number.
- *ex inf.* (for *ex informatione*, meaning 'from information provided by …') is used to acknowledge personal help given in conversation or correspondence.
- *et al.* (for *et alii* meaning 'and others') is a device for saving space by minimising a string of authors' or editors' names. It is normally employed where more than two authors or editors are responsible for a particular work:

EXAMPLE:

E.A. Wrigley *et al.*, *The Population History of England ...* (instead of E.A. Wrigley, R.S. Davies, J.E. Oeppen and R.S. Schofield, *The Population History of England ...*)

Bibliographies

A substantial piece of written history should include a bibliography, listing all details of the manuscript and printed sources which have been consulted. Items should appear in the following order, with appropriate sub-headings and with primary sources coming before secondary:

- Manuscripts (by custom, the British Library is given pride of place).
- Printed primary sources (for example *British Parliamentary Papers*, or the volumes of record societies)
- Books
- Articles in journals
- Unpublished works, such as academic theses.

NB: In a bibliography, the surnames of authors and editors should *precede* initials or forenames.

EXAMPLE:

Borsay, Peter, *A History of Leisure: the British Experience since 1500* (Palgrave Macmillan, 2006)

Appendix 18

Abbreviations in historical references

In references words are commonly abbreviated in order to save space but, to avoid misunderstandings, this should be done as consistently as possible. The list below recommends abbreviations for words frequently used when citing printed and manuscript sources. They are mainly based on the *Oxford Dictionary for Writers and Editors* (2000) and Maney & Smallwood, *The MHRA Style Manual* (2002).[1] A few other words which are often shortened in references have also been included, and are shown without italics. Note that where an abbreviation ends with the same letter as the original, a full-stop has not been used.

abbr.	abbreviated, abbreviation
abr.	abridged
Abstr.	*Abstracts*
Acad.	*Academy*
Agrar.	*Agrarian*
Agric.	*Agricultural*
Ann.	*Annals*
Antiq.	*Antiquarian, Antiquary*
app.	appendix
Archaeol.	*Archaeological, Archaeology*
Architect.	*Architectural, Architecture*
Assoc.	*Association*
Bibliog.	*Bibliography*
bk	book
Brit.	*Britain, British*
Bull.	*Bulletin*
Cal.	*Calendar*
cent.	century[2]
ch./chs	chapter/chapters
col.	column

---

[1] In preference to the 'Standard list of abbreviated titles of current periodicals' in *Signposts for Archaeological Publication …* (CBA, 3rd edn, 1991), App. A, pp. 59–70. The latter includes some odd features, including a total lack of punctuation (e.g: *J Brit Soc Master Glass Paint*).

[2] In references numerals are often used to save space: '17th cent.' instead of 'seventeenth century'.

Coll.	*Collections*
Dist	*District*
Doc.	*Documents*
Eccles.	*Ecclesiastical*
Ecol.	*Ecological, Ecology*
Econ.	*Economic, Economy*
edn	edition
Eng.	*England, English*
fig./figs	figure/figures
Fld	*Field*
fn.	footnote
fol./fols	folio/folios
Geog.	*Geographical, Geography*
Geol.	*Geological, Geology*
Hist.	*Historical, History*
Ind.	*Industrial, Industry*
Inst.	*Institute*
Jour.	*Journal*
Leg.	*Legal*
Mag.	*Magazine*
ms/mss	manuscript/manuscripts
Med.	*Medieval*
Misc.	*Miscellany*
Mod.	*Modern*
Mus.	*Museum*
n.d.	no date
n.s.	New Series
N&Q	*Notes & Queries*
Occas.	*Occasional*
o.s.	Old Series
p./pp.	page/pages
Pam.	*Pamphlets*
Pap.	*Papers*
pt./pts	part/parts
pl./pls	plate/plates
Pop.	*Population*
Proc.	*Proceedings*
Publ.	*Publications*
Rec.	*Record, Records*
Rel.	*Religion, Religious*
Rept	*Report*
Res.	*Research*
Rev.	*Review*

Roy.	*Royal*
ser.	Series
Sociol.	*Sociological, Sociology*
Soc.	*Society*
Stud.	*Studies*
supp.	Supplement
Trans	*Transactions*
Univ.	*University*
vol./vols	volume/volumes
Yearbk	*Yearbook*

Examples:

Agrar. Hist. Eng. & Wales	*Agrarian History of England and Wales*
Econ. Hist. Rev.	*Economic History Review*
Jour. Eccles. Hist	*Journal of Ecclesiastical History*
Loc. Pop. Stud.	*Local Population Studies*

Notes:

Place-names (including names of counties) and personal names are normally spelt without abbreviation:

Trans Halifax Antiq. Soc.	*Transactions of the Halifax Antiquarian Society*
Sussex Archaeol. Coll.	*Sussex Archaeological Collections*
Trans Thoroton Soc.	*Transactions of the Thoroton Society*

A few exceptions:

Certain well-known sources, or those used repeatedly in a particular study, are often referred to simply by initials. Nowadays, to avoid excessive spottiness, full-stops tend to be omitted. It is of course necessary to explain such acronyms in a special key (as on p. ix, above):

VCH	*Victoria County History*
ODNB	*Oxford Dictionary of National Biography*
REED	*Records of Early English Drama*
TLH	*The Local Historian*

Appendix 19

Compiling a glossary

Readers of all kinds, ranging from general to specialist, can find valuable guidance and stimulation in well-constructed glossaries. The purpose is, of course, to explain the forms and meanings of words encountered in original sources. Nearly all record publications need glossaries, even those dealing with modern texts. In addition, many other books and articles might profitably include glossaries or glossarial footnotes, especially when they contain technical, legal and other specialised terms which are not familiar to all their readers (for example, 'headborough', 'navigation', 'First Fruits' and 'Incorporated Hundred'). While some editors and authors miss these opportunities altogether, the glossaries which do appear in print are often inadequate – even in volumes issued by well-respected record societies. In compiling a glossary the following steps need to be considered:

- If a word was spelt in several different ways in original documents, as often happens, give the variants in alphabetical order, e.g. HEYER, HEYIR, HEYYR (hair). However, one sometimes has too many variants to include them all, in which case it is important to give those which affect the first syllable or two, e.g. MAUZEY, MAWZYN (Malmsey wine). Major variations in spelling the first syllable may well necessitate the use of cross-references, e.g. STYKKES: see Stekes.
- If the old spelling of a word is different from today's, always give the modern equivalent before attempting a definition, e.g. MESTELYN: maslin. This is often forgotten, yet is the vital key for readers who want to pursue the subject further.
- A definition or explanation of the word, such as you might find in a dictionary, is frequently needed, e.g. MESTELYN: maslin, a mixture of wheat and rye. Make sure that you give the definition which is strictly relevant to the usage in your text. Do not merely copy everything a dictionary may say about a particular word.
- If a word was used in more than one sense, each needs to be carefully distinguished, e.g. STOUNE: 1. stone (as building material); 2. mill-stone; 3. measure of weight which varies by commodity from 8 to 24 lbs, but often 14 lbs.
- If a word appears once or only occasionally in the original document or record publication, one should help the interested reader by giving references to the relevant page(s) or folio(s), e.g. HODE: wood (131v).
- Where a word is rare or specially important, one should similarly give helpful references to dictionaries and word-lists which yield the necessary explanations, e.g. TWIDDLES: pimples, a Suffolk term (Halliwell).

- If you make purely editorial comments, put them in square brackets. It is astonishing how many historical words, English and Latin, appear to mean 'unidentified' or 'obscure'!

Finally, give thought to the typography, punctuation and layout of your glossary, so that it is clear and attractive without wasting space. With the help of modern software, it is easy to experiment with such details. Glossaries in books sometimes appear before the text and sometimes after. Either way, they should of course feature in a paginated List of Contents.

Historical dating

Answers to dating exercises on pp. 144–5

1. 23 April
2. 23 June
3. 21 Oct. <u>or</u> 22 Aug.
4. 20 June
5. Thursday after Trinity Sunday
6. 20 Nov. 1275–19 Nov. 1276
7. 22 June 1397–21 June 1398
8. 22 Apr. 1546–28 Jan. 1547
9. 29 May 1660–29 Jan. 1661[1]
10. 5 April 1309
11. 6 Sept. 1336
12. 20 Oct. 1397
13. 27 Aug. 1460
14. 31 Jan. 1376 [*leap year*]
15. 9 Jan. 1705 [*New Style*]
16. 6 Feb. 2007–5 Feb. 2008

---

[1] The reign of Charles II is counted from 30 January 1649 when his father was executed.

Index